BECOMING FOLLOWERS
OF JESUS

A PEOPLE'S APPROACH TO
WHOLISTIC SPIRITUALITY

BECOMING FOLLOWERS
OF JESUS

A PEOPLE'S APPROACH TO
WHOLISTIC SPIRITUALITY

BARBARA PALECZNY SSND
and
MICHEL CÔTÉ OP

TRINITY PRESS
Burlington, Ontario, Canada

ISBN 0-919649-58-0

© 1983 by Barbara Paleczny

Trinity Press
960 Gateway
Burlington, Ontario
Canada L7L 5K7

Printed in Canada.

For those who have shown us that co-operation and responsible participation are at the heart of a better world. We are grateful for the taste of joy, truth and love that real community brings; it makes us laugh, sing and dance even with wounded legs!

IN GRATITUDE

The development of this work was similar to the growth of a gospel in that it emerged from reflection on communities' experience of the Lord and his power at work in us and needs of our time:

1. All of the members of the Christian Life Communities in Ontario have contributed to this book in their own way, but especially through sharing what helped and hindered them as they formed communities during the last eight years. Since 1975 when four couples and John English SJ began the first Christian Life Community here, many laity, sisters and priests have prayed and planned together, led groups, reflected on our experience, revised and adapted approaches. From our initial four years' co-operative efforts and insights, I assembled and developed the *Growing Together in Christ* manual. During this time, we formed communities, prepared people for the Spiritual Exercises of St. Ignatius and then directed them, generally throughout a year. Our goal was to form basic faith communities, committed to following Jesus today within the real concerns of family, work, civic and ecclesial realities, and to do this with breadth of vision because we live in a global village. We found that the best world-wide community of laity with whom our groups could relate in all these aspects is the "Christian Life Communities"; our communities decided to form an English-speaking Canadian federation with them. Who, then, formed these Christian Life Communities? It is with love and gratitude that I cite the founding communities as St. Michael's and Our Lady of Lourdes parishes in Waterloo, and a community in Brantford, Ontario. Our co-presidents, Barbara and Peter Peloso, as well as Helen and Louis Drago, Lois and Kuruvila Zachariah, Frances Morrison, Geraldine and Walter Dorsey, Desneiges and Art Walter, Helen and Frank Sullivan and Dan Phelan SJ were some of the initial members whose commitment inspired much growth in the area. While Harry Sommerville and Ruth Cornwell CSJ worked mainly with

the Exercises, Patricia Mansfield SSND, Bernice Kroetsch SSND, Shirley and Bob Gatchene focused more of their efforts on Growing Together in Christ groups and facilitators' workshops; John Veltri SJ supported these ministries with much initiative and creativity.

John English SJ has been in constant dialogue with these communities, leadership programs and entire ministry in significant ways; namely, by sharing his insight, by taking initiative with obvious hope and perseverance, and especially by calling forth and trusting others' gifts for ministry. John's *Communal Graced History, A Manual of Theology and Practice*, is the basis from which the sixth unit is adapted.

The Christian Life Communities encouraged me to write more on the experience and insights of the last years; they also gave many suggestions as I wrote it and strove to integrate this with relevant studies and experience. Michel Côté OP became a colleague with this.

2. During the last few years, Michel Côté OP and I have worked together to understand and develop liberation theology for our society. We probed questions such as, what is needed in our society and how is change effected. Our hope was to create a tool which might assist people in wholistic growth that required integration on the personal level as well as in the realm of society because of its great impact on us: we are both grounded in and called forth from our society. Michel's analysis of the Canadian scene (advertising and myth in particular) and his experience of being with the marginalized also have very significant influence in this book; they helped us root insights in today's realities. He generously co-operated in writing articles and critiquing the units. His humour and incessant questioning were inspiration and discipline as we developed, sorted out and clarified material. We realize that liberation theology will emerge as people decide and act in faith and love, reflect on their experience and share their insights.

3. My Notre Dame Sisters and the postulants have been part of all this process "from the inside", even doing the typing and distribution of the original *Growing Together in Christ* manuals. These women are for me a true community of friends and, as such, a treasured and challenging way of knowing the Lord and being formed for others. Bonnie DuHamel did the final typing. It is a variety of ministries that we celebrate!

4. We are grateful to those who wrote articles specifically for this book, allowed us to reprint articles, or agreed to our printing the substance of their presentations.

5. A real joy for us is experiencing the wealth of friendship and "coming together" of the gifts of married and single Christians, priests and religious. It is a community called church! All of us are grateful to all those who have influenced us toward following the Lord!

> Joyfully,
> Barbara Paleczny
> School Sister of Notre Dame
> Easter, 1983

BECOMING FOLLOWERS OF JESUS

TABLE OF CONTENTS

PART ONE: A MINI-JOURNEY

UNIT I: COMMITTING OURSELVES TO BECOME FOLLOWERS OF JESUS

PART TWO: THE JOURNEY

UNIT II: ON BEING HUMAN AND INTEGRATING MATTER AND MEANING

UNIT III: INTEGRATING FEELINGS AND FAITH IN DAILY LIFE: A HEALING PROCESS

UNIT IV: INTEGRATING FAITH AND JUSTICE – HEALING OUR COLLECTIVE EXPERIENCE

UNIT V: INTEGRATING GOD'S VISION OF RIGHT – THE KINGDOM IN THE MAKING

PART THREE: FROM WORDS TO ACTION

UNIT VI: INTEGRATION THROUGH DECISION-MAKING

PAGE

ARTICLES

INTRODUCTION

Humans alone on this earth have the ability to ask the all-important question "Why?". Why are we here, being what we are and doing what we're doing? Why are things the way they are? This little word, why, invites our minds, our hearts and hopefully even our feet on a pilgrimage, a quest for truth.

Luckily we are not the first ones to walk down this road. Many have taken up the journey before us and are now able to show us the way. Christianity, for example, before it got its official name was simply known as "The Way". People were called to follow the steps of a man named Jesus on the path of light and life, the fullness of which resolved for many the dilemma of the original 'why'? Jesus alone took both creation and God seriously enough to highlight the truly complete *human* venture of our existence: his incarnation was essential to his salvific mission (Col. 1:12-20). Through him, people discovered that to be God-like was to develop fully the human potential that the Creator put into each of them, to share the divine life. In fact, they realized that the glory of God was visible in persons fully alive in the image of Jesus Christ. The followers of Jesus called themselves '*christ*-ians' and accepted a simple yet difficult task: integrating their physical, emotional and social beings into the plan (or vision) that God imagined ("image"-ined) for them ever since the beginning of time:

"God created man *in the image* of himself   (vision)
in the image of God he *created him,*   (matter, biology)
male and female he created them.   (sexuality, psychology)
God *blessed* them, saying to them: (compassion)
be fruitful, *multiply,*   (social)
fill the earth and *conquer* it.   (politics, economics)
Be masters of the fish of the sea, the
birds of heaven, and all *living* animals
on the earth . . .   (ecology)
God saw *all he had made,* and indeed
it was very good."   (spirituality)
(Gen. 1:27-28,31 emphasis added)

The followers of Jesus came to experience that in Christ, all life, matter and relationships, in fact the entire cosmos, could be transformed. "Spiritual" life, therefore, encom-

i

passed every aspect of persons and society; it became life that is energized or transformed by the Spirit of the risen Lord. It is life that is offered to people of all races, a life that invites them to an intimate relationship with the all holy Lord of history who not only cares for the stranger, down-trodden and outcasts but actually dwells among his people and shows them 'The Way'.

The process adopted in this book seeks to examine and integrate the many facets of our created beings (the physical in Unit II, the psychological in Unit III, the socio-politico-cultural in Unit IV, and the spiritual in Unit V) that are in constant tension with one another throughout our daily lives. The approach emphasizes self-discovery of the creative gifts that brings us to individual and corporate wholeness. "Now I am making the whole of creation new". (Revelation 21:5) May your journey be filled with the Lord's ever-surprising presence!

PROCESS

While weaving the various aspects of our lives into each unit, the process will be like a spiral that returns to experiences from a variety of perspectives according to the particular focus of the unit while gently moving deeper into understanding life's mysteries and our individual places within it; for example, in the first unit there is gradually more use of imagination, especially in remembering personal life experience. This is repeated in Unit II as we focus on individual, societal and church symbols but only dealt with explicitly as a theme in Unit III when it is suggested as an aid for contemplating the gospel, for understanding our own and others' emotions and for grasping our collective imagination in myths. As the following units unfold, we again develop our imagination in coming to know the Body of Christ (community) today, co-operating in building his presence among us, celebrating both our life and the Lord's victory together and making decisions appropriate for our times. This same spiral process is true of all the main themes.

The community approach incorporates the following premises and beliefs:

1) The great gift that Jesus left us is community.

2) God is love. We experience the tangible presence of God in our relationships with others around us, — in our communities. The manifestations of God are multifarious because we as individuals are all unique. Each of us perceive things separately and privately within our own minds. We show each other what we learn, as was done in the past when the teachings of God were first recorded. There, in the Bible, we see the many ways in which God was revealed to people. God is the Father in some cases, the Holy Spirit in others, and Jesus Christ, a man, as well. In every case, though, God is a single, all- embracing consciousness whose appearance is formed by limited human perceptions. We describe God in personal terms that are meaningful to us because our language is inadequate; we are faced with the option of focusing on the single, personal term 'he' (or she), or the plural 'they' that includes the trinity of Father, Son, and Spirit. Addressing God's manifestations as 'they' and 'them' is particularly appealing because the plural form recognizes the diversity of God's mysterious and omniscient will that cannot be categorized by human beings. The plural forms 'they' and 'them' also help us to acknowledge the communal presence of the Trinity in all things. Thus, the tangible presence of God's love that we experience in our community relationships is actually similar to the community of all living things that God represents. We live 'in the name of the Father, the Son, and the Holy Spirit.'

3) Mutual trust within a group is one of the most effective ways to help a person do the following:
   – realize his/her own worth
   – be open to change in behaviour
   – become more aware that social consciousness happens as we recognize that everyone has a basic potential for growth that must be respected and called forth.

   The energizing quality of community life creates hope for its individuals and helps to develop their social consciousness and their ability to minister to the needs of others.

Reinforcing the individual's strengths, the community has a life which is greater than the contribution of any one person or even of all the members. "Where two or three meet in my name, I shall be there with them". (Mt. 18:20)

4) A community can use its own wisdom and good sense to respond to individuals or invite them to particular growth as they are ready. This complete trust allows members to grow and change their behaviour patterns without the pressure to reveal underlying causes. A community need not ask members' motivation but may gently invite people to share what a feeling means for them if they want to do that.

5) Sharing experience in a group allows a sense of community to happen. Focusing on both the inward journey and their external thrust enables people to experience the spiritual and psychological intimacy so needed today, and to be church with all the strength required for this.

6) Listening to the experience of others and to the work of the Spirit in them helps us to deepen:
   – our sense of awe and gratitude toward God
   – our appreciation of the very ordinary aspects of our daily lives
   – our respect and trust of others
   – our awareness and communication on many levels; growth in individual and communal discernment
   – our unity in obvious diversity
   – our growth in realizing that this community is the Body of Christ and how, as Risen Lord, he communicates with us at this time in this community, this flesh, this church. His presence is real in community, in his word and sacrament.
   – our ability to accept our gifts and weaknesses honestly
   – our desire to give and receive both love and forgiveness
   – our openess to new experiences of prayer, empathy, mission and ministry, insight into our times, celebrating. It helps to deepen our appreciation for the Eucharist.

Sharing personal experiences can also help members to

clarify and appreciate them, and then be ready for new depths.

7) We are happiest when we are forgiving, loving people, loving God and neighbour generously with all the freedom and responsibility this implies! We become conscious that being God's people and building the kingdom even here is life and full identity. This is what our call to be saints (followers of Jesus) is all about!

8) Adult learning happens most effectively as people reflect on and share their experiences and participate as equals in the process. Within this approach to becoming more human and Christ-like, both social justice and celebrations play an important role. We become a community of disciples with a new heart and mind as we follow Jesus.

Perhaps the discipline, fidelity and openess required to listen well and take time for this commitment are part of the following of Jesus that is needed to support our faith, make good decisions for ourselves, our family and society, to foster the readiness to be flexible, to do whatever he tells us (John 2:5) and go wherever he leads us, through his body, the community known as church.

FACILITATION, NEW MEMBERS, AND THE FORMAT OF THE EVENING

It is important that facilitators have a solid foundation in spirituality; personal experience of the complete Spiritual Exercises is recommended as part of this. OF COURSE, LEADERS AND GROUPS MAY ADAPT, BE CREATIVE, AND USE ANY OTHER GOOD SKILLS IN FACILITATING GROUPS AND FORMING COMMUNITIES. As a community assumes responsibility for its spirit, direction and choices, members gain confidence in taking even more initiative.

Preparation for the evening is most essential. This is a facilitator's book and is meant to be used as an aid. DO NOT GET LOCKED INTO IT! The primary concern is community life and adult growth; the key is facilitation. If the leader is familiar with the purpose of the unit and the evening and the discussion questions s/he may select aspects according to group need and time. Each phase may be one evening or occasionally more than one, although it is not necessary to exhaust any topic before moving on because of the spiral approach used. The group simply needs to be aware of when they may be proceeding too quickly or too carefully since people may be overwhelmed by the amount or threatened by the probing and depth. Since the community will return to topics in ever-increasing depth, new members who have not completed the previous units could be welcomed as a group begins any of the first three units.

The format of each evening is basically
  1 hour   Prayer and sharing on past week.
  10 minutes Break
  1 hour   Discussion (any input from the facilitator would be included here if relevant.)
  20 minutes Preparation for the prayer of the week.
             Journal or reflection on the evening.

Be flexible to suit your community needs and wisdom.

Spontaneous prayer, quiet reflection and singing can be introduced at emotionally significant moments for an individual or the group. Obviously, some groups will be more at ease with these. Do what is good for them! The "Prayer for the Week" is a suggested list only. Leaders are free to change references, encourage repetition and follow individual needs. As a facilitator's book, this contains all that is in the participants' book. The latter reprints the table of contents, overview and for each week, the suggestions for prayer and the articles.

By focusing mainly on two gospels, we hope to grasp a little more clearly their spirit and message. At some point, facilitators may need to talk with the group about the problem of random selection of scripture passages as a usual way of choosing a reading; namely, we miss the context and thrust and total message of the gospel letter or book. If we select some passages and ignore others according to our own purposes, we may be distorting the work of the Lord.

PREREQUISITES AND COMMITMENT OF MEMBERS

It is helpful (but not an absolute requirement) if participants have had some previous group experience in deepening faith; such as, Scripture study, Genesis II, cursillo, marriage encounter, or retreat(s). Basic mental health, that is, being in touch with outer reality but also willing to let inner experiences surface if needed, as well as a readiness to interact with the group. Obviously, members' freedom to choose the amount and depth they share is sacred. This should be an explicit value for every group of this kind.

Commitment to the weekly meeting and daily prayer are basic. During this formation period, members are asked to commit themselves to these for each of the first units. By this time a community may be ready to commit themselves to each other in weekly meetings for a year or more. Ten or 12 people (including the leaders) meet in a home; each should bring a bible, the participants' book and his/her journal every week.

If it is possible, an occasional renewal day or week-end could facilitate better understanding and easier communication.

USE OF THE PROGRAM

This approach has emerged after working with many groups in a variety of ways. It can be used for renewal within groups; such as Cursillo ultreyas, charismatic meetings, follow-up for Renew, or for religious communities, seminarians or priests. More often, priests, sisters and brothers have participated in or led groups with married and single Christians; this enriches their experience of church for all. Basic communities in parishes have used it. Some have adapted sections for days or week-ends as well.

It was developed mainly for initiating new members and for renewal in Christian Life Communities. We have used it as a preparation for doing the Spiritual Exercises of St. Ignatius, mostly according to annotation 19; that is, throughout the year instead of in a closed retreat of thirty days. We suggest that at least Units I-VI be used before the Exercises. A few criteria to determine readiness for them include: a personal desire and commitment and self-discipline to make it a priority, ability to pray with Scripture, spend time in solitude and to talk about what is happening interiorly, generosity and a desire to integrate one's life experience and prayer in order to be a disciple building the kingdom with the Lord and his people. The remaining units could be continued (possibly adapted) while some or all members do the Exercises with a personal prayer guide, or they could be used as follow-up. Another excellent option for follow-up is *Building Christian Communities for Justice,* by Paul Roy, SJ (Paulist Press, 1981).

BY DOING ANY PART OF THIS EXPERIENCE, YOUR GROUP IS IN FACT DEVELOPING AS A CHRISTIAN LIFE COMMUNITY. An aim of these communities is to integrate their lives in all its aspects and constantly grow by being a community in mission, by sharing their values in ways that penetrate the superficiality of consumer societies, by maintaining a clear bond with similar communities in our global village; the latter is growing in importance because of both good communications and urgent crises that require cooperative effort. If your group desires to explore, unite with and celebrate their common interests with the world community of Christian Life Communities at any time during this formation (preferably early!) they should contact their local or national center. Information and addresses for Christian Life Communities are included in VI-14-16.

Those who desire to use this book for formation in Christian Life Communities would need to add more of the history and dynamic spirit of the movement; this is done best through contact with members. Those who are familiar with the Spiritual Exercises of St. Ignatius of Loyola and may want to use this approach as preparation and/or follow-up to the Exercises will recognize many elements; for example, unit II is based on the principle and foundation as well as the two standards, particularly in the impact society has on us. This unit also faces the identity question, "Who am I?". There is gradual exercise of the imagination before it is formally introduced in unit III when participants contemplate the Jesus of the gospels and look at myths of our society; in units IV and V, it is expanded to contemplation of the body of Christ today in our streets, and of possibilities for a new world order. Focus on God's mercy and compassion, and putting on the mind and heart of Jesus ministering, crucified and risen also penetrates the entire process.

One of the key approaches is reflecting on our experience in the light of faith, or the awareness exercise. It is introduced informally in units I and II, and then formally in unit III. This is done on the individual and communal level, including local and global awareness. From this, discernment grows and there is possibility for more effective co-operation, decision-making and action. Throughout the entire process, we emphasize adult, responsible participation, being in touch with our own and the community's affective movements as well as the realities of our societal and global situations, and the importance of responding to the Lord's mission in wholistic, but specific ways. These are all aspects of healing and our call to be for others in ways that bring about effective social change.

Our real hope is that communities will grow together, reflecting on their faith in Jesus and their experience in society and that out of this openness, the Lord will not only liberate them but also show them what is needed in our time. For this reason, WE SUGGEST THAT THE LEADERS KEEP A JOURNAL OF THEIR DISCERNMENT OF THE GROUP INSIGHTS AND MOVEMENTS. We invite you to share any of this with us.

A FEW BASICS ABOUT SHARING DURING THE GATHERINGS

1) Since it is important to leave time so that all may share something if they want to, it is most important to remind members to be selective regarding what they will share. IT IS THE INNER EXPERIENCE, not the details of the external circumstances, and especially not the names or descriptions of others, that give rise to faith and are the substance of the sharing. Occasionally a member will need to share at length but it is inappropriate for the leader to allow one or two people to monopolize the group attention consistently.

2) Since most of the communication process is non-verbal,

look at the person who is speaking! Respond at least non-verbally or in a brief acknowledgement unless further clarification is appropriate. A mature group can invite and challenge its members further but most of the initial sharing should simply be received gratefully. Loyalty is obviously essential. In the second half of the meeting there is time for discussion, but here too the facilitator needs to be alert to the right(s) of all to participate.

3) Some points that may facilitate sorting out what is happening in a group:

a) Giving messages . . . verbally and non-verbally: What is the purpose of the message? Am I (or is another member) sending double messages? Words may say something different from what the non-verbals seem to convey. Clarify regarding these and re: mixed emotions. Simply state what they are even if they seem to conflict with each other.

b) Listening does not need to mean that you are agreeing or disagreeing. Listening involves hearing, understanding, and clarifying what the speaker meant.

c) Watch for a tendency to jump to conclusions. Since words often have different meanings for different people, it is important to listen to the context and ask for clarification. Wait: pauses do not necessarily mean that the message is finished. Listening reduces stress and can clear tension and anger.

d) Ponder:

i) What the other is trying to say about the topic or him/herself;

ii) Listen for HOW a message is given. Is there any emotion? What might emotion or lack of it indicate?;

iii) What reaction is going on in me, or others? Are we threatened by another's status, education? Are we fearful or irritated?

iv) What does my reaction indicate? Is some tender territory of mine under attack? Or am I being encouraged? Or is there something in the group that needs to be faced?

e) Are the other's premises stated or implied?
f) Is the facilitator or group expected to make a response or just understand the position? If in doubt simply ask.
g) Ask yourself, 'What is the content of the message, — fact, opinion, feeling? What is most significant now?' Respond to that.

Growth is possible where there is listening love.

Note regarding the journal

We encourage participants to express their personal and/or community awareness in personal journals, in music, plays, television or theatre, poems, dance, short stories or any other art form. These are an effective means both of expression and of effecting social change.

UNIT I

COMMITTING OURSELVES TO BECOME FOLLOWERS OF JESUS

Thrust: Any persons about to undertake a trip or wishing to pursue a goal, usually assess their resources before setting out. By our baptism, we christians have been called to follow the road Jesus walked before us. This is our objective. But the Father did not leave us stranded resource-wise: with the Spirit of Jesus and with each other we have what we need to reach that objective. The purpose of this first Unit is to present an overview, a first run-through of the pedagogical spiral that this book invites us to follow: how God loves us in the full reality of our everyday lives. Hopefully, this integration of our faith might enable us to respond more generously and gratefully to the call of our vocation: the sharing of Jesus' mission to fully humanize (and thus divinize) our world.

Process: By examining some elements of our faith option, elements which present basic points from Units II to V (the core of this program), the participants should, at the end of this Unit, be able to decide whether or not they wish to continue their christian journey within the group in following this program over a period of two years. These nine weeks are therefore, a mini-journey of the more expanded units to come.

> Week 1 Introductions, Overview Of This Approach, Exercises To Become Aware Of God's Presence
>
> Week 2 Short-Term Contract With The Group; Reflecting On Experience. Prayer As Relationship
>
> Week 3 Praying With Scripture: Disposing Skills And Aids

Week 4 Reflecting On Socio-Cultural Influences (re Unit II)

Week 5 Becoming Aware Of Faith History (re Unit III)

Week 6 Appreciating Our Own And Others' Faith History (re Unit IV)

Week 7 Further Integration Of Our Life-History And Faith (re Unit V)

Week 8 Reflecting As Community: Decision-Making (re Unit VI)

Week 9 Sharing Decisions About The Future And Celebrating

Goals:

- a willingness to grow and to accept our own/ others' worth by developing an atmosphere of trust and respect
- the enabling of each member of the group to discover, esteem and learn from others
- the developing of knowledge about and love for the scriptures
- the discovery/discernment of the revelation of God in our everyday lives
- the formation of community through these encounters.

INTRODUCTIONS, OVERVIEW OF THIS APPROACH, EXCERCISES TO BECOME AWARE OF GOD'S PRESENCE

Purpose: The purpose of this first meeting is simply to facilitate groupbuilding by finding out who is in the group and by presenting the format which will be used during the upcoming meetings. "Who are we?" and "What are we doing here?" are two questions whose answers will allow the members to focus on a common goal.

A first prayer reminds the group that it is the Lord who brings them together as they are. An overview of the meeting gives direction. Presentations and expectations clarify where people are coming from. An overview of Unit I provides longer-term vision. The break offers time for non-structured, social encounters. Learning how to use scripture references provides a practical tool and puts everyone at the same advantage. An experience of God's presence allows the group to discover something new together and to create their own "history". An evaluation of the meeting helps to keep the direction clear by making needed corrections. Finally the preparation for the upcoming week provides the direction, the motivation and the continuation between meetings. Elements of this format will be constantly used at all meetings, though with great flexibility.

Minutes

5   1. Open with a hymn and/or prayer which includes:

a) recognition that the group comes together with a wide variety of experiences, gifts, concerns, hurts and joys

b) remembering the Lord's promise to be with us

c) asking for the Lord's light and grace to continue to open our hearts to him and to teach others.

10   2. Give an overview of tonight's format.

15   3. Introductions (even if there is only one newcomer to the group this is extremely important!) Do a) or b).

        a) Any approach that will help people know the others' names and begin to appreciate who they are can be used here; for example, possibly share the following with one partner. After the sharing, each will introduce the other partner to the group.

          i) What is one thing you enjoy doing?
          ii) What is one topic you enjoy reading? What music?
          iii) Married, single, separated, widowed, priest, religious?
          iv) If married, what is your spouse's name? Any children?
          v) What is one quality you like about yourself (or what others like about you)?
          vi) What is your work?

        b) If participants know each other quite well, omit the above and share points such as:

          i) What is one way you have changed over the last months?
          ii) What is one thing about yourself that others don't seem to realize?
          iii) What are some questions you have about the meaning of your life, your successes and failures: When did these questions arise?

30   4. Take a few minutes to reflect on the following questions, and then share, simply going around the group without discussing others' responses until all have had an opportunity to share. Of

4

course, they are free to 'pass' on any of the points.

Write the responses of 'c') to 'f') on a chart for use in Unit I-Week 8, #1 d) to see if expectations were met.

a) What are one or two of your interests and commitments?

b) What is one thing that helps to give meaning to your life?

c) What is one reason you have for coming to this group? Is it your only reason?

d) What are three qualities that you think are most important for a group like ours?

e) What is one thing you would like this group to avoid?

f) What are your expectations for this group, this experience?

10   5. Give an overview of the coming weeks (Unit I) and books needed: *Becoming Followers of Jesus* (participants' book), Bible, and note book for a journal.

10   **BREAK**

10   6. Finding particular books of Scripture: Check that all are at ease with using the table of contents, abbreviations, Old and New Testament, names of books, way of writing chapter and verses.

(Throughout all the time together, it is always okay to ASK ANY QUESTION, regardless of how 'simple' or 'obvious' you may feel it is! This promotes trust and real learning within the group.)

15   7. One person leads one or more exercises that can help people be more aware of the Lord's love for them. Take a few moments of quiet with each; for example,

a) Close your eyes and place fingers on wrist or neck to feel your pulse. Relax and let each pulse be a reminder such as 'gift of life' or 'I love you' from God our Father and he continues to give it until you are ready to have him embrace you with the fullness of that life, face to face with him.

b) Be aware of the sounds you hear. Listen to them. Our God desires to be closer to you than the sounds you hear.

c) Be aware of the feel of the clothes you wear. Our God desires to be closer to you than your clothes. Possibly read Jeremiah 13:11.

d) Be aware of your breathing. Is it fast or slow, deep or shallow? Let it quietly deepen and slow down. Imagine that, with every inhalation, light and healing fills every fibre of your being; every time you exhale, imagine all tension and fear leaving you.

e) After a few moments quiet: continue to let your breathing be slow and deep and now let your consciousness gradually move down to rest at the heart of your personality where God dwells with you. We'll take about five minutes quiet just to relax in the presence of the Father, Son, and Holy Spirit since they are at home with you.

f) At the end of the time for these exercises, suggest that people open their eyes as they are ready, gradually becoming aware once again of others around them.

15   8. Share anything of what they felt; e.g., relaxed, awkward, loved, sleepy, angry, . . . *Any* feeling is valid!

10   9. Give opportunity to share anything they felt during the entire evening.

10   10. Ask members to bring a notebook for use as a

journal, that is, for any exercises we do in the group and especially for their personal reflections. Have them write down the names (first and last) of everyone in the group so that they can pray for them and their families. Talk over the points for reflection and prayer (below) and their implementation for the week.

5   11. Sing a hymn as a concluding prayer for the evening.

Reflection and Prayer for the Week:

1. Decide if you will make the commitment for the next eight weekly meetings and for daily reflective prayer of about 15 minutes; we will provide guidance for this. Let the leader know 2-3 days before the meeting if you will not be coming.

2. Go for short walks (at least). Notice a little more of nature (sounds, colour, what is happening).

3. Listen to some music you like.

4. Notice some things that others like.

5. Take some time each day to do some of the exercises of being aware of God's presence as we did during the meeting. Respond to God, the giver of life, in your own way. Write down what you felt in these experiences.

6. What has helped you to pray in the past? Be prepared to share any approach, particular prayer or question you have had. Remember that there are *many* ways to pray! Talk over with the Lord how you pray.

SHORT-TERM CONTRACT WITH THE GROUP; REFLECTING ON EXPERIENCE PRAYER AS RELATIONSHIP

Purpose: The purpose of this meeting is basically to allow members to enter into the Trinity's way of seeing and of loving. In the same way that the Lord has established a covenant with his people, members will be called to commit themselves to the group for seven more meetings. This stance will be followed by two exercises on how we feel the Trinity relates to us and on how we relate back to them. The prayer for the week will maintain this theme.

Minutes

5   1. Overview of the evening.

10   2. To begin, ask each person to write down what feelings they have experienced in the last day or so. Leave them anonymous and put the papers together. With a spirit of prayerfully accepting the gift of each person, read each paper aloud; lead a prayer remembering that we usually don't know what another is feeling unless s/he tells us, that the Lord is with us in these feelings and desires that we respect others in their 'mystery of life' with its ups and downs.

Ask what they notice in this sharing. Sing a hymn that suits the moment.

10   3. Note that since coming here means you are committing yourselves to the group, we will recall names and celebrate this by having each one say his/her intention or desire aloud; for example, "I am *(name)* and I commit myself to you for the next seven meetings. I intend to take time for reflective prayer each day". For each person sing an appropriate refrain.

15   4. Lead one of the exercises from Week 1 (#7) to remember God's love for each of us and to pre-

8

pare for the following prayer: Remember moments of appreciating a sunset, fire, water, particular person(s).

How does God regard nature and people?

Recall some moment when you felt anger, pain or compassion in the midst of an evil situation. How does God feel about this situation?

Ponder the fact that: when you appreciate and care for people and nature, you share the Lord's way of seeing and appreciating it! You share his mind and heart! When you are grieved and act against destruction of people and nature, you again share God's way of seeing. "You shall not kill". When you desire unity and appreciate each person regardless of status (or lack of status) you share the mind and heart of God.

Jesus commissions (mandates, sends or commands) us to love one another as he has loved us. When we do that, we "put on the mind and heart of Christ".

When we accept and love ourselves, we share God's way of relating to us. When we refuse to be put down by another's reflection of us (or our own self-judgment), we share God's reality and vision of us a little better.

Read Deuteronomy 30:11-14

Spend 5 minutes quietly pondering this mystery, grateful for the ways you have shared God's life, even when you didn't realize it!

45   Share some aspect of what you felt or realized during this time, some experience of the prayer from last week, or something that has helped you to pray in the past.

10   BREAK

40   5. Discuss the following as a way of reinforcing

that prayer is a relationship:

a) Think of a person whom you love; e.g. wife, husband, friend. Remember the many different ways you relate together, different feelings, expressions of love, fear, joy, reconciliation, anger.

Discuss what relating to others involves.

b) The Lord desires that we be fully human in relating to him. What would that mean for me?

c) God desires to communicate with each of us personally. What does this mean to me?

d) Take a few minutes to remember quiet moments by a fire, by water or any moments that were simply 'still', 'staring' or pondering after which you felt better. Then read the following:

> When we relate to the Lord, we need to 'come as we are', not as we hope or pretend to be. We can pour out our angers, griefs, fears, worries and concerns to the Lord; we can bring him our complaints, hectic schedules. We can come in joy and hope, sharing what we have enjoyed. We can savour moments of our day with him. We can simply be quiet with the Giver of Life, one who 'thought up' the universe and people and not only keeps us in existence but desires to relate with us. It is also important to allow quiet time with him so that we don't do all the talking!

> One way that the Lord communicates with us is through the events and word of Scripture. He spoke to a people, Israel, and to his disciples. We are called individually and together as his people to hear his word for us today in our time and circumstances. We can put in our own name, our family,

our nation instead of 'Israel' (or others!) and let the Lord's love into us, let him enlighten and direct our way in this decade and in the real situations of our life and world.

10   6. Prepare for prayer during the week by talking about the suggestions below.

5   7. Conclude with a hymn/prayer.

Prayer for the Week:

Begin each time asking to experience and recognize the Father's unconditional love and caring for you and for those you love.

On three of the days, take about 15 minutes just to sit and relax quietly by yourself or with another. If you need to discuss something with the Lord (or another) before you can be quiet inside, do it! But take time for quiet as well! Respond to him in your own way!

We need to take time to be with those we love, including God!

On three other days, take 15 minutes to ponder the Trinity's word for you in order to let them communicate their love for you. Begin by asking for the grace (above) remembering their desire to love you, possibly using an exercise which we did together in Week 1. Read the scripture passage once or twice and then ponder or savour it with the Lord who loves you so much. Respond in your own way.

> Isaiah 43:2-4
> Hosea 11:1-4,9
> Psalm 139:1-18

Throughout the entire week:

Do others in your family, work etc. know your esteem for them? How do they know it? Ask for the grace to esteem each person you meet and show it by the way you look at them, listen, speak and act with them.

11

PRAYING WITH SCRIPTURE: DISPOSING SKILLS AND AIDS

Purpose: This meeting is a first attempt at entering the group's individual and collective sense and practice of prayer. An exercise in relaxation and prayer will be one way of bringing out the experience of prayer. This experience will be shared with others. The included article presents a summary of collective wisdom on the question of prayer. Again sharing and questioning should help everyone see that there are no magical, mysterious ways to prayer: it is an act of trust and love. The following week attempts to offer concrete experiences in this respect.

Minutes

5   1. Open with a hymn and/or prayer which includes remembering the Lord's loving presence, asking for his light and grace.

20   2. Do the following relaxation exercise for about five minutes.

Sit quietly in a comfortable position. Close your eyes. Relax all muscles starting with your feet and moving up to your face. Remain very relaxed. Breathe deeply, quietly, slowly through your nose. Be aware of your breathing. As you breathe out, let a word such as Spirit, or Jesus, slowly accompany it, easily and naturally. At the end of the time, ease out of the exercise gradually to listen to the word of the Lord for us. Jeremiah 31:3.

After pondering this scripture passage for about 10 minutes, write down what you felt during the time of quiet, because of this and/or other experiences today.

60   3. Share:
       a) Were you able to take time for prayer this week?

    b) What helped you do this? (for example, tak-
ing time for prayer before doing tasks, parents alternating taking responsibility for children, doorbell and phone while the other has
time for prayer. At some time, parents and
children pray together, not parents' 'hearing'
their prayers; all pray!)

    c) When and where is best for you?

    d) What posture is best for you? Why?

    e) How did you get started with your prayer?
(Ways we have shared, others you have discovered?)

    f) What is something you felt during those
times of prayer or in our quiet time this evening?

    g) What are some different ways we can re-
spond to the Lord in prayer? Remember
ways you use to respond to others and ways
you like others to relate with you. Do these
help you in relating to the Lord? Why or why
not?

    h) Can you remember very well what you expe-
rienced each day and what you felt because
of this experience (or lack of experience)?
Discuss the importance of noting some
reflection at least briefly *after* each time of
prayer. Suggest that they include the date,
unit, week and scripture reference each time.

10   BREAK

30   4. Share attitudes and/or approaches that you have
found helpful for praying with Scripture.
Quietly read the article which is included at the
end of this week. Think about what is helpful
for you and if you have any questions about it.

    Discuss any of the above.

5   5. Prepare the Prayer for the Week. Remind all to
bring their journals each week.

10   6. Conclude the evening with a hymn or prayer as it is appropriate for the group.

Prayer for the Week:

Ask the Lord each day to be able to listen to him and know his love. *Use one passage each day.* At the *end* of your time of prayer, write down in your journal what you experienced even if it seems like nothing! What was the mood? Did time go fast or slow? How are you with that?

Luke 10:25-28   Commission or mandate to love.
Luke 11:1-4   The Lord's prayer.
Luke 11:5-11   The persistent friend.
Luke 11:9-131   The Father's desire.
Luke 12:22-32   How much more are you worth?
Luke 12:31-32   It has pleased your Father.

PRAYING WITH SCRIPTURE

God Speaks To Us First

This fundamental truth makes it possible for us to pray to the Trinity. They have been concerned for each of us long before we became concerned for ourselves.

They desire communication with us.

They speak to us continually, revealing themselves to us by various modes:

– through Jesus Christ, His Word;
– through the Church, the extension of Christ in the world (because we are joined together in Christ, God speaks to us through other people);
– through visible creation around us, which forms the physical context of our lives. (Creation took place in His Son, and it is another form of God's self-revelation);
– through the events and experiences of our lives;
– through Holy Scripture, a real form of the Lord's presence. This is the mode of communication we are most concerned with in prayer.

14

They Invite Us To Listen

Our response to the Lord's initial move is to listen to what He is saying. This is the basic attitude of prayer.

How To Go About Listening

What you do immediately before prayer is very important. Normally, it is something you do not rush right into. Spend a few moments quieting yourself and relaxing, settling yourself into a prayerful and comfortable position.

In listening to anyone, you try to tune out everything except what the person is saying to you.

In prayer this can be done best in *silence* and *solitude*. Find the passage from Scripture. Read it through a few times to familiarize yourself with it. Put a marker in the page. Try to find a quiet place where you can be alone and uninhibited in your response to God's presence. Try to quiet yourself interiorly. Jesus would often go up to a mountain by himself to pray with his Father.

In an age of noise, activity, and tensions like our own, it is not always easy or necessary to forget our cares and commitments, the noise and excitement of our environment. Never feel constrained to blot out all distractions. Anxiety in this regard could get between ourselves and God.

Rather, realize that the Word did become flesh, that he speaks to us in the noise and confusion of our day. Sometimes in preparing for prayer, relax and listen to the sounds around you. God's presence is as real as they are.

Be conscious of your sensations and living experiences of feeling, thinking, hoping, loving, of wondering, desiring, etc. Then conscious of the Trinity's unselfish, loving presence in you, address them simply and admit: "Yes, you do love life and feeling into me. You are present to me. You live in me. Yes, you do."

Remember your littleness and need as well as the Lord's great desire to share his Spirit of courage, love, wisdom, and hope with you. God is present in you through the Spirit who speaks to you now in Scripture, and who prays in you and for you.

Ask the Lord for the gift of being able to listen to what he says or for any other interior need you have today.

Begin reading Scripture slowly and attentively. Do not hurry to cover much material.

If it recounts an event of Christ's life, be there in the mystery of it. Share with the persons involved; for example, a blind man being cured. Share their attitude. Respond to what Jesus is saying.

Some words or phrases carry special meaning for you. Savour those words, turning them over in your heart. Feel their power in you. Stay with any meaning even if it is somewhat obscure, any image, melody or other sensation.

Treat the words of Scripture as holy, as spoken by God to you right now, as love and effective; be reverent, full of awe. Feel the mystery of the words, which are deeper and higher than merely rational meanings, revealing the overwhelming God who is intimate to you. Do not try to control the Lord, but let him act in you.

When something strikes you, for example,
- You feel a new way of being with Christ. He becomes for you in a new way (e.g., you sense what it means to be healed by Christ).
- You experience God's love.
- You experience new meaning.
- You are moved to do something good.
- You are peaceful.
- You are happy and content just to be in God's presence.
- You are struggling with or disturbed by what the words are saying.

This is the time to pause. This is God speaking directly to you in the words of Scripture. Do not hurry to move on. Wait until you are no longer moved by the experience.

Don't get discouraged if nothing seems to be happening. Sometimes the Lord lets us feel dry and empty in order to let us realize it is not in our own power to communicate with him or to experience consolation. The Trinity is sometimes very close to us in seeming absence (Ps. 139:7-8). They are for us entirely in a selfless way. They accept us as we are, with all our limitations, even with our seeming inability to pray. A humble attitude of listening is a sign of love for them, and a real prayer from the heart.

At these times remember the words of Isaiah:

> "Yes, as the rain and snow come down from the heavens and do not return without watering the earth, making it yield and giving growth to provide seed for the sower and bread for the eating, so the word that goes from my mouth does not return to me empty, without carrying out my will and succeeding in what it was sent to do." Isaiah 55:10-11.

Spend time in your prayer just being conscious of the Trinity's presence in and around you. If you want to, speak with them about the things you are interested in or wish to thank them for, your joys, sorrows, aspirations.

Summary of the Five P's

1. Passage from Scripture. Pick one and have it marked and ready.
2. Place. Where you are alone and uninhibited in your response to God's presence.
3. Posture. Reverent, relaxed and peaceful with back straight (sitting, lying down, kneeling). A harmony of body with spirit.
4. Presence of God. Be aware of it and acknowledge and respond to it. When you are ready turn to the passage from Scripture.
5. Passage from Scripture. Read it very slowly aloud and listen carefully and peacefully to it. PAUSE.

Read aloud or whisper in a rhythm with your breathing, a phrase at a time, with pauses and repetitions when and where you feel like it.

Don't be anxious, don't try to look for implications or lessons or profound thoughts or conclusions or resolutions, etc. Be content to be like a child who climbs into his/her parent's lap and listens.

Carry on a conversation with the Lord concerning what you hear. (Hearing in this context is an 'inner sense', just as one might say 'I see' when s/he understands something. 'I hear' means 'I know' or 'I am aware'.)

After the period of prayer is over it may be helpful to reflect back over the experience of prayer. This review will help you notice what the Lord is doing in your experience.

Adapted from articles by
A. Nigro, SJ and J. Wickham, SJ

REFLECTING ON SOCIO-CULTURAL INFLUENCES

Purpose: The first part of the meeting will focus on examining what went on with the prayer experience of the past week. This format (revision or seeing again) will often be used in the upcoming Units: the discovery of one meeting is tempered by a week of prayer and then reflected upon by the group before advancing on to the next step. Here, for example, after having experienced a certain form of prayer, we will now be invited to start including ourselves and our roots more into our prayer. The process will involve looking at "where I came from" and possibly sharing "where we came from" to see what influences were (are?) at play within us. Opinions on this will be recorded in a personal journal and the meeting will end with preparation for Prayer of the Week (integrating the experiences of our lives into our prayer).

Minutes

5   1. Begin the evening by leading the following 3-5 minute exercise:

"Close your eyes and relax. Lord we ask with bold confidence for light to see your gifts to us and to be grateful, and to accept ourselves as you do, with love, in the full reality of who we are and have been. (Pause). Picture yourself preparing a gift or surprise for someone and remember how you felt. (Pause). Imagine the Lord giving you gifts: of life, your personality, faculties, sight, hearing, other people, companionship, faith, his love for you, his forgiveness, his invitation to you in your vocation. Let gratitude fill your whole being." End with Ps. 103: "Bless Yahweh, my soul, bless his holy name, all that is in me! Bless Yahweh, my soul, and re-

19

member all his kindness . . ." Sing a hymn.

10   2. Read and take time for quiet personal reflection using the following:
   a) Were you able to take time for quiet and/or Scripture prayer daily?
   b) What helped/hindered you in that?
   c) What spot have found that is best? Time?
   d) What is one thing that you experienced in this time?
   e) Is there anything you experienced?
   f) What is one difficulty you experienced?

50   3. Share on the experience of prayer this week.

10   **BREAK**

50   4. Since our background (familial, cultural, regional, social, etc.) affect us very deeply, take about fifteen minutes to remember the following:
   a) Place(s) where you grew up: rural, urban (inner-city or suburb), immigrant, mobile, nature of the land (mountains, prairie, port), amount of space available for your use, proximity to rivers, lake or ocean, climate, environmental problems (pollution, traffic tie-ups, earthquakes, floods). How are these a part of you even in attitudes that you have; for example, your sense of work, play, friendships?
   b) Family size (single parent, number of children, others sharing the home, group home, problems such as alcoholism or abuse) customs, ways of relating within the family, male or female domination, attitudes about money, sexuality, religion. What are some frequent slogans or sayings that you heard? How has this influenced you?
   c) Social, political, economic influences: How did involvement and knowledge (or lack of

it) in these influence you? Was there any high risk level or stress in parents' work; for example, mining, police duty, professional decisions, monotony, widespread unemployment? How did you as a family and as an individual face it? Who were your friends? How did you relate to neighbours and strangers? How do you feel about this background?

Share anything of your background that you choose; obviously, you are free to be selective in what you share. It is important, however, that you can recognize these influences and reflect on what they mean for you *with at least one other person.*

10   5. Write in your journal:

What emotions concerning prayer and concerning influence in my life did you feel this evening? Do you know what sparked them? Gently note them and ask during the week: "I wonder what that means for me?" Let the Lord give you his light!

What was our group spirit like tonight?

10   6. Prepare for the Prayer of the Week and conclude with prayer and/or song.

Prayer for the Week:

Each day focus on some aspect of the influences on you life. Remember it and ask "Lord, how were you with me in this? How do you want to make this a gift for me?" (e.g. of healing, feeling compassion for others, learning wisdom, courage . . . ?)

To end your time of prayer each day, read one of the following passages reflectively and then note briefly some of what happened in you in your journal.

Deuteronomy 1:31; 2:7
Luke   2:1-8   Nazareth and Bethlehem
Luke   2:19   Mary pondered these
                                 things in her heart

Luke	2:46-52	Jesus' youth
Luke	5:29-32	Jesus' dinner friends
Luke	4:16-22, 28-30	Jesus wins approval

Optional reading:

THE SIGNIFICANCE OF OUR SOCIO-CULTURAL CONTEXT

I will discuss the relationship between our self-awareness as persons, our self-identity, our self-image, and the socio-cultural context that we live in. This is extremely important for us. I would suggest that it does make a difference that the process of formation that we are engaged in happens in Canada, not in Latin America, and not in the United States. It makes a difference whether it happens in Toronto, or in Quebec, or in the Maritimes, or in the West. It really does make a difference.

If we reflect on the parable of the sower and the seed, often we tend to meditate on it in terms of our own personal experience. Is my soul an open ground for God's Word? What about my weedy little heart? Am I all dried up, and busy about many things? But we can also reflect on it in terms of our whole society. Is it a welcoming society? a welcoming ground for the Word of God? a weedy ground, mixed up with many things? These are some of the questions that I want to explore.

You are probably aware of the important part that personal relationships play in the development of a person's self-identity or self-image. For better or worse, we are influenced by our family, by our friends, by our peers, by our community, by those with whom we work. These relationships are factors which no formation process can ignore. They can enable personal integration, or they can hinder it; they can affirm a positive self-image or they can create a negative self-image.

Yet, how often do we consider the significance of our social and cultural context in the formation of our identity as persons? We spend a great deal of time in formation helping people reflect on their experience, but it is often a very limited experience, our work or community experience. Very rarely does our reflection go on to encompass our experience within our country or within our province or within our region. And it is my conviction that it is this limited self-awareness, this lack of social self-awareness, that prevents us from becoming effectively engaged in mission.

Our language, our categories of thought, our values, our view of nature, our sense of reality, our notion of happiness, our status, our roles, – all of these are profoundly affected by the social context we live in. Every change in our social structures reverberates in the internal personal existence of each individual, and affects our awareness as persons. There is, on a very personal level, a kind of jiggling of our sense of security, because of world events. Our expectations of ourselves and of others, what we do, and how we are to do it, – all of these are attitudes which are influenced by the society that we live in.

Our identity as persons evolves as we go more deeply into ourselves, and as we broaden our relationships and go more widely beyond ourselves.

The Difficulty of Naming Our Reality

There is at least one significant reason why Canadians have found it so difficult to name their own reality, to reflect on their own experience. We are and we always have been a colony. We have been a colony first of France, then of England, and now we are an economic colony of the United States. Psychologically, to a greater or lesser extent, we have the mind-set of a colonial people. As Northrop Frye, the most penetrating critic of Canadian culture, has said: Canadians know that the head office is elsewhere. They know that all the basic decisions affecting their lives will be made elsewhere, in Paris, in London, in New York and Washington, and more recently, in Frankfurt and Tokyo. The centres of art and culture and education are elsewhere. Our point of reference has always been elsewhere. And so, says Frye, we have not taken our own context seriously. The question, he says, is not what is happening there, but "Where is here?", a very difficult question for colonials to answer. And this question which is being asked of the nation as a whole is being asked even more urgently by the colonies within our colony, by the Indian people, and the Quebecois.

Many words in social justice seem like foreign imports. They seem strange. It is as if we have to learn a whole new language. So also some Canadian women look to American women to be the spokes-persons of the feminist revolution. What is going on there is important. But we take their analysis, we take their strategy, and then wonder why so many Canadian women remain unmoved by the issue. They feel that is is coming from out *there* and that somehow it has nothing to do with us *here*.

I am not saying that we should not be in touch with the tremendously significant movements in Latin America and among American women today. I am saying that these movements, these awarenesses, exert a particular temptation for those of us with a colonial mentality. We tend to feel that the action is anywhere else but here. And so we remain in our private worlds, caught up in our community concerns, busy about many things in the hectic routine of our work, and always with a nagging sense that what we do does not matter too much, in any global sense.

One of the dominant themes of Canadian Literature is that of the struggle against the forces of nature, the wind, the snow, the forces that seem so uncontrollable. Very often these natural forces are identified with the Indian people. It is a struggle which has marked much of our Canadian history, and some regions more than others. Certainly, coming from the prairies, I have a sense of the extent of this struggle, the 30's, the winter, 40 below!

Margaret Atwood has suggested that it is perhaps the result of this struggle with nature that one of the dominant attitudes in the Canadian psyche, if there is such a thing, is that of survival. The early settlers and explorers, faced with this vast, cold land, did not want to win, did not want to dominate, but simply to survive. It was a case of mere survival and the victory lay simply in enduring, nothing more. And so in our literature we find many examples of those who have survived: the whooping crane, the Canada geese, the Hutterites, the ponies on Sable Island, and perhaps last but not least, the Quebecois. They have survived. And it is this attitude of survival which we

24

have carried with us into many areas of life. But it is no longer mere survival, it is grim survival. We will endure. We will just keep plugging along, "hanging in". Our political question to-day is not "Is our country going to win?", but "Will our country survive?" Again, it is grim survival.

In this struggle for survival against the forces of nature, Canadians developed certain social virtues: frugality, caution, discipline and endurance. They also developed what Northrop Frye has called "a garrison mentality." Against the vast un-consciousness of nature we erected our little fortress, our little civilization. We erected physical and psychological barriers which protected our small and isolated communities. And what is crucial is that within the garrison we developed an overwhelming respect for law and order. It protected us. Law and orderheld our communities together. In this closely-knit and beleaguered society, the greatest sin was pulling away from the group, rebelling, being different. And today some people would say that Canada is simply a multiplication of gar-risons, of groups, each with its own psychological barriers: a cultural mosaic in which there are not two, but many solitudes, which very rarely enter into dialogue with one another.

Let us continue to explore. We cannot conclude that the images and attitudes I have mentioned are clearly dominant in Canadian life. On the one hand, there is some evidence that we no longer believe that it is good enough merely to survive. It is significant that the United Church's study on a theology of nationhood was entitled "More than Survival". On the other hand, it is quite clear that in most places in Canada, we are no longer struggling against the threatening forces of nature. Na-ture has more or less been tamed, and the paintings of the Group of Seven depicting nature in its stark and terrible beauty are a form of exorcism in which the demons of nature are set down and therefore tamed. With snow-blowers and ski-doos we have shown that even winter will not hold us back. Through technology we have conquered nature and made our-selves at home in this land. Through tracks and telegraphs and telephones and television we have created a web of communi-cation in which we somehow have a sense of our country or our region in relationship to others. (It is significant that Canadians make more telephone calls per person than any other people in the world.) Technology has enabled us to conquer the demons which we formerly saw in nature, and nature has become for many of us a play-ground, where we go with campers and tents. It is a refuge from the city, because the demons which have gone from nature now inhabit our centres of civilization, our cities, our social systems, our politics. Civilization is now the place where one wages a battle against those forces which threaten life.

Technology, which enabled us to dominate our environment, has now come to dominate us. The systems of economics and politics which we so easily accept dominate us. The problem is, of course, that the demons are not as obvious as they used to be.

The taming of nature coincides with a new period and a fairly recent one in our history and in our literature. It is a period marked by a sense of the breakup of the old order which was present in nature, and present in our defensive stance against it. There are several reactions to this breakup which are discernible. The first reaction is a sense of guilt that we have lost our belief in the old order, our belief that "God's in his heaven, All's right with the world". The second is a sense of "realistic involvement" whereby we accept the absurdities and ambiguities of a life with a sense of vacuum. It is a vacuum within us personally and within our country as a whole. There is a sense that we as persons, as communities and as a country have yet to come to birth. And so there is a search for what has been called a "vital truth", for a personal and social raison d'être, and our personal raison d'être is closely bound up with that search for a social raison d'être.

I am now going to talk a little more about our history, and about something in our social structure which both helps and hinders our action for justice and our mission.

I think that somewhere in the back of our minds there is that feeling that Canadian history is not that interesting or that important. However, if we take Scripture seriously, particularly the Hebrew Scripture, I think we are invited to believe that God's call comes to us not only as individuals but as a people, as members of social groups, as members of a political reality. And as we have been reminded, there is a very intimate connection between the call of the people and the land.

It is this kind of contextual call that I think we are called to affirm, called to remember and called to believe in as Canadians. When we think of the people of Israel, when they tried to discern the action of God in their history, we see that they discerned his action primarily in terms of their peoplehood, their nationhood. They saw his action in events. In reflecting on former events, they understood later events; in reflecting on later events in their history, they understood former events. There is this constant back and forth movement in their history of interpretation and event. What is most crucial is the utter seriousness with which they believed that God was acting in their history.

There are many ways of interpreting the dynamic of our history, and one of the more recent interpretations is that our history is one of conflict between rich and poor.

Our culture, our society and our history have been controlled by a very small group, an economic elite probably numbering no more than 60 people. It is a kind of club that it is extremely hard to break into. There are interlocking business interests, social connections and educational background. People like Peter Newman are beginning to tell us what this power is in our society. Whether we agree with them or not, what is interesting is that for the first time we are beginning to see the faces of the people who control much of our economy. We are becoming more conscious of the kind of economic realities which are operating in our country.

If there were once two solitudes, two national groupings, there are now many, many ethnic groupings within Canada. Perhaps the more central conflict now is between the regions and centralism.

For a long time in our history the metropolis was Europe and Canada was simply a vast hinterland which was exploited for its natural resources. More recently, Canada has become a hinterland of the United States. But within Canada I think many would say that this tension exists between what has been called the Golden Horseshoe of Toronto- Hamilton, and the rest of the country. We are hearing voices from the hinterland announcing that the centre of power is beginning to shift. That geographical tension is another way of describing the conflict in our country.

Also, two very different ways of life have grown up in Canada; one is the way of life of the large urban centre, the other that of the closely-knit rural community. I think you will have to ask yourself which of these interpretations helps you to understand your own reality.

While there are no heroes in our history there is still a kind of collective heroism. It is the group or groups of people who somehow engage in significant action. The history of the C.P.R., for example, teaches us something of the tenacious heroism of those who built it. When we speak of Brebeuf, we usually speak of Brebeuf and his brethren, – not just the man, but a group of men who together came to the wilderness. When we speak of the Quebecois and of how they have preserved their culture, we are speaking of a group of people, and of a kind of group heroism.

In Canada, there was no definitive break with the "old world", no rebellion, no passionate will or desire for freedom, our nation evolved from within a tradition and presents as supreme values law, order and good government. No drama such as the Exodus exists in Canadian history (unless we look at the Exodus as a 200 or 300 year search!).

Canada is passing through a crisis in history, only coming to some kind of political and social self-consciousness. We live beside a powerful giant, this affects our self-image. Forms of mass consumerism and advertising are destroying ethnic and cultural differences when we are hardly beginning to appreciate them.

The Canadian theologian Douglas Hall has said that what we need now is not nationalism in the old sense, but care for the nation; and what we need is not internationalism, but vigilance for humanity. And this search for new forms of human groups on a large political scale is also present in many of our efforts to create neighbourhood communities, co-operative forms of life, food co-operatives, etc. These are all part of the same movement against the vicious centralizing tendencies in our world today.

One of the implications of the fact that there are no heroes in our literature is that we might be able to act as communities in bringing about change. The pattern of Canadian action always seems to be communal. I think we can draw on that as something acceptable in our culture, and something to transform it. I spoke about what a negative thing a garrison can be; but in a metropolis, a city, a civilization, a garrison can also be a very positive thing. It can be a counter-culture. We have different values from the consumer culture, the mass culture; and so there is a whole tradition we can draw on there in terms of change, of challenge, and perhaps of prophetic witness.

It will be important how we deal with authority; whether it is presented in a way that is truly liberating, or in a way that makes us spiritual colonials.

Perhaps, too, in our communities we need to find ways of dealing with conflicts. The great Canadian way is to smother and to muddle through. I think we have to admit that this is not a good thing. Conflict must be faced and must be dealt with.

In closing, I want to speak about the Christ who has already embraced our socio-cultural context in a most radical way. There is the New Testament story of the leper who asked Jesus to heal him, and Jesus" response was, "Of course I want to. Be cured!" That "Of course I want to!" is so reassuring! For any of us who are talking about personal and social change, this is a fundamental and important belief. Just as we see that *of course* Jesus wants to heal the leper, we believe too that *of course* he wants us to love and have peace. He does! And so when we work for change in our culture or elsewhere, we need to participate in the action of Christ who says, "Of course I want to heal the world." The more we are united in his action and in his intention, the more we will experience a liberation, a healing, that is both personal and social. Then the energies we draw on will be the transforming energy of Christ. Through him and with him we can engage in action which will at once transform us and our socio-cultural context. It is in Christ that we will enter more deeply into the human condition of our culture. Through him we join in his activity of transforming our socio-cultural context into a more just, a more loving and a more peaceful reality. He is already rooted in our reality and it is from there that he calls us to a radical mission.

Excerpts of presentations given by
Mary Jo Leddy N.D.S.

BECOMING AWARE OF OUR FAITH HISTORY

Purpose: Again, after prayer, we will be given a chance to reflect and share on the influences brought to bear in our lives in the course of last week's prayer. We will then be invited to express our faith history (and feelings) through symbols and see how other factors influenced us also. We will conclude by noting our feelings regarding this process in our journal. Prayer will center on personal faith experience.

Minutes

5   1. Begin by leading the following 3-5 minute prayer: (Relax)

"Father, we come togther in Jesus' name this evening and ask with great confidence that we may recognize your gifts to us, especially your love for each of us personally and the life you give us. Fill us with gratitude that we may experience deep wonder and awe at your goodness. Imagine the Lord desiring to love you, drawing you to himself, being with you in every aspect of your life with all the good and sinfulness that this includes." (Pause)

10   2. Read Deuteronomy 10:12-21 aloud and reflect on the following:

– What did you experience in prayer this week?
– Focus on one part of this.
– What does it mean for you?

50   3. Share any experience of prayer this week.

10   BREAK

15   4. Give out paper and crayons. Read Deuteronomy 1:31 and 2:7. Ask each person to divide the paper in four or five sections and use symbols, sketches or lines to show the main periods of his/her history. Include moments of pain, feel-

ings, and healings. How is it influenced by other factors (topics outlined in Week 4 #4). Do this as silent reflection.

35   5. Share any of this. How can your life experience help you to be more with Jesus for others?

5   6. Write in your journal:
     What did you feel and/or realize this evening? What is happening in our group?

10   7. Prepare Prayer for the Week and conclude with prayer, and/or singing in praise and gratitude for members of the group and others.

Prayer for the Week:

DAY 1   Recall the more confident times in your life. What helped you in that time? What were you like? How does this relate to your faith in Jesus?

DAY 2   Remember yesterday's prayer and read Deuteronomy 32:10-11. Be with the Trinity and let them show you their love in view of these experiences of your life.

DAY 3   Recall times that were very difficult yet somehow growth-filled even as you went through them. What were some of your attitudes at the time?

DAY 4   Remember yesterday's prayer and read Deuteronomy 31:6-8. Be with the Trinity and let them show you their love in view of these experiences of your life.

DAY 5   Recall times in your life when life was not 'together' for you. What were some of your attitudes then?

DAY 6   Remember yesterday's prayer and read Deuteronomy 7:7-9. Be with the Trinity and let them show you their love in view of these experiences in your life.

Reminder: Bring your journal to every meeting.

APPRECIATING OUR OWN AND OTHERS' FAITH HISTORY

Purpose: During this meeting a well-known follower of Jesus, Peter, will be presented and his journey will be examined to see where he came from, who he was and how he behaved in faith in respect to Jesus and others. This should allow us to see how even the most chosen ones had their ups and their downs just as we do, but that they (the chosen ones) allowed themselves to be constantly loved into growth by God.

Minutes

5   1. Lead the following 5 minute exercise:

Close your eyes (or focus on one object; e.g., a candle) and relax.

Lord, we ask to recognize how you have always been with each of us whether we knew it or not. We ask for this light and for the gift of gratitude. (Pause) Imagine the Lord loving you from the moment of your conception in your mother's womb, through birth, infancy, childhood, teenage, and adult life. Image his accepting you in your worst times as well as your best.

10   2. Read aloud Deuteronomy 4:7 and ask the Lord for the grace to recognize how he is with each of us personally and leading us within the reality of our particular life.

Take ten minutes for silent reflection on this.

50   3. Share one insight of the past week. If you desire to add what it means to you or how you see it relating to your faith in Jesus, you are welcome to do so.

10   BREAK

50   4. Read the following aloud and reflect on them briefly:

Mark 8:27-31; 1:16-18; 10:28-30; 14:26-31; 14:66-72.

Discuss:

a) What are some of the apostle Peter's very real weaknesses and ways of showing his very real generosity and love for Jesus and for others (leader of group)?

b) How did Jesus show his unconditional love and affection for Peter?

c) What experiences drew Peter closer to Jesus? Why? Did anything separate him from the Lord? Why or why not?

d) Read Romans 8:28,38 to see how God views our ups and downs.

e) What is one example from your life of something hurtful or painful that has helped you to grow?

f) Read the article "Peter the Saintly Sinner"; it is included after the prayer outline.

10   5. Prepare for Prayer for the Week by reading the suggested approach and clarifying as needed.

6. Conclude with hymn, prayer. If participants are not at ease praying aloud, simply ask if there are any needs they want all to remember and then lead them as it is appropriate.

Prayer for the Week:

Begin by remembering the Lord's presence and love for you. Ask to experience deep wonder and awe at the Father's care for you personally and at the special significance of your life for others. Reflect on the word of scripture and the question. Talk with the Lord about it in a way that is natural for you; take some moments for quiet with him too! Afterwards, jot down what you felt and thought in this time.

DAY 1   Mark 1:16-18. Remember moments in your life when you felt drawn to the Lord or to choose the good. Talk with the Lord about his desire to have you follow him.

34

DAY 2 Mark 8:27-30. Who is Jesus for you? Talk it over with him.

DAY 3 Mark 10:28-30. "What about us?"

DAY 4 Mark 14:26-31. Is there any way that you are like Peter?

DAY 5 Mark 14:32-42. When in your life have you been close to another in a distressing time?

DAY 6 Mark 14:53-54, 66-72. Has anything really separated Peter from the Lord? Why or why not?

During the week: Listen well (with the heart) to others about anything they care to share regarding their opinions, feelings, experiences. For anyone who is left out in any way by society, this is particularly important; for example, the unemployed, those who have experienced family breakdown, rejection, loss or death.

PETER: THE SAINTLY SINNER

Last impressions are often lasting ones. Because we observe a final positive outcome to some event, we often conclude that the effort undertaken was always successful. We seem to forget that those who apparently ended their lives fruitfully had first of all to grope and make mistakes. Saints are of this category: had they only to nod at the right times and places, for heaven to be theirs? The gospels don't believe so. The first saints are simultaneously every bit as called, as earthy and as sinful as we are. Even the experience of the Risen Lord wouldn't change their personalities; not even if they had been especially singled out by Jesus, as was the case for Peter.

Peter's real name was Simon, son of Jona; but Jesus gave him a nickname, Rocky (petros). He most likely came from Bethsaida (i.e., "House of Fishing") a small town on the east side of the Sea of Galilee, heavily under Greek influence. He was a fisherman, an uneducated layman, who worked in collaboration with James and John. He married and eventually lived in Capernaum (on the west side of the lake). Though it is said that he left everything to follow Jesus, he went back to his trade from time to time and his wife accompanied him in his later travels out of the country. With his two partners, James and John, he was part of the innermost group of the apostles and certainly the one most in the forefront, often acting as spokesman for the group or taking particular initiatives. It probably did not take Jesus long to observe Peter's zeal, exuberance and daring: but Jesus was also aware at the time of Peter's clear lack of understanding and of his cowardice when under attack.

Two events during the public ministry of Jesus and one after his resurrection will suffice to show how various social influences were at play in Peter's personality, influences to which we can probably relate as followers of Jesus.

1) "And who do *you* say I am?" asks Jesus (Mark 8:29). Peter very affirmingly answers back "You are the Christ" that is, the Messiah or the Saviour who is to come in power. Every Jew knew that God was going to send someone to straighten things up on this earth, a real fire-brand leader who would have God and might on his side; Peter truly believed that Jesus was the one the Jews expected. But when Jesus tries to indicate that the Christ must suffer, Peter attempts to play God and remonstrates Jesus for thinking such thoughts. Clearly the future events suggested by Jesus did not fit into Peter's program: Peter was not in this to lose and even less to suffer. That is why Jesus rebukes him so sternly: "Back, Satan!" Being called "Satan" by a friend makes one stop and think. Whose influence should be followed? My family and my culture? Or this man Jesus? Needless to say this temptation of power over the call to suffering service has been a source of controversy and division throughout the ages, not only personally but also collectively.

2) "You too are one of them" said the bystanders. "I do not know the man" answers Peter (Mark 14:71). This response is all the more surprising that Peter, just a few hours before, had stated: "Even if I have to die with you, I will never disown you." Yet here he is, doing exactly what he said he would never do. One might better understand his position if he had been physically abused into denying, or

36

threatened by some instance of power. But surprisingly it is a servant-girl and some bystanders who put him to rout. When the time comes for Peter to express not especially his faith but simply his solidarity, his friendship, for the one to whom he had been so close, he cannot pull it off. He breaks down under anonymous social pressure. Influences that he was not even aware of made him betray his promise.

3) "When Peter came to Antioch, I (Paul) opposed him in public, because he was clearly wrong" (Gal 2:11). Even after the Lord had risen, even after he had appeared especially to Peter, even after Peter had spoken bravely to the crowds and to the ruling elders, even after having had a personal vision from God concerning the entry of the pagans to the kingdom, even after all of this Peter still remains Peter. He can still be influenced into adopting cowardly stands. Life is never simple: not even in the Spirit-filled first communities. Peter finds himself in an awkward position. On one hand the Jews from Jerusalem (his close friends and associates, under the guidance of James, the "brother" of the Lord) at that time expect new members of the faith to be circumcized. On the other hand Peter has seen how the Spirit has touched the pagans, even without circumcision. Will he bow under social pressure or state the truth? Which side will he take? In accordance with his personality he tries both. But more and more he gives into social pressure. And that is why Paul chastizes him. Peter is operating under double standards. "His (Peter's) custom had been to eat with the pagans, but after certain friends of James arrived, he stopped doing this and kept away from them altogether for fear of the group that insisted on circumcision. The other Jewish brothers also started acting like cowards along with Peter. When I (Paul) saw that they were not walking a straight path in line with the truth of the Gospel, I said to Peter in front of them all: You are a Jew, yet you have been living like a pagan, not like a Jew. How, then can you try to force pagans to live like Jews?" (Gal. 2:12-14). By his attitude Peter was creating two classes of christians and jeopardizing the whole mission to

the pagan Gentiles.

If then Peter, the Rock, went wrong, why can't we? If in spite of all this Peter was still touched by God, why wouldn't we? If Peter needed the full community to follow Jesus, why not we?

FURTHER INTEGRATION OF OUR LIFE-HISTORY AND FAITH

Purpose: Getting it all together is no easy task. But it needs to be faced squarely. This will be the main theme during the prayer, the revision and after the break, the discussion. An exercise will then allow each member to enhance what s/he likes about the other, in such a way that each person represents a mosaic of affirmation. Feelings about this will be included in the journal and reflected upon during the week.

Minutes

5   1. Lead the prayer for light:

Father, you give us Jesus to be the light of the world, to be our way, truth and life. We confidently ask you therefore, to give us your Spirit of light abundantly. Enlighten us that we may see ourselves, our daily lives with our various relationships and circumstances as you do, that is, with love and wisdom. Let us see the truth of who we are before you, your loved ones, people who are weak and sinful but profoundly and intimately loved. Set us free in the knowledge of this truth that we may put all our trust and confidence in you and not in our own talents or anything else we have.

10   2. Silent reflection on Mark 10:32.

50   3. Share from your experience of Prayer for the Week.

10   BREAK

35   4. Reflect quietly for a few minutes on the following questions and then discuss them:
        a) i) What does it mean to "have it all together?" Consider different models or images

of what being human means; for example, being in control, superhuman, without suffering or weakness . . . or . . . ?

    ii) When and how did the disciples of Jesus "have it all together?"

    iii) When and how did Jesus "have it all together?"

b) What does it mean to say that the Word was made flesh? How is he 'made flesh' today?

c) What does it mean when we say that Jesus is Lord of history? Of our history?

25   5. Giving and receiving affirmation are ways of helping participants "get it all together": for each person in the group, write some statement of gratitude and affirmation; for example, I want to thank the Lord and you for . . . or, I appreciate your . . . When you finish these, give your papers to the respective persons. Read these (quietly) and write how you are feeling now in your journal. As it is appropriate, pray and sing together.

5   6. Prepare the Prayer of the Week. Remind them about continuing to use their journal after the time for prayer and bringing it to the meeting.

10   7. Conclude with a hymn/prayer.

Prayer for the Week:

Each day ask for a sense of gratitude that you are called to share the mission of Jesus.

DAY 1 Which of your personal qualities and activities bring you most alive, help you appreciate your life and strengthen you? Let the Lord show you! These are important for you as you share his mission!

DAY 2 Remember yesterday's prayer and use 1 Corinthians 12:3.

DAY 3   What kind of encouragement, praise or other interaction with others helps you most? Talk with the Lord about this and in gratitude remember ways you have affirmed others.

DAY 4   Remember yesterday's prayer and read 1 Corinthians 12:3-7.

DAY 5   What kind of remarks or actions tend to destroy your confidence or bring out the worst in you?

   What hurts or fears do they touch within you? Talk with the Lord about this and possibly about how you have acted this way toward others.

DAY 6   Remember yesterday's prayer and read Mark 10:32 and Mark 16:7-8.

REFLECTING AS A COMMUNITY: DECISION-MAKING

Purpose: For seven meetings now the group has experienced, in summary form, a rapid overview of the total proposed program. Each one of us has had the chance to 'touch base' with ourselves, the others and the Lord. This is but a possible first step in following Jesus. Much more is involved. For those who wish to go on in *this* way, much more is required: decisions need to be taken and will be at the next session. The purpose of this meeting will be simply to *help* us come to a reflective, prayerful decision, be it to continue or not! Therefore, help will be provided so as to allow clearer decision-making: attitudes, exercises and suggested reflections. The feelings of this process will be included in the journal. This process may also prove useful for us in other circumstances of life.

Minutes

15   1. Hymn and prayer: presence, light, gratitude. Lead any of the reflective exercises from Week 1 #4. Ask for the grace to appreciate the value of your group in the Lord's eyes, its significance for you and for others.

With silent prayerful reflection, ponder (scripture) these questions:
   a) What has happened in our group during the last two months?
   b) How has this experience affected your relations with your family, colleagues at work and others you meet, including those on the fringe of society?
   c) How have our gatherings affected your desire to grow as a Christian?
   d) Contrast expectations with original expectations [Week 1 #4 c) to f).]

50   2. Share responses to the questions (above).

10   BREAK

50   3. Some aids for decision-making.

     a) i) What are some attitudes that you think are necessary for good decision-making?

        ii) Compare your list with the following attitudes:

          – Deep belief that God is active in my own unique history; that God does in fact communicate with me very personally.

          – An awareness and belief that God himself brings me to spiritual freedom, to follow whatever way I see as God's desire.

          – Deep desire to serve Jesus and a readiness to act against my own sensuality and selfishness.

          – Realistic appraisal of the data underlying the decision.

          – Dynamic memory – with an awareness of the touch- stones in my life which gives me a sense of what comes from God. It seems to fit or does not fit according to my unique history.

     b) Check out the objectives of your decision:

        i) Presentation of overview of Units II-VI. Refer to initial process (table of contents).

     c) Introduce the following exercise to help people prepare for decision-making.

I will continue with this community for the next Unit of Weeks		*I will not continue with this community*	
Advantages for me	Disadvantages for me	Advantages for me	Disadvantages for me

15   4. Decision making.
        a) Give quiet time to do it (except the conclu-
           sion).
        b) Ask if there are any questions. Note the ad-
           vantage of considering it from different per-
           spectives:
            i) of putting yourself into each one, to 'try
               it on', to see if it fits.
           ii) that the advantages and disadvantages
               are 'for me', as a family person, mature
               adult christian. Therefore, you can in-
               clude what is truly best for your spouse,
               family and colleagues as good for you.
               What is truly good for you is also good
               for others. The Lord does not work
               against himself. Is it physically good, eco-
               nomically and socially beneficial?
          iii) just as you can gain a different perspec-
               tive from seeing a city as you go away
               from it out to sea or going in the opposite
               direction from sea into the city, so the
               different approach gives a little better in-
               sight and appreciation of that position.
          iv) sometimes we go back and forth from an
               advantage to disadvantage and find it
               more confusing to know what we think
               and feel. This way can help us to sort out
               our thinking.
           v) sometimes we *know* what decision is
               needed, or best, without doing this at all.
5   5. Journal: What did you experience interiorly
        this evening? What does this mean for
        you in the light of your faith in Jesus?
5   6. Prepare Prayer for the Week.
5   7. Conclude with prayer and/or a hymn together.

Prayer for the Week:

Ask for the gift of recognizing good and poor decisions in your life and for the ability to choose well according to the Lord's call for you.

DAY 1 Remember a good decision in your life. Why do you think it was a good decision? Talk it over with the Lord.

DAY 2 Galatians 5:16-26.

DAY 3 Recall a bad decision in your life. Why do you think it was a bad decision? Be with the Lord.

DAY 4 Colossians 3:5-17.

DAY 5 Be with the Lord remembering how he loves you and leads you; make a decision about continuing with this group or not.

DAY 6 Philippians 2:1-5.

SHARING DECISIONS ABOUT THE FUTURE AND CELEBRATING

Purpose: This is the last meeting of Unit 1. The group is at a turning point. "What have we accomplished? Where are we at? Where are we going?" These are questions that need to be answered. In an atmosphere of prayer, members will share their decisions about continuing. Then, during the Eucharist, we will also express in our own way our gratitude for the bonding and the growth that occurred among us in our individual and collective life of faith.

Minutes

15   1. Hymn and prayer: light, presence, gratitude.

Ask to appreciate how the Lord is leading each person in this group for the good of that person and others.

Quiet reflection on scripture that will be used in the liturgy later tonight.

50   2. Share: What decision did you come to regarding continuing with this group or not?

How did you come to this decision?

After each has had a chance to share, take time to share present feelings about these decisions.

Note: the decision to stay or not should NOT be judged by others. It may be more honest for some to grow elsewhere in Christ.

10   BREAK

3. A Celebration of Eucharist: Gratitude For The Nine Weeks. Include some special prayer for those leaving the group and that those staying will also truly grow together in Christ. Pray thanking for the bonding of the group and growth of faith.

Prayer for the Week:

Choose 'favourite' passages from the last few months.

UNIT II

ON BEING HUMAN – INTEGRATING MATTER AND MEANING

Thrust: Over the last months we have come together to discover more of what it means to become a follower of Jesus. We have had the opportunity to experience how God works within the reality of our lives. Our purpose in the first Unit was to open ourselves in order to appreciate the Trinity's love for us and for others, to let their revelation shed light on our lives and to do this as a group so that we could gain confidence in the resource the Lord gives us: the presence of Jesus among us. Jesus left us community!

In Unit II, we will attempt to see what being human means for us, how we express that which is most meaningful for us, individually and collectively, both within society and within the church. This approach will include reflection on the value of material reality in our lives, sorting out what is humanizing from what is dehumanizing. We thus hope to let the Trinity have their rightful place and creatures theirs, knowing and choosing more clearly what helps us to follow Jesus and rejecting what is destructive.

Since God took human and material reality seriously enough for Jesus to be the Son Incarnate, we too are invited to express our faith externally: as we grasp more the significance of the gift of all creation, we hope to discover new ways of celebrating tangibly our gratitude. This thrust includes awareness of imagination, feelings and society's impact on us; as such it becomes gradual preparation for Units III and IV.

Process: The process simply involves reflection on our own experience to see how symbols (images or signs of our physical reality) emerge in our own lives, in society (through advertising) and in the church. We will look at these in the light of the gospel values incarnated by Jesus and conclude with a common celebration.

Week 1 Reflecting On Personal Symbols

Week 2 What Does It Mean To Be Human?

Week 3 Reflecting On Society's Symbols As Presented In Advertising

Week 4 Who Decides Society's Way Of 'Being Human'?

Week 5 Comparing Society's Way Of 'Being Human' With The Gospel's

Week 6 Taking Human And Material Reality Seriously: Incarnation

Week 7 How The Church Helps Us To Be Human

Week 8 Community Reflection And Celebration Of 'Being Human' Through Preferred Symbols

Week 9 Celebration Of Gratitude With Preferred Symbols

Goals:
● to support each other in trust, to be encouraging so that members will be strengthened, to take time for prayer

● to become more aware of what being human means for us and how we can express this symbolically

● to recognize how our symbols help us to know that which is a value for us and that they reinforce these values

● to become more aware of society's symbols and the attitudes they convey so that we may choose with greater understanding/freedom which way to follow

50

- contrast society's standards, promises and ability to fulfill hopes with the gospels' way of life since they seem to appeal to two different realities within us
- to appreciate the worth of all material reality and to treasure it as gift from the Creator for all rather than making an idol of it
- to integrate our interior life with our external realities; to realize that our outward expression is the real test of what we say we believe.

REFLECTING ON PERSONAL SYMBOLS

Purpose: At the last meeting, the members expressed publicly their decision to continue or not to continue. Now those who wish are invited to formalize their decision to remain through a prayerful commitment. The members are then presented with a general overview of Unit II: all of us, individually and collectively, carry God's image in us inviting us to become completely human, like Jesus. Unit II stresses the role of created goods in our lives. What happens when they have meaning beyond their actual use or worth: such as a coloured cloth that becomes a flag one is willing to die for. Material reality then takes on the value of a symbol. What are these symbols that shape our lives, hopes and dreams? How are we affected by them? Can they be used to make us richer/poorer persons? How did Jesus react to them? These are some of the questions that will now be examined. An article is included for extra background reading.

Have a Christ candle and enough other candles (any size) to represent the number of participants in the group ready for use in the introductory commitment. Have some objects on a table; for example, plant, pine cone, dollar bill, ring.

Minutes

5   1. Sing a hymn and lead a prayer asking to be filled with gratitude: for all that has been meaningful for you, gratitude for the great gift of your life, and gratitude for the ability to think, remember, cherish, feel various emotions, communicate, choose, be sorry, and generally, for being human!

5   2. Give an overview of this unit (see introductory thrust and process). Pause briefly.

5   3. Group contract: As a sign of your commitment to the group for this journey and to daily prayer,

we invite you to light a candle and place it near the Christ candle. Sing or play some music while doing this.

50 4. Reflect on and discuss:

a) Think of something that is meaningful to you; for example, a ring, an anniversary, sitting by a fire on a river, seeing a tree blowing in the wind, a picture, a meal with a loved one. Choose anything you like and simply remember how it came to mean something to you. Let your imagination capture it again and let your feelings emerge.

b) What do you think 'symbol' means? How does it relate to what we just discussed? Possibly read paragraph 3 of the article on 'Symbol' (see end of week) and comment on it.

c) What are some personal symbols that help you appreciate, understand and express yourself and your relationships (clay vessels, old slippers, new car, a trophy, a song, etc.).

d) Has any symbol lost or changed its meaning for you?

e) What are some universal symbols?

10 BREAK

15 5. Read Mark 2:15-17 (meal); Luke 11:33-36 (lamp), 4:26-29,30-32 (seeds); and Mark 12:41-44 (widow's mite).

Ponder quietly for about 10 minutes what symbols seemed to be meaningful to Jesus. Ask him! Focus on one that appeals to you and be with Jesus as he tells you about it.

10 6. Share examples of symbols he used and how he spoke about them. List these.

20   7. Journal: What did you experience interiorly this evening? What does this indicate for you? How would you describe what the group experience included tonight?

Share these briefly.

20   8. Prepare Prayer for the Week by discussing the options given in 'A' and reminding all about review of prayer and journal.

10   9. Conclude with prayer.

Prayer for the Week:

(A) Possibly take a few days for each of the following ways:

i)   Remembering one of your symbols and talking it over, sharing it with the Lord, express your gratitude, joy, sorrow or regret as it is appropriate for you.

ii)   Read one of the following scripture passages. Ask to know Jesus and his love for you. Imagine how Jesus is feeling. Picture yourself with him and share it with him quietly or talk over something that reminds you of that from your life.

      Scripture: Mark 2:15-17
      Mark   4:26-29
      Mark   12:41-44

iii) Ponder and savour a word that means a lot to you.

(B) Review of prayer/journal. In summary, note particularly any way in which you were drawn to some words, or irritated, or anything you felt.

Possibly read the following article:

THE REVIEW OF PRAYER

After the formal prayer period is over, review what happened during that time – not so much what ideas you had, but more the movements of consolation, desolation, fear, anxiety, boredom, and so on – perhaps something about your distractions, especially if they were deep or disturbing, or what you were pondering when they started. Questions like the following may help:

- What went on during the period of prayer?
- What struck you?
- How did you feel about what went on?
- What was your mood, changes in mood?
- What did the Lord show you?
- Is there some point you should return to in your next period of prayer?

During this review, thank the Lord for his favours and ask pardon for your own negligences.

This review is an instrument to help you reflect upon the experience of the prayer period. It helps you notice your interior experiences. Thus it enables you to be spontaneous during the actual prayer time and to go with the flow of experience. If you were to monitor yourself during the period of prayer, you would be interfering with the Lord's communication. Let happen what is happening during the prayer time; afterwards take a look to see what the Lord is saying in all this.

It is helpful during this review to jot down a few reflections that strike you so that you can more easily prepare for your next period of prayer. The Lord may be inviting you to go back to a point where you were moved. St. Ignatius says, "I should remain quietly meditating upon a point UNTIL I have been satisfied" i.e., until the movement has been completed (the insight completed; the struggle resolved; the consolation ended; the meaningfulness finished . . . . for now).

Jotting down your reflections during the review is also a help for you to discuss your prayer experience with the spiritual director.

It is also helpful at the end of a prayer period to indicate the difference of this review from the prayer period by some change of place or posture: the activity of *review* is different from the activity of the prayer period.

John Veltri SJ

For extra reading:

SYMBOL

Today we hear a lot about being fully human, about our desire and need for fulfillment and self-realization. We desire to be human, not just numbers or robots. We are more than animals and meet frustration when we find ourselves just 've-getating'.

We are body-persons, one reality. Being human involves a profound simplicity and wholeness even as it encompasses a wide range of complex marvels: body, spirit, emotions, conscious and subconscious, rational and intuitive intellect, individual persons, collective identity and interdependence. (The latter will be developed in Unit V). Because of this and the fact that growth is gradual, we are constantly discovering what it means to be human. It is a mystery. As we give of ourselves in love, whether this is verbally or non-verbally, we come to discover ourselves as well as deepen what is within us. Expressing externally what is within us completes and expands ourselves. It harmonizes because the interior and exterior 'worlds' are then the same. Tears, for example, show that something is happening inside; they may spring from a person's compassion, sense of awe, self-pity, exhaustion, union with God, healing, discouragement, and so on. The experience itself may be what reveals to the person what the source is! They come spontaneously from experiences that we may not be able to understand or explain or control but they express some reality within us; they can bring healing and wholeness as our inner and outer realities are one. They can bond us to others as well. Tears are an example of what we call symbol.

Symbols may be gestures, actions, pictures, images, music, objects, or any external reality (for example, tears, a smile). They tend to arise spontaneously from significant moments, relationships, tradition, surprising coincidences, meaningful experiences. We may discover that some experiences are simply too rich to describe, or we cannot explain it or we have not grasped the meaning of them yet. But there are ways we remind ourselves and share with others that go beyond words (though words too are important symbols!). The expression of what is deepest in ourselves is what we call symbol. Our bodies, for example, actually express our inner realities. It is natural for us to create symbols. They not only embody in time and space what is meaningful for us and who we are; they strengthen the initial awareness, appreciation, knowledge or love in us. They also become means of communicating with others.

Receiving is obviously important too. We 'become real' in knowing and by receiving others' expressions of their knowing and loving. We affirm others or support their being more human when we recognize their symbols.

Jesus is the symbol of God. A children's song captures this, "Jesus is God's show and tell"; Jesus reveals God is present with us (Col. 2:9). These statements explain what we mean when we say that Jesus is the sacrament (making present) of God.

In Unit III we will center our attention on knowing the historical Jesus.

In Units IV and V we will ponder more of the mystery of the body of Christ today, his kingdom and our celebration of these realities.

In this unit, we want to remember how the Trinity expresses themselves in all creation, humanity, and all our history; we gradually realize that we ourselves are symbols of their presence; we are made in the image and likeness of God. Their presence is real in us and in others for us. As a symbol or expression of their life, *all* creation is inseparable from the reality they are.

WHAT DOES IT MEAN TO BE HUMAN?

Purpose: As creatures, we were put on this earth for a purpose: to become human. But the picture of what
this entails is not very clear. All too often, humans
present themselves as no more than a mass of
needs. The purpose of this meeting is for us to filter
out our true calls and needs from the chaff; this will
be done by succinctly examining various levels of
needs as presented by psychology, advertising and
the Gospel. Elements of this examination would
then become part of our prayer.

Minutes

10   1. Begin by leading the following exercise:

Lord we ask for light to realize what being human means to you. (Pause)

Imagine a potter fashioning a clay vessel that is
very special to him/her and how s/he delights in
the creation.

Let us remember the poetic image of our creation, an image that has been retold for generations:

Imagine God creating the universe, all of
nature, and finding it all very good. Imagine the Trinity taking clay and forming persons who are of the earth (pause); yet they
breathe their own life into them. (Pause)
They delight in making man and woman in
their own image and as companions for
each other and God walks in the garden
with them (Pause). They are God's people
and God entrusts the care of all the rest of
creation to them making them stewards and
co-operators in the divine expression of
love. God is with them and finds them very
good. This lord of the universe, our creator
is with us now and desires to be God for us!

5   2. Quiet reflection on the above.

40   3. Share any part of your experience of prayer last week.

10   BREAK

70   4. Discuss:
    a) What are your hopes and expectations in life?
    b) i) What does it mean to be human?
       ii) What are some of your needs that are already being met?
       iii) How do we distinquish between needs and desires?
    c) What are two or three messages of the gospel that you consider most important?
    d) i) Explain briefly A. Maslow's pyramid of needs.

Self-actualization

(which includes being for

others, loving, bringing

about peace, justice)

Esteem

Belonging

Safety

Physiological Needs

(food, shelter, clothing)

People must have the elementary needs of adequate food, shelter, clothing, and safety met before they will be concerned about higher needs of belonging, esteem and justice. When each need is met, it is natural to move further up the scale and to find satisfaction there. The fact that people are concerned about the esteem of others suggests that their physiological needs are being adequately met. Health and body fitness are other physiological needs that must be met but are sometimes given excessive attention today (in North America, at least) by some. The greatest fulfillment even on a natural level comes when people are self-actualized; that is, motivated from within to be for others, to love, to work for peace and justice, even when there is suffering involved (and possibly loss now of other 'basic' needs). It is inherent in our nature to move toward these. When we say this is unreal, we close off our real humanity and God's desire to work through us.

Since we are in the midst of a great amount of family breakdown and rugged individualism there seems to be a real lack of a sense of belonging and esteem in our society. Advertising appeals to our need for esteem, intimacy and peace but suggests that these can be bought. Purchasing superfluous amounts of initial human needs (richer fashions, luxurious eating, exclusive furnishings, 'body beautiful'), it is suggested, will give us human fulfillment. It becomes evident, however, that this excessive focus of our time, energy and resources locks us into the first level of human needs and leaves us there, — dissatisfied.

ii) How do your responses # a), b), and c) compare with Maslow's hierarchy of needs?

e) i) What does advertising say it means to be human?

ii) What does advertising promise us?

iii) To what do ads appeal and how do they suggest that needs be met?

f) What does the gospel say it means to be human?

g) Compare b)i), e)i), and f).

5   5. Journal and brief sharing: What did you experience and realize this evening?

5   6. Prepare Prayer for the Week and invite members to bring in ads for II-3, #1 and #3 a).

5   7. End with prayer and a hymn.

Prayer for the Week:

Scripture Prayer.

Read one of the following scripture passages. Ask the Lord to give you his Spirit of wisdom and love that you may recognize what helps you to grow, especially in cherishing relationships (with the Trinity and any people you meet this week).

Mark	1:14-15
Mark	12:13-17
Mark	12:28-34
Galatians	5:1,2,13
Philippians	3:7-14
Colossians	2:2-3

WHAT DOES 'BEING HUMAN' MEAN?

We are body-persons. It was unthinkable for the Hebrew to consider being without a body; even after death, we would be transformed into a new spiritual body (I Cor. 15). We express both the good (the wholeness) and the conflict (or disintegration) that are in us in and through our bodies. Rooted in the world, we are present to things and they to us through the senses. So others and all material reality affects us, our inner reality through the body. We belong not just to ourselves but to the world in mutual interdependence. Even our actual freedom depends on the extent to which we will accept each other in love and respect.

Being human means that we are not God. We share the life of the Father, Son and Spirit and can relate intimately with them because of their initiative. Being human means that we have definite gifts and limitations. On the other hand, being human distinguishes us from animals. "Human" implies heart, intelligence, will, conscience, openness to the divine. It means being able to communicate, to be compassionate, wise, humble, caring, responsible, forgiving, interdependent, and trusting. This is far from any definition that limits being human to bursts of temper, theft and competition, addiction of any kind, especially when these are promoted as goals or criteria of acceptance.

So, being human includes being temporal, weak, dependent on God and interdependent with others; it involves gradual growth in all aspects. We become more and more human as we develop our potential, individually and collectively in the Lord. "The glory of God is person fully alive in the image of Jesus" (Irenaeus).

In fact, the Christian reality is that God became a particular man, Jesus of Nazareth, and because of this, Jesus is the criteria for what is human and reputable.

REFLECTING ON SOCIETY'S SYMBOLS AS PRESENTED IN ADVERTISING

Purpose: This meeting (as well as the next) will give us a chance to integrate the content/discoveries of the last two meetings at a societal level now rather than at a personal one. Society has many mirrors of itself: the arts, the media, the school curricula, advertising and others. Because of its scope, penetration and resources, advertising offers us an excellent source of analysis.

Others' symbols affect us profoundly, particularly if they are shared public symbols such as those in advertising and media. The effects of these common symbols are also multiplied and extended when we communicate with each other about them; this is particularly true if the shared experiences are part of the public domain. Advertising symbols and slogans become a familiar part of our culture and generally leave us accepting them without much conscious decision.

Personal and societal symbols can be humanizing or dehumanizing depending on their motivation, mode of expression, intent and effects. Members are therefore invited to examine the impact advertising has on their lives and to integrate this in their prayer.

Minutes

15 1. Hymn and prayer. Ask for light to recognize what society is telling us, especially in the ads you brought and for wisdom to know how it is humanizing or dehumanizing.

Reflect quietly on your experience of prayer and daily events of the past week in the light of Luke 14:7-11.

45 2. Sharing of some awareness in prayer and daily living.

63

10 BREAK

60 3. Advertising and us.

a) Use ads brought by the group to see how advertising uses each of the following: the body, age, success, status, the individual (me) and time (immediate self gratification), emotions, products as a credible substitute for human growth and as a replacement for relationships (home, family, colleagues).

(The general article and examples included this week provide background on this.)

b) How does the gospel value each of these? (Of course you are welcome to refer to other gospels and letters as well as these from Mark and Luke.) These examples are only indicative of gospel values:

Security
Mark   8:34-38   "win world and lose life?"
Mark   12:13-17   "Give to Caesar"
Luke   12:13-21   "On hoarding possessions"
Luke   16:13-15   "Use of money"

Sexuality
Luke   6:43-45   "Good tree, good fruit"
Luke   7:36-50   "Loved much"
Luke   16:18   "Adultery"

Sociability
Luke   14:7-11   "On choosing places at table"
Luke   14:12-14   "On choosing guests to be invited"
Mark   1:14-15   "Kingdom of God"
Luke   12:22-32   "Kingdom of God"

c) i) In what ways does advertising shape our attitudes?

ii) Does advertising actually help us in setting our priorities? To what extent?

iii) What makes us so vulnerable to advertising?

64

10   4. Prepare Prayer for the Week.

5   5. Reflection: What are some things you felt tonight? During the week, simply wonder what
they indicate for you.

5   6. End with prayer and a hymn.

Prayer for the Week:

Take an ad (T.V. or magazine) and reflect on it in view of
our human needs (see: Unit 2, week 2). What does it mean to
be human in this question? Read and ponder a scripture passage as it sheds light on this for you. Ask to recognize what society and the gospel are saying and to ask to be strengthened in
choosing what leads to life.

Mark 8:34-38   Luke 12:13-21
Luke 16:13-15 Luke 7:36-50
Luke 14:7-11   Luke 14:12-14

THE ADVERTISING MACHINE: PACKAGING PLASTIC HUMANS

To keep the consumer market going, people must be
aware of what is available. In Canada, a budget equivalent to
the education grants for all universities in the country is spent
each year to get people to buy. This of course is a hidden cost
which we, the consumers, pay for: we pay to be informed and
even more, we pay to be cajoled into opting for one product
rather than another. To sell, products must touch us in our
weaknesses, in our fears or in our hopes and expectations. Advertising mostly, though not alone, tells us what and who to
be, how to act and survive in society. It highlights our models,
our images and our symbols. Ultimately it teaches us our value
system. Advertising mirrors our society and must therefore be
taken very seriously: billions of dollars each year don't lie. Advertising shows us pretty, perfect bodies that we should all
have: as if God messed up creation each time any of us were
born, because we certainly don't seem to fit the image (but
then the product will give it back to us). Everybody must be a
success: if we are not up there in the social ladder, it's because
we are not wearing the right product, or we are misinformed.
Of course aging is not tolerated: people who age gracefully

don't need to buy. So by making the inevitable a problem, the market wheels spin, and so do the profits: for everybody has been taught to fear the worst part of aging, death. Products are geared to *you* and to *me:* those wonderful companies have only us specific individuals in mind when they manufacture, for example, 40 billion hamburgers. But we are so gullible; we lack self-esteem to the extent that we fall for it. Or else, the product (cars especially) promise us strong emotions that will fulfill us as human beings. Then of course, there are all those ads that humanize the product and make humans objects. Products will replace all those needs for friendship, intimacy, lasting relations, faithfulness and security. Humans can't do this as well as material objects anymore it seems. Quality has been given over to quantity, for quantity sells. Advertising does not tell us any more where we are at, but rather where we should be. Ignoring our reality, it dictates and entices our desires, fanning them into deceptive compulsions, making them appear as urgent needs. Advertising is not neutral. In some of its worst forms it can be violent and degrading, leading us to an ultimate society of plastic dolls, in constant search of new wardrobes.

Some Examples of How the Advertising Machine Gets to Us

In the same way that education was based on the three R's, our human instincts are based on the three S's: security, sexuality, and sociability. To sell their products, advertising zeroes in on creating 'needs' in these last elements. Here are some examples. It would be easy to find your own . . .

a) SECURITY: "Be *sure* with . . ." "Wake up a better person with . . . (mattress)". "At . . . (muffler) you're a *somebody*". "This pad (hygienic) will make you *feel better* 25 days a month"; to promote this for *general* use is an attempt to create a need. "Feel in tip-top shape with . . . (mineral water)". "We won't love you and leave you (computer)".

By having all, acquiring all, we become god-like and control everything. Fears are created, played upon and then solved with a product, now seen as a need. Preservation (security) becomes a power-game rather than the acceptance of our vulnerability which needs to be supplemented by the vulnerabilities of others. "I can't seem to forget you, your . . . (perfume) stays on in my mind". The product becomes so overwhelming that it replaces us. The product becomes the reality and we become the illusion. Additive products not only express our personalities, they actually replace us. The security the product promises is nothing but an illusion.

b) SEXUALITY: "Men can't help acting on . . . perfume". "Jeans for lovers". "(a shirt on him) . . . the next best thing to skin (now on her)". "I'm more satisfied (cigarettes)". Relationships between men and women are now worked out to the fine art of the *mating* game. No pain, no commitment, just instant attraction as long as it works out. It is mindless, involving no use of intelligence nor creativity and it is heartless, involving no deep interpersonal relationship. Sex, with all its nuances for that companionship of the prince or princess charming, sells; especially, it gets people to look twice at the product and at least subconsciously to expect its promise.

c) SOCIABILITY: "Do you want a meaningful relationship? One that won't tie you down? Then buy . . . radio". "Do you want to improve your social life? Try . . . (punch)". The same is said of lipstick, beer, cars, etc. "Friends wherever you go . . . (hotel chain)". "Fill your child's room with 'friends' not just with furniture . . .". "A home away from home (credit card)". "This (photocopier) seems to like Fenwick". "Toys that will love you back".

One of the greatest unspoken ills of our society is loneliness. We have forgotten how to relate gratuitously with one another; our relationships are formal or efficiency-oriented. Because relationships appear more complicated, we replace them with simpler ones, pets or things. Things ultimately clutter up and mask our loneliness. But at the same time, things become more important than people (our T.V., our computer, our car, our collection, our house, etc.). We tend to define the interpersonal by the *things* we can talk about: we value a child by the pretty dress or suit worn. And advertising constantly feeds the need we have to be appreciated.

For further reflection, read Wisdom 13,14,15.

WHO DECIDES SOCIETY'S WAY OF 'BEING HUMAN'?

Purpose: Prayer gives understanding and courage to face some disturbing realities. The meeting opens up with such a prayer and an invitation to share the past week's high and low points. The topic then turns to: who decides that which society expresses as being human? Why? This topic will surely challenge us and feelings should be allowed to be expressed openly or in the journal. Prayer and time may be needed to heal gently the changing vision of the world this meeting might bring about.

Minutes

15   1. Hymn, prayer: presence, light and gratitude.

Ask for a great and growing confidence in the power of the Holy Spirit to give us wisdom, understanding and courage as we face society's impact on us.

Quiet prayer with Mark 10:35-40.

50   2. Share from your reflection during the week.

10   BREAK

50   2. Discuss the following:
a) How does the size and pervasiveness of the advertising effort touch you?
b) Who controls advertising? The producer? The consumer? How?
c) Who benefits from advertising? The producer? The consumer? How?
d) If advertising convinced us completely, what would the world look like? How human would it be? would we be?
e) How does advertising succeed in filling our essential human needs? Why can't it?
f) What does advertising do to our faith? What are some of today's idols?

69

g) What are some criteria for good advertising?

10   4. Reflection:

What was happening within you and in the community this evening? Share briefly on this.

Minutes

10   5. Prepare Prayer for the Week and conclude with prayer and hymn.

Prayer for the Week:

Ask daily to be open to the Spirit and both gentle and generous in your response.

DAY 1 What do you think/feel about our discussion with the community? Ponder with the Lord: what does this mean for you?

DAY 2 Psalm 115:2-9

DAYS 3 and 4

Read and ponder the following excerpt from the letter "Redeemer of People" by Pope John Paul II, 1979.

DAY 5 Wisdom 12:15-18

DAY 6 Business is based on maximization of profits. The scripture approach is maximization of prophets. Where do you fit now? Be with the Lord and talk over your concerns.

PROGRESS OR THREAT

If therefore our time, the time of our generation, the time that is approaching the end of the second millennium of the Christian era, shows itself a time of great progress, it is also seen as a time of threat in many forms for us. The Church must speak of this threat to all people of good will and must always carry on a dialogue with them about it. Our situation in the modern world seems indeed to be far removed from the objective demands of the moral order, from the requirements of justice, and even more of social love. We are dealing here only with that which found expression in the Creator's first message to man and woman at the moment in which he was giving them the earth, to "subdue" it. This first message was confirmed by

70

Christ the Lord in the mystery of the Redemption. This is expressed by the Second Vatican Council in these beautiful chapters of its teaching that concern our "kingship", that is to say our call to share in the kingly function of Christ himself. The essential meaning of this "kingship" and "dominion" of people over the visible world, which the Creator himself gave us for his task, consists in the priority of ethics over technology, in the primacy of the person over things, and in the superiority of spirit over matter.

This is why all phases of present-day progress must be followed attentively. Each stage of that progress must, so to speak, be x-rayed from this point of view. What is in question is the advancement of persons, not just the multiplying of things that people can use. It is a matter — as a contemporary philosopher has said and as the Council has stated — not so much of "having more" as of "being more". Indeed there is already a real perceptible danger that, while our dominion over the world of things is making enormous advances, we should lose the essential threads of our dominion and in various ways let our humanity be subjected to the world and become something subject to manipulation in many ways — even if the manipulation is often not perceptible directly — through the whole of the organization of community life, through the production system and through pressure from the means of social communication. We cannot relinquish ourselves or the place in the visible world that belongs to us; we cannot become the slave of things, the slave of economic systems, the slave of production, the slave of our own products. A civilization purely materialistic in outline condemns us to such slavery, even if at times, no doubt, this occurs contrary to the intentions and the very premises of its pioneers. The present solicitude for humanity certainly has at its root this problem. It is not a matter here merely of giving an abstract answer to the question: Who are we? It is a matter of the whole of the dynamism of life and civilization. It is a matter of the meaningfulness of the various initiatives of everyday life and also of the premises for many civilization programmes, political programmes, economic ones, social ones, state ones, and many others.

If we make bold to describe the situation of people in the

modern world as far removed from the objective demands of the moral order, from the exigencies of justice, and still more from social love, we do so because this is confirmed by the well-known facts and comparisons that have already on various occasions found an echo in the pages of statements by the Popes, the Council and the Synod. Peoples' situations today are certainly not uniform but marked with numerous differences. These differences have causes in history, but they also have strong ethical effects. Indeed everyone is familiar with the picture of the consumer civilization, which consists in a certain surplus of goods necessary for persons and for entire societies — and we are dealing precisely with the rich highly developed societies — while the remaining societies — at least broad sectors of them — are suffering from hunger, with many people dying each day of starvation and malnutrition. Hand in hand go a certain abuse of freedom by one group — an abuse linked precisely with a consumer attitude uncontrolled by ethics — and a limitation by it of the freedom of the others, that is to say those suffering marked shortages and being driven to conditions of even worse misery and destitution.

This pattern, which is familiar to all, and the contrast referred to, in the documents giving their teaching, by the Popes of this century, most recently by John XXIII and by Paul VI, represent, as it were, the gigantic development of the parable in the Bible of the rich banqueter and the poor man Lazarus. So widespread is the phenomenon that it brings into question the financial, monetary, production and commercial mechanisms that, resting on various political pressures, support the world economy. These are proving incapable either of remedying the unjust social situations inherited from the past or of dealing with the urgent challenges and ethical demands of the present. By submitting us to tensions created by ourselves, dilapidating at an accelerated pace material and energy resources, and compromising the geophysical environment, these structures unceasingly make the areas of misery spread, accompanied by anguish, frustration and bitterness.

We have before us here a great drama that can leave nobody indifferent. The person who, on the one hand, is trying to draw the maximum profit and, on the other hand, is paying the price in damage and injury is always a human being. The drama is made still worse by the presence close at hand of the privileged social classes and of the rich countries, which accumulate goods to an excessive degree and the misuse of whose riches very often becomes the cause of various ills. Add to this the fever of inflation and the plague of unemployment — these are further symptoms of the moral disorder that is being noticed in the world situation and therefore requires daring creative resolves in keeping with our authentic dignity.

Such a task is not an impossible one. The principle of solidarity, in a wide sense, must inspire the effective search for appropriate institutions and mechanisms, whether in the sector of trade, where the laws of healthy competition must be allowed to lead the way, or on the level of a wider and more immediate redistribution of riches and of control over them, in order that the economically developing peoples may be able not only to satsify their essential needs but also to advance gradually and effectively.

This difficult road of the indispensable transformation of the structures of economic life is one on which it will not be easy to go forward without the intervention of a true conversion of mind, will and heart. The task requires resolute commitment by individuals and peoples that are free and linked in solidarity. All too often freedom is confused with the instinct for individual or collective interest or with the instinct for combat and domination, whatever be the ideological colours with which they are covered. Obviously these instincts exist and are operative, but no truly human economy will be possible unless they are taken up, directed and dominated by the deepest powers in us, which decide the true culture of peoples. These are the very sources for the effort which will express our true freedom and which will be capable of ensuring it in the economic field also. Economic development, with every factor in its adequate functioning, must be constantly programmed and realized within a perspective of universal joint development of each individual and people, as was convincingly recalled by my Predecessor Paul VI in Populorum Progressio. Otherwise, the category of "economic progress" becomes in isolation a superior category subordinating the whole of human existence to its partial demands, suffocating people, breaking up society, and ending by entangling itself in its own tensions and excesses.

It is possible to undertake this duty. This is testified by the certain facts and the results, which it would be difficult to mention more analytically here. However, one thing is certain: at the basis of this gigantic sector it is necessary to establish, accept and deepen the sense of moral responsibility, which we must undertake. Again and always human person.

This responsibility becomes especially evident for us Christians when we recall — and we should always recall it — the scene of the last judgment according to the words of Christ related in Matthew's Gospel.

This eschatological scene must always be "applied" to human history; it must always be made the "measure" for human acts as an essential outline for an examination of conscience by each and every one: "I was hungry and you gave me no food . . . naked and you did not clothe me . . . in prison and you did not visit me". These words become charged with even stronger warning, when we think that, instead of bread and cultural aid, the new States and nations awakening to independent life are being offered, sometimes in abundance, modern weapons and means of destruction placed at the service of armed conflicts and wars that are not so much a requirement for defending their just rights and their sovereignty but rather a form of chauvinism, imperialism, and neocolonialism of one kind or another. We all know well that the areas of misery and hunger on our globe could have been made fertile in a short time, if the gigantic investments for armaments at the service of war and destruction had been changed into investments for food at the service of life.

This consideration will perhaps remain in part an "abstract" one. It will perhaps offer both "sides" an occasion for mutual accusation, each forgetting its own faults. It will perhaps provoke new accusations against the Church. The Church, however, which has no weapons at her disposal apart from those of the spirit, of the word and love, cannot renounce her proclamation of "the word . . . in season and out of season". For this reason she does not cease to implore each side of the two and to beg everbody in the name of God and in the name of people. Do not kill! Do not prepare destruction and extermination for people! Think of your brothers and sisters who are suffering hunger and misery! Respect each one's dignity and freedom!

Pope John Paul II
Redeemer of People #16

COMPARING SOCIETY'S WAY OF BEING HUMAN WITH THE GOSPEL'S

Purpose: During the past meetings there has been an attempt to examine what value we place on things and how we associate this with becoming human. Much of this depends on our vantage point. As christians, everything needs to be viewed through the filter of the Gospel. This will be the thrust of the next two meetings. In particular, this time, there will be an effort to contrast social goals and attitudes with those of the Gospel, allowing us to be more critical of the way in which we say and wish to follow Jesus.

Minutes

15   1. Begin with a hymn and prayer, remembering the presence of the Father, Son and Spirit, asking for light and giving thanks.

Ask for the grace to experience what the way of the Gospel involves today and to be strengthened in following Jesus.

Quiet prayer, reflecting on the experience of the week and my response to it in light of Mark 8:34-38.

50   2. Share any of this.

10   BREAK

50   3. Alternate activities. Choose a), b), or c). The article at the end may assist you in this.
a) Use chart paper to compare the consumer way of life with the Gospel way of life.
b) What in our culture is truly humanizing but is not supported in advertising and media? Why is it not supported?
c) Discuss how a christian vision on consumerism (prayer, community, life-style, social justice and tithing of time, etc.) could radically transform our present culture.

10   4. Reflection and sharing on what happened in you
     and in the community this evening.

10   5. Prepare Prayer for the Week.

5   6. Conclude with praying and/or singing.

Prayer for the Week:

Ask daily for a great and growing confidence in the power
of the Holy Spirit to give you wisdom, understanding and
courage as you face society's impact on you.

1. What do you feel about our discussion with the community? Ponder with the Lord: what does this mean for
   you?

2. Do you now desire to follow Jesus, to be christian? What
   does this mean for you in our time?
   Mark 10:14-45 (leadership with service)

3. Reflect on the article "On Slavery and Freedom in the
   Commodity Way of Life".

4. Mark 12:13-17 (Give to Caesar . . . God)

5. Consider the persons in your community and family. Is
   there any way you can share some of your insights and
   searching with them? Be with the Lord who loves them.

6. Remember a moment of joy, fear, hope or anger you felt
   in relation to advertising. Ponder with the Lord how he is
   leading you in that.

ON SLAVERY AND FREEDOM IN THE COMMODITY WAY OF LIFE

When asked what they wish to be freed from the most,
people usually answer: fear. Fear of the unknown, fear of tomorrow, fear of what other people think, fear brought about
by insecurity. As limited human beings, we cannot manage to
control everything: surprises, some more interesting than
others, keep on popping up in our lives. So we set about building buffer walls, acquiring things that will make us less vulnerable, and become fortresses unto ourselves. Once secure, we

have no need for anyone. "I am a rock, I am an island", sang Simon and Garfunkel, "and an island feels no pain. . .". We have just made ourselves into gods, and we are our own idols. Or maybe our material and structural props, our status or prestige (whatever 'wealth' it is based on), power or pride (religious or secular), have become our idols. Whether our addiction is high or low class, it matters little. Yet, in our attempt to be gods, we have become slaves! Is this the only way out . . . ?

> "Everyone moved by the Spirit is a child of God. The spirit you received is not the spirit of slaves bringing fear into your lives again; it is the spirit of children, and it makes us cry out, "Abba, Father".
> (Rm. 8:14-15)

The choice is very simple. We get sucked into the commodity way of life and await its salvation, its freedom, its way of "being human". Or we accept the invitation to live as children of God.

> "After saying this, what can we add? With God on our side who can be against us?" (Rm. 8:31)

But most of us prefer not to opt, not to choose but just to let things slide because it would demand a risky leap in faith. And how can we compare the assurance of the comfortable 'now' with the possibility of the painful 'tomorrow'? Yet,

> "Nothing can come between us and the love of Christ, even if we are troubled or worried, or being persecuted, or lacking food or clothes, or being threatened or attacked." (Rm. 8:35)

The choice is very simple: either a visible limited deceptive yet immediately gratifying security, OR an invisible, faith-based, unlimited, life-giving relationship.

> "For no one can follow two masters." (Lk. 16:13)

To see how attached we are to our 'pet idols' and securities, we need only ask how ready we would be to become nomads (travellers) again like the people of God were in the desert. How many suitcases would we bring along? What would we really feel is essential? Would we even be ready to divest ourselves of all our 'extras' and trust God alone as the provider of our "mannah" (food) and water? How really free are we of the consumer goods in our lives? and how could we develop as children of God? Read Gal. 5:13-26 and 1 Peter 2:16.

TAKING HUMAN AND MATERIAL REALITY SERIOUSLY: INCARNATION

Purpose: One of the main reasons christians suffer a body/ soul split or a Monday/Sunday split is because there is not sufficient awareness of the fact that the Creator Lord is also the saving Lord. Salvation is part of creation and not vice-versa. This meeting hopes to open us up to the beauty of material reality and especially of our troubled, battered planet by reflecting on the reality of incarnation, on its fascinating mystery (Phil. 2:6-7) and on the effect that this awareness could have on our lives.

Minutes

15   1. Hymn, prayer: presence, light and thanks.

Ask to appreciate all of creation in its rightful place so that we may praise, reverence and serve the God of creation, incarnation and redemption in all aspects of our life.

Quiet prayer using John 1:1-5, 9-14.

40   2. Share some of your experience of prayer and daily life, especially how each affects the other.

10   BREAK

50   3. Reflect on and discuss:

     a) What does the word incarnation mean? (Possibly refer to the article.)

     b) Read John 1:9-14 and 18, Romans 8:19-23. What does incarnation mean in our faith.

     c) What would taking the incarnation seriously mean for us?

     d) What is the role of material goods in salvation (wholeness)?.

     e) What does this mean for issues of ecology, pollution in our global village? (Gen. 2:15)

10   4. Reflection and sharing on what you heard and felt this evening. How well did members listen,

and confidently share their views? Share your responses; encourage all!

5   5. Prepare Prayer for the Week and conclude with prayer, song.

Prayer for the Week:

Ask daily to appreciate all of creation in its rightful place so that you may praise and serve the God of creation and incarnation in all aspects of our life.

1. With the Lord, reflect on your participation with the community. Express your gratitude and concerns to him and ask how he is calling you to further growth.

2. Lk. 1:26-38.

3. Be aware of your body, of creation, the world (material reality) around you. Thank the Lord for each.

4. John 1:9-14.

5. What would taking the incarnation seriously mean for you?
Colossians 1:15-20, 2:9.

6. What place do material goods have in your life?
Wisdom 11:21-27.

INCARNATION

Consider . . . Our whole attitude toward material reality also profoundly affects our understanding of religion and what living our faith means. Spirituality for example, cannot be only a privatized, interior experience without manifesting (incarnating) this love in all relationships, social structures and way of using all created things. Spirituality encompasses all of life; in authentic spirituality, people allow themselves to be more and more dominated by the Spirit of the risen Lord and to be brought together in him. Spiritual life is life dominated by the Spirit bringing us to life in Christ, one with Father, responsible for our human community.

Religion that over-spiritualizes is as heretical as a consumer model that insists only on a god of things. Both realities are important: *God in flesh*. We can have symbols, therefore, not with things as ends in themselves but as expressions of ourselves and as arrows to the creator. We need to celebrate the godliness of all things because they are gifts and signs of God. They give rise to gratitude and meaning in us. In letting the Lord have his rightful place in our lives, we can (and must) take material reality seriously as creature rather than idol; material reality too is godly. Concerns of ecology are directly related to *living* our faith (as are the areas of social services and politics). Because we believe in the God of creation, incarnation and salvation (wholeness of the universe with him), we oppose both materialism and spiritualism.

God is incarnate (made flesh) with us. Jesus was present (body-person) for compassion, healing, hugging. How is God present to others through my body (senses, presence). How important is my body in expressing compassion? Do I use symbols to express compassion?

The church is human and needs symbols, visible signs. The church is a people called to be aware of gifts and to know the reality they symbolize.

HOW THE CHURCH HELPS US TO BE HUMAN

Purpose: Going one step further, if material reality is good and at the service of the humanization process, how can the Church use these elements in its symbols so as to foster a clearer sense of compassion among the followers of Jesus? Material 'goods' are only truly 'good' in their common destination for all (com-passion) and not in their particular hoarding by some (passion). Time will also be allotted here to reflect and to prepare a celebration expressing our awareness of material reality in our lives.

Minutes

15 1. Hymn, prayer: presence, light, thanks.

Ask to appreciate all of creation in its rightful place so that we may praise, reverence and serve the God of creation, incarnation and redemption in all aspects of our life.

Quiet prayer using Wisdom 11:24-27.

50 2. Share what is happening to you in prayer and life especially as it is related to interior deepening and/or change of attitudes in regard to being human.

10 BREAK

60 3. Reflect on and discuss:
   a) What are the symbols the church uses? List many (for example, water, fire, a married couple, particular gestures . . .).
   b) How did they become symbols for us? Do they still have meaning for us today?
   c) How important is the body (all the senses) earth, all creation in the church?
   d) What are some examples of how Jesus used his senses and creation? How did Jesus use his body in his relating to others? Express compassion, healing, touching?

83

Examples:

Mark 1:31 he took Peter's mother-in-law by the hand

Mark 1:35 long before dawn, he got up . . . went off to a lonely place and prayed there

Mark 1:41 Jesus touched him (leper)

Mark 2:16 eating with sinners

Mark 4:38 he was in the stern, asleep

Mark 7:34 he put his fingers into the man's ears and touched his tongue with spittle

Mark 8:23 he took the blind man by the hand . . . then putting spittle on his eyes and laying his hands on him . . .

Mark 10:16 he put his arms around them

Mark 10:21 Jesus looked steadily at him and loved him

Mark 11:15 he upset the tables

– – – any parables

e) How is the church, the body of Christ, present to the world in the same way Jesus' body was present to the world i.e., in compassion?

f) How seriously is the church taking incarnation? (Salvation of the whole world) How do we include material realities in the celebration of our faith?

g) What new symbols would you use for the church today?

10   4. Reflection and sharing on what is happening in you and the community.

10   5. Prepare Prayer for the Week.

10   6. Conclude with praying and/or singing.

Prayer for the Week:

Ask to appreciate all of creation in its rightful place so that we may praise, reverence and serve the God of creation and incarnation in all aspects of our life.

1. Ponder with the Lord what you heard and felt during the community gathering. Ask the Lord how he is leading you in this. Respond in your own way.

2. Romans 8:20-23.

3. Ponder with the Lord how you can 'translate' your insights to practical experience within your relationships and daily life; e.g., if you have come to know the Lord of light possibly put candles on the table for supper. 'Speak' in language other family members are interested in.

4. Romans 8:35-39.

5. Reread the article "Incarnation" from Unit II Week 6. Ponder it with the Lord.

6. Romans 1:18-22.

COMMUNITY REFLECTION AND CELEBRATION OF 'BEING HUMAN' THROUGH PREFERRED SYMBOLS

Purpose: The time has come for an integration of all that has gone on over the last months. There will be a period of evaluation and a celebration expressing gratitude for being human, i.e., materially-rooted creatures. The proposed celebration should not take the form of a eucharist, but be the result of the common creative imagination of the group.

Minutes

15   1. Hymn, prayer: presence, light, and gratitude.

Ask the Lord for his Spirit of confidence, wisdom and courage for this community so that you may respond to the Lord's invitation for you in the particular circumstances of your life.

Quiet prayer using Colossians 3:5-17.

50   2. Share any inner experience that you experienced in prayer or in daily life as it relates to last week's theme.

10   BREAK

50   3. Reflect and share:
   a) What have you found most helpful in these weeks?
   b) What have you found least helpful in these weeks?
   c) What are some needs for development and growth that you have?
      What steps can you begin to take to fill them?
   d) Would you call our group a community? Why/why not?
   e) How could we celebrate next week using symbols that we have reflected on in this unit? Plan it. Do we want to invite any

others? Whom? (Partners, family, pastor, other christians, others?)

15   4. Reflection and brief sharing on what happened in the group this evening (and/or individually).

15   5. Conclude with praying/singing.

Prayer for the Week:

Ask daily for the Lord's Spirit of confidence, wisdom and courage for yourself and the community so that you may respond to the Lord's invitation for you in the particular circumstances of your life.

1. Colossians 3:5-17.
2. Possibly reread some of your journal for this unit. Remember moments of insight with gratitude.
3. Recall any tension you felt during these weeks. How is the Lord leading you in that?
4. Wisdom 13:1-9.
5. Decide with the Lord whether you will continue or not with this group and what are you willing to invest in it. What hopes would you have?
6. Mk. 10:16.

CELEBRATION OF GRATITUDE WITH PREFERRED SYMBOLS

Celebrate what you prepared last week! (Refer to II-8, #3 e).

UNIT III

INTEGRATING FEELINGS AND FAITH IN DAILY LIFE: A HEALING PROCESS

Thrust: In Unit II, our purpose was to become more aware of our personal symbol-making, how we spontaneously express ourselves in external signs, how both humanizing and dehumanizing tendencies in us and those around us become concretized in society expressing and reinforcing these tendencies as well as the attitudes that emerge from them. Our ability to imagine and to feel obviously play an important role in all of this and, because of their importance, will become the focus of Unit III. Used intuitively, imagination and feelings can bring new insight into reality, release potential and hidden sources of energy; they can help us be open to new experiences, link previous concepts and images, and express ourselves creatively. Imagination and emotions are gifts that can be used for healing, and for growing in awareness, gratitude, understanding ourselves and others, as well as in relating with our God. As such, they can help bridge the gap between our faith and daily life; they can enable us to move more easily to new avenues of creativity and relationships. It is a healing process. Yet we are not healed in isolation. Our corporate need for healing deeply affects everyone. As we become more conscious of what we need to be liberated from, we can look at prevailing myths of our society which both express and reinforce attitudes for better or for worse. Can society and its vision provide the source of freedom, growth and happiness for which we long?

Process: We begin by focusing on how we can use imagination in prayer, not only to know Jesus better and be aware of our images of God, but as an effective tool in our own personal development. This leads us to consider how understanding our emotions and inner experiences can lead us to greater awareness that is the basis for integrating our faith and life, for good decision-making. While all of this is healing in itself, the last weeks touch on our need for corporate healing and how we have grasped at deceptive myths in our society.

Since this approach is becoming a way of life, we invite you to meet with and explore possibilities of linking your communities with the Christian Life Communities. (Refer to the Introduction and VI, 14-16.)

Imagination:
Week 1 Using Our Imagination: Gift Of God
Week 2 Fear: Humanizing Or Dehumanizing?
Week 3 Imagination And Our View Of God
Week 4 Gospel Images Of God
Week 5 Gospel Images Of Jesus

Emotions, Awareness Exercises:
Week 6 Emotions: Gift Of God
Week 7 Emotions And Attitudes
Week 8 Interior Experience
Week 9 Signs Of The Presence Of The Holy Spirit
Week 10 Interpreting What Happens Within Us
Week 11 How Jesus Faced His Emotions

Healing:
Week 12 Happiness According To Society (1)
Week 13 Happiness According To Society (2)
Week 14 Happiness According To Society (3)
Week 15 Reflecting On Various Ways To Happiness
Week 16 God's Vision Of Mercy, Sin And Forgiveness

Goals:
- to integrate our faith and life
- to develop and use our imagination and emotions in humanizing ways
- to know Jesus as the Gospels reveal him
- to become aware of our images of God and how Scripture reveals Father, Son and Spirit so that we can better relate to them
- to find healing of past hurts
- to become aware of our deep desires, affections and inner urges and what is causing them, so that we can interpret how the Lord is leading us within particular circumstances (awareness exercise)
- to become aware of society's vision of life and reality so that we will grasp how it can influence us and also so that our collective hurts can be healed
- to introduce formally the prayer of imagination, review of prayer, repetition, awareness exercise (individually re: societal myths)
- to celebrate the Lord's presence and action with this community

USING OUR IMAGINATION: GIFT OF GOD

Purpose: By remembering different experiences in our lives, we discover how we use a variety of senses. This is all the work of imagination and it can be used in humanizing ways for personal growth and in prayer. The latter is introduced this week. Have a picture or some card ready with the statement, "I commit myself to participating in the next 17 meetings with you and to daily prayer." Let all sign it and pray the "Our Father" while standing together in a circle.

Minutes

50 1. Hymn and prayer asking to appreciate all our gifts, how they are given to us for our own and others' good. Lead any (or all) of the following exercises: Close your eyes and relax.

a) Remember a joyful, peaceful, trusting, tender or grateful moment that you experienced in the last month. Can you hear again any words, music, sounds that were part of it? Picture again who or what you saw, touched. What feelings come now as you remember that moment? See yourself thanking person(s) involved and God for the experience. (Leave a few minutes quiet.)

b) Remember one or two different scents: special dinner, some flower, hay, perfume, . . . do they seem real again for you? (Brief quiet time).

Share any of a)and b): What did you experience?

c) Remember an experience of anger and conflict or someone's repeating a slogan that disturbs you; e.g., "you never listen . . ." or "hurry up . . ." or "she's so messy . . .". Can you hear it again? What feelings come? (Pause)

d) Picture children coming in from playing in the snow (yourself as a child, your own children or others). What do you see, hear, feel? Or remember a novel or movie when you identified with someone. (Pause for reflection)

e) Play some classical music and let whatever images or feelings that come to you emerge.

Share any of c), d), or e). What did you experience?

10   BREAK

40   2. Discuss:

a) Which senses are easiest for you to imagine?
b) What is imagination and what impact does it have on our lives?
c) What is one example of how imagination can be used in a humanizing way?
d) What is an example of how imagination can be used in a dehumanizing way?
e) How have you ever used imagination in prayer?

20   3. Lead the following for the group:

"Close your eyes and relax. Ask to know Jesus better that you may love him more and share his way of thinking, feeling and serving . . . Let yourself see, hear and feel what is happening as you hear part of the Gospel: Luke 13:10-13. (Read it aloud and pause for a few minutes of quiet reflection.) Now I will read it again and leave about five minutes for your own quiet prayer. This time, include yourself as part of what is happening, at least at a distance in the crowd, apart or up close. (Quiet prayer) Respond to Jesus in your own way because the

Lord is always present to you. (At the end of the five minutes:) Gradually become aware again of those around you. You are invited to share anything you experienced, as well as ask any questions about this approach to prayer".

15   4. Prepare for the Prayer for the Week by reading the suggested approach (below) and discussing any questions that emerge.

10   5. Journal: (quietly)

What did you feel during the meeting? If you felt encouraged, challenged or angry, impatient, irritated, what was the particular point being discussed at that moment? Was it the content spoken or the person saying it that sparked the feeling? It is very *important* for you to take that point or attitude to the Lord and ask what it means for you!

5   6. Conclude with a song or prayer.

Prayer for the Week:

The following points may help you with your daily Scripture prayer:

Each day *prepare* for prayer: come as you are. If you are tense, angry, etc. pour it out to the Lord . . . choose a reverent, open and relaxed posture.

Relax (possibly doing some exercise as in I, 1, #7) to help you be more open and trusting. Give all your loved ones and concerns to the Lord.

Consciously remember the Lord's presence with you, his unconditional love for you and how he desires to communicate with you, to be with you today in some way that is good news for you.

Desire Him:

Ask for the grace to experience how Jesus relates to others and to you personally (or ask for any other grace you need). Slowly read the gospel passage.

Be with Jesus:

Forget about looking for meanings, implications, conclusions, resolutions.

Use your imagination to see and/or hear, feel what is happening as Jesus relates to others. Notice how he feels about them, talks with them, touches them.

Let him look at you and speak to you, touch you, forgive, strengthen, console you . . . Let him take you through dryness and darkness if he prefers; trust yourself to him. You are completely dependent on him and he is totally dependable! (Some may find it easier to go as a child to meet Jesus.)

Respond to him in your own way. Be genuinely yourself and respond honestly, freely, spontaneously, reverently. Speak what is in your heart, even if you feel like complaining. Remember that when you do not know what to say, the Holy Spirit prays in you and for you.

> (These points are adapted from articles by A. Nigro, S.J. and J. Veltri,
> S.J. in Orientations I ibid p. 5-6)

Scripture: Use a passage for as many days as it is helpful:

Ask daily to experience how Jesus relates to others and to you personally.

> Luke 13:10-17
> Luke 5:29-32
> Luke 5:12-14

After the time of prayer, take time to reflect on your experience and note it briefly in your journal. Begin your prayer the next day with that part of Scripture.

Further reading:

THE ROLE OF THE IMAGINATION IN GOSPEL CONTEMPLATION

Use of imagination allows us to be present both in our conscious world and the world beyond our ordinary consciousness.

We perceive reality through our senses; we *know* something when our imagination changes the sense perception into a mental image or conscious idea. Any image in us, then, is composed of a *memory* of something experienced, together with *emotions* and *thoughts* that accompanied that sense experience.

Although all our inner senses can be involved in mental images, seeing and hearing tend to predominate over smelling, tasting and touching. All images are permanently retained within us, most often unconsciously.

Emotions and attitudes connected with experiences are often unconscious but can generally be surfaced by allowing images to speak to us. When we do this, experiences tend to be opened up even further.

Besides receiving impressions from the outer world, the imagination has a thrust, dynamism, and purpose of its own.

Occurring within us at all times, imagery can lead toward what is best; for example, our present imagination may open us up to only one possibility from which to take a stand; if, however, we use imagination to its full potential, it may present other options that will give us more possibilities through which we humanize our lives. As a gift of God, imagination is good and needs to be both developed and guided by reason, through the intuitive and rational intellect.

Imagination simply presents and juxtaposes multiple aspects of life; at times, this enables us to touch the deepest meaning of things. Since its dynamism is closely allied with the sense of play, it tends to express itself dramatically.

Ignatius of Loyola had deep insights into the importance of imagination in developing our relationships with God and others. His valuing of this function was based on assumptions such as these:

1) There is a *mystery* in life which lies just beyond our ordinary awareness. Although this mystery is available to everyone, it is present to each person in a unique way.

2) One of the human means for contacting this mystery is the *imagination*. As an instrument and place of presence, the imagination must be used wisely so that we do not let it become more powerful than the mystery.

3) To contact the deeper meanings and power behind imagery and symbols we must have *faith* that they can contain the dynamic presence of the mystery.

4) The mystery is concerned with our development as persons. Thus it is advantageous to *dialogue* with the images of the mystery – even the apparently inadequate ones.

5) Before further development of our personalities can take place, it is usually necessary to experience some *healing* or strengthening of weak areas.

6) Each of us has an *active* role in our own development towards greater wholeness.

7) There are advantages to having a *director* or guide at certain times during the journey within ourselves.

8) Imagery often takes a dramatic form. One can *enter the drama* and even change it.

9) In all use of the imagination it is important to really know and experience what we are *feeling*.

10) The insights gained through imagery need to be *grounded* in our external life.

11) *Reflection* on an imagery experience adds a new dimension of wholeness to that experience.

12) There is a special usefulness in consciously re-presenting a particular symbol or scene to ourselves in imagination. Such a *repetition* is always a moving forward.

These assumptions can be applied more specifically to prayer. In doing so we also need to keep in mind these basic facts of Christianity:

1) The symbols of Christianity are of central importance to a believer. The historical drama of Christ's life provides us with particularly meaningful scenes and symbols for interaction with the Trinity. In a very real way we all are at various places in the gospel story. Where we are and who we are at any given time God will reveal to us when we ask.

2) One of the main purposes of prayer is that through it we might choose the better way to act. The gospel message can enlighten our choices.

3) In the gospel, the pattern of death leading to life is found over and over leading up to its culmination in Christ's death – resurrection. By focusing on this mystery in prayer we become aware that the healing pattern of Christ's death – resurrection is also present in different degrees throughout our lives.

4) Our moving forward in development involves moving outward. Service to others and responsible action in the world are signs of the christian and, for Ignatius, the goal of prayer.

The new testament stories are a record of the effect Jesus' life had on the early christian community years after his death. Acutely conscious of Christ's risen presence, these people reflected on their life experiences and left us their conclusions. Their writings have become for us a major source for understanding how Christ moves through all time and space, including ours. Through imagination, we can place ourselves in these gospel scenes.

Since Christ is still living out the paschal mystery in each of us, we can discover our personal position in this mystery at any given time through imagery.

Such an exploration requires trust in the Lord, belief in the power of imagery to communicate ultimate reality, and relaxation which will allow the imagery to unfold in its own way even in contrast to the gospel message. Then we might see more clearly where we really stand in relation to Christ rather than where we would like to think we stand.

Besides the relaxation necessary to allow our personal symbolism to merge with that of the gospel, there is need of great trust that there is a "hidden self" in us through which God's power, ". . . can do infinitely more than we can ask or *imagine*." (Eph. 3:16,20). While it may at first be our surface mind and heart which is attentive to what is going on in the imagery, it is the "hidden" self which gradually grows stronger and takes over. As this happens we are called to let go of old ways.

God the Father has always intended that each of us, like Christ, surrender to becoming a true ". . . image of the unseen God." (Col. 1:15). Each of us holds within us as our "treasure" (2 Cor. 4:7) at least the seed of a unique image of the perfect Image of the invisible God.

As ". . . stewards entrusted with the mysteries of God." (1 Cor. 4:1) we could use our imaginative faculty to enter any gospel scene and discover what God cares to reveal about it in our lives at the time. In doing this, we may be surprised to find people we know among the crowd, that the background is a familiar childhood or current locale, or that Jesus has the face of a specific friend or enemy. If we bring our whole selves to prayer, it is probable that we will discover some of our "subpersonalities" in the various people and aspects of the scene and learn much through identifying with them in the imagery. For example, in contemplating the scene in which the centurion asks Jesus to heal his servant (Mt. 8:5-13), we may discover a "compassionate centurion" in ourselves. Or we may find ourselves drawn more to the sick servant and, by identifying with him, learn something about a part of ourselves that needs healing.

We can dialogue with images of negative parts of ourselves – our fear, resentment, jealousy, arrogance. We could, for instance, ask the dead daughter of Jairus in us (Mk. 5:22-24, 35-43) who she is. We may hear in reply a description of some delightful and useful quality of our childhood which we have allowed to die. We also could inquire of the mutinous tenant farmers who murdered the heir (Lk. 20:9-18) who they are, thus surfacing what lurks in us which unchecked would strangle our true life. By continuing in dialogue with images such as these, we could learn of some of the more subtle ways we deny life or hold out on God. Similarly, we could discover unsuspected and thus unaffirmed beautiful parts in ourselves; for example, accepting the "unselfish Andrew" in us who introduces his brother to Jesus (Jn. 1:42), or recognizing and affirming the "searching Nicodemus" (Jn. 3:1-21), or the "forgiving father" of the prodigal son (Lk. 15:11-32) in order to define some of our own attitudes, values, or roles.

Sometimes we may uncover emotions such as fear, anger, and jealousy which have been repressed out of the mistaken notion that they are "wrong". When unexpected emotion is uncovered, expressing it in some appropriate way, discharges some of its excess. This may at times involve anger with the Trinity who understand our feelings and love us as we are. By drawing us to themselves, they heal our fears of being disrespectful or of receiving punishment. In the very expression of the anger or whatever emotion is involved, we will probably free ourselves to move forward and discover how well God, another person, or an object involved in the imagery can "take it".

Being accepting and kind to weak parts of ourselves is not leniency. Nor is affirming and being pleased with concrete signs of the Spirit's presence in us pride or self-centredness. The overflow benefit of recognizing and releasing repressed feelings, ministering to our own hunger, alienation, and nakedness (Mt. 25:40), loving both the weak and good parts of ourselves is always a proportionate growth in love of our neighbour (Lk. 10:27).

There are more direct ways in imagery of improving our relationships with others. Practising a certain movement in imagination activates corresponding emotions and body responses in us. Thus, in time we could build up and reinforce attitudes and habits in ourselves. Identifying with a person such as the good Samaritan (Lk. 10:20-37), asking and allowing to surface what he is feeling, sensing, thinking, and doing is one way. Another is to be oneself in the imagery, being creative about one's own responses in a gospel scene. If we are never able to feel and act in imagery, we may need to question what lies behind this resistance and remove some obstacles which stand in the way of our relating to others. We could also be creative about who or what is in the imagery by bringing a specific person to Christ – who needs healing or is hurting us – and listening in on the conversation. We might take the other person's place at some point and be surprised at the change in perception that occurs.

It is especially important also to relate to the Christ in our imagery, in order to learn how to follow him better. Matthew tells us: "It is enough for the disciple that he should grow to be like his teacher" (Mt. 10:25). Such a growth can occur while imagining ourselves accompanying him to the "lonely place" where he prayed to his Father (Mk. 1:35) or sitting down to talk to him privately after the crowds leave. Jesus will teach us much through such dialoguing with him even if the image through which we encounter him is incomplete as in the "baby" Jesus. Sometimes it is good to identify with Christ in the scene, feeling, sensing, thinking as he might have while healing, praying or suffering. We watch him and let our attachment to him grow. While identifying strongly with Christ, we may then look at ourselves. For example, in contemplating Jn. 21:15-17, we might identify with Peter answering the Lord, then with the Lord speaking first to Peter in love, and after that to ourselves with the same love. Doing this identifying might help us realize more and more with St. Paul the truth of, "I live now not with my own life but with the life of Christ who lives in me." (Gal. 2:20).

Each "death" in our lives is joined to Christ's death ". . . so that as Christ was raised from the dead we too might live a new life." (Rom. 6:14).

In the dying, we find life. Sometimes we know the paralysis, illusions, complexes, blindness, and demon from which we need to be healed or freed; at other times we need to ask to know the area of woundedness and unfreedom. In either case it is helpful to stand before Christ, experiencing our pain and frustration, and to ask for and expect the relief and new life that only he has the power to give.

A special way to facilitate our awareness of the Christ in people around us is to accompany or identify with those in scripture who recognized the risen Lord. It is energizing to share the burning hearts of the disciples on the road to Emmaus (Lk. 24:13-35) or Mary Magdalene's joy when she realized who the "gardener" was (Jn. 20:11-18). The Lord may reveal himself in our imagination under the appearance of someone whom we had been seeing more superficially.

Following Christ more closely as a disciple leads us to understand more and more that he is not separate from us. We share his life, his mind and heart. Asking Christ to reveal who he is, allowing him to direct us, identifying with and living according to our images of him, all lead to the same reality; namely, that we are particular expressions of Christ's life in the world. Each person is a *unique* expression; the *full* image of the risen Lord is incomplete inasmuch as we are not true to our selves or another. Thus, imagination leads us to the image. Trusting, treasuring and aligning ourselves with the good, the true, and the beautiful in ourselves, others and all creation, enables us to recognize Christ among us (Col. 1:27), and ultimately the Trinity.

Patricia Mansfield SSND

FEAR: HUMANIZING OR DEHUMANIZING?

Purpose: By sharing from our experience of prayer in the last week, we can help each other be open to using imagination in order to help us sense Jesus' presence in some way. A discussion on when fear is humanizing and when it becomes dehumanizing can help us on our journey as we realize the extent to which we can let our imagination be a source of growth or a paralyzing influence in our lives. A further exercise in imagination can help us 'dismantle' some 'bomb' within us and allow ourselves to imagine new ways of relating.

Minutes

15   1. Hymn and prayer: presence, light and thanks. Ask to experience how Jesus desires to heal your fears and deepen your trust. Quiet prayer using Luke 13:10-17.

50   2. Share from any experience of prayer this week:

Is there any way that you sensed Jesus' presence with you?

10   BREAK

30   3. Discuss:
    a) What are some of your fears?
    b) What happens in you when you are afraid? (An image might help you express this.)
    c) When is fear humanizing? "Fear of the Lord is the beginning of wisdom." (Rom. 8:14-17)
    d) When is fear dehumanizing? "Fear is useless, what is needed is trust." (Mk. 5:36) Fear that cripples, turns us in on ourselves and paralyzes us, is essentially lack of faith in God's love and power.
    e) How can the energy generated by anger or sexual desire be directed in healthy/unhealthy ways?

f) Are emotions ever to be feared? Why do you say this?

20   4. Lead the following:

Just as we can be with Jesus in experiences of his life, we can also invite him to share with us any moments of our own lives. Today we hear so much about war and peace, bombs and active pacificism. Let us now take time to look within ourselves at these same realities. Close your eyes and think of some 'bomb' within you, any attitude of self-destruction, crippling fear, hostility, resentment, hurt, an unforgiven incident. Remember what sparked it, what was said and done, how you felt. (Pause) Let Jesus come and be with you in it. Gradually dismantle that bomb together. (Pause) Forgive the other or ask forgiveness in your imagination . . . or talk over with Jesus your inability to do it. (Pause) Let him strengthen, heal and empower you. (Pause) Imagine relating to yourself and/or others in a new way without that bomb. Let Jesus be part of this new relationship. Ask him to give you trust in God, in the gift of your own and others' lives. We will now leave about 10 minutes quiet for your own reflection and response to the Lord.

Are there any groups of people; such as, a nation, a company, a racial, or income group against whom you have a bomb? Dismantle it with Jesus (follow a process similar to the above).

Imagine one nation asking, receiving and/or offering forgiveness of another. Imagine how they would relate without bombs.

These imageries are based on experiences led by Patricia Mische (Global Education Associates)

104

10   5. Prepare for prayer during the week by reading it over and checking if there are any questions.

10   6. Journal: Note what you felt during this meeting. What were you thinking, imagining or hearing when you felt that? Did your feelings change at any time? What brought the change? What does this mean for you?

5   7. Conclude with prayer and/or singing.

Prayer for the Week:

Each day, ask for the grace to face fears with Jesus and to be filled with trust. After your time of prayer, note in your journal what you experienced interiorly (the questions on "Journal" in the meeting this week may help you).

1. Use your imagination again either to dismantle another bomb in you or to continue what you started during the meeting. Do you need to talk and pray with someone about this? If so, who?

2. Mark 10:32 – Imagine yourself with them on the road. What were they feeling?

3. Remember what you experienced yesterday in prayer. Begin prayer today with some moment of meeting Jesus or some feeling (irritation, fear, joy, anger, gratitude) that you had in that time of prayer.

4. Remember people with whom you live and work. Imagine trusting them deeply and what your relationships would be like if they are based on trust and love. Read Mark 5:36. (Fear is useless, what is needed is trust)

5. Mark 14:32-42. Imagine what Jesus felt in the garden. Be with him.

6. Remember yesterday's prayer and continue praying on some moment with Jesus; or: remember a time of fear in your own life and invite Jesus to be with you in it.

IMAGINATION AND OUR OWN VIEW OF GOD

Purpose: By sharing our experience of prayer, we desire to be a healing community and to help each other relax with prayer using any of the 'inner senses' in imagination. We will now see that what we imagine the Trinity to be like affects our relationship with them, how we pray and what we expect of community. By reflecting on this and naming it, we can become more open to true scriptural revelation of God. We are invited to know God intimately, as mother and father, as the all holy, as community of love in our midst.

Minutes

40   1. Hymn, prayer: presence, light and thanks.

Take only a few minutes quiet now to remember God's presence with us and to prepare for the sharing about one interior experience in prayer or daily life of the past week as it relates to your prayer.

Sharing.

20   2. Lead the following exercise:

"Close your eyes and relax. Remember God's presence here with us and especially with you personally. Imagine yourself with God . . . what setting are you in? What is God like for you? What is happening (action, conversation, expression . . .) between you and God? How do you feel in this meeting? How does God feel about you?"

Take 5-10 minutes to be quiet with God and simply let any images surface. Respond in your own way. Continue to take quiet time but now go back with the Trinity to see how your image of God has changed throughout your life.

15   3. Remain in this reflective mood and use crayons to draw or form symbols of different ways you have pictured God and your relationship with God throughout your life and now.

10   BREAK

45   4. Share any of the above that *you choose.*

5   5. Prepare for prayer this week by reading it over.

10   6. Journal: What did you notice most about yourself and our group during this meeting? Ask the Lord what that means for you.

5   7. Conclude with prayer and/or singing.

Prayer for the Week:

Ask each day to experience personally who the Lord is and to share his mind and heart in your life.

1. Remember both the quiet prayer and sharing during the meeting. Select one moment that you were most involved and come to God with that. Read Psalm 113.

2. Be with the Trinity as you remember your image of God throughout your life. Ask them to show you which views are true to who they are and which are false. Let them reveal, correct and heal you. End with reading Psalm 146.

3. Answer each sentence as honestly, and spontaneously as you can. Then talk them over with the Lord.
   a) For me, God is . . . .
   b) I seldom ever think of God as . . . .
   c) I feel more "in touch" with God when . . . .
   d) One "moment" in my own life when I was most aware, most conscious that God's power was working in me beyond my own limits was . . . .
   e) My prayer to God is most often . . . .
   f) For me, Jesus is . . . .
   g) I have felt the Holy Spirit active in my own personal experience when . . . .

h) What I want most of all to share with someone about my God- experience is . . . .
i) When I am "in-touch" with my own personal sinfulness, I think of God as . . . .
j) What delights me most about God is . . . .
k) When I think about God's love for me personally I am . . . .
l) For me, the surest sign of God's presence in my life is . . . .

4. Remember a false image you have (or have had) of God. Imagine yourself with God who loves you so profoundly. Together go back to how these false slogans and images grew in you and let God correct them and strengthen you in truth. Imagine yourself relating to God without that image. End by reading Psalm 68:3-10 or Wisdom 9:9-18.

5. Imagine yourself relating with God, the loving mother: Isaiah 49:15 or God, the prodigal Father: Luke 15:11,32.

6. What images of God did Jesus use? Be with Jesus as you remember them.

7. Who is the Spirit of Wisdom, or the Spirit of Love that draws us together? How has she been active in your life? Read Wisdom 9:9-18.

For further reading:

OUR EXPERIENCE OF GOD

Christianity is experiential. The mature christian lives on the word of God. All authentic christian spirituality is based on the experience of God in Jesus Christ, and until there is real encounter with Jesus Christ, until he is a person to us and we to him, we will remain at the level of a religion of law and ritual. Creeds and codes and rituals have their place. We must "live up to" the demands of faith. But it is imperative that we "live the faith". It is necessary that we move from "head knowledge" i.e., rational, factual knowledge *about God*, to *heart knowledge*, i.e., *personal insight* and commitment *to God, to Jesus as Lord, to the Spirit.*

We are the only living authority on our personal experience. We know better than anyone else what our personal experience of God is. It is important that we be aware of what our experience of God is, that we reflect on it and be able to name it.

Images of God, Images of Self, Images of Prayer

1. We are dealing with *Spiritual Awareness* (consciousness).

   Spiritual awareness is not the same as holiness. The journey of the spiritual life is not the same as the consciousness of that journey.

2. We want to be able to ALLOW God to touch our mystery.

   God is Mystery – the other. God respects our mystery. We are invited to know God intimately, as our Mother and Father, as the all holy, as a community of love in our midst.

3. Sometimes we try to reduce mystery by stereotyping the other.
   When this happens, the other is not free to communicate: feelings are filtered and twisted; noticing is prejudiced; communication is received wrongly. We prevent God from revealing His word in our experience through FALSE IMAGES.

4. Images not only influence our affective responses but they influence our expectations.

5. What is an image of God? An unreflected spontaneous attitude that influences my responses to the Lord. Hence it can be a caricature, a stereotype, a hidden belief. It is tied up with our attitudes towards life and others. It is like an imprisoned affective response. Example: think of the image a person has when s/he has been told early in life, "God is going to punish you for being bad."

   Some possible false images: tyrant, police, Santa Claus, movie director, puppeteer, chess player, architect, cat and mouse, etc.

   Example of having a false (non-biblical) image of God as a grand designer or architect and how it affects self-concepts, expectations in personal prayer and in group.

109

Image of God:	as an architect with a completed, master plan. God is impersonal, efficient, a hard ruler.
Image of God's will:	finding our way alone through a maze or completing a jig-saw puzzle. "He knows exactly what to do and how to do . . . and we don't. If only he would tell us, it would be so simple."
Image of self:	since this is the most perfect of all designs, we must work to fit into it by hard work and super efficiency. There is only one way and no room for error in self or others. Encouragement and approval of others are extremely important because worry and, nameless fears tend to paralyze. Self becomes more robot-like. There may be guilt for not 'measuring-up'.
Image of prayer:	pray as if answers are magical. Prayer is mainly pleading, uninvolved with God in a personal way, generally based on fear. It has nothing to do with experience.
	Consolation and the gift of healing of this false image may include a call to trust, to use one's own insights, to co-operate with others, to relate as a free adult with God and others.
Image of group:	people expect results, clear answers, security and rational interactions (feelings don't matter). Freedom does not fit in well and is an intellectual question. May expect others to accept the same rigid standards or to be very understanding of personal defensiveness because 'trying so hard' covers all errors.

110

On the other hand:

When a false, non-scriptural image of God is described, it is not difficult to see how it could have developed from a true insight; an analogy or image of God, however, was taken in isolation of the rest of scripture and pushed to apply to all aspects of the image instead of those intended by the authors. It is the partial-truth twisted out of context of other revelation that causes the deception. There is often projection onto God of other people's qualities especially if they are significant in our lives.

Using the previous example of God as an architect, we remember Paul's delight, "We are God's work of art, his building", but we forget the original image of the Trinity creating us as thinking, loving, social human beings befriended by them, responsible with them as co-creators for the earth. Scripture clearly reveals that God's will for us is to love God and our neighbour. The Trinity clearly promises to be with us. The history of God's people is one of relationship, of God's involvement in history, in working with us in the midst of whatever good and evil we have moved toward, and in working it all for good. We are participants, as friends, made apostles, enlivened with the Spirit of God and called to be compassionate toward all. Thus we strive together in an atmosphere of trust to discover how to live out God's will today.

6. In order to receive God's communication correctly in our own experience we have to be free from false images. Spiritual leaders should learn to recognize false images at work in dealing with others on a one-on-one or in a group situation. For example: persons insisting that they have to share everything they have experienced and have to keep talking over and over again may in fact have an image of self as an inferior person seeking the approval and strokes of the group. The image of God may be of one who has been displeased with their life choices — the image of the group may be one of having to work through their whole feeling life. If on the other hand the purpose of the group is to analyze a given situation, one can see how their images and

111

expectations can interfere with the purpose of the group.

False images can mean that the group is not free in the decision making process.

A spiritual leader should be in touch with her/his own images and expectations that flow from these; then s/he can begin to recognize these operating in others.

7. THE IMAGE OF GOD is the Risen Lord.

All images in the bible must be corrected by the IMAGE of Jesus risen. The so-called negative images that are found in the bible are examples of how disobedient and alienated people project their own alienation upon God's love; for example, a disobedient child may experience a loving father in a tyrannical way.

8. A schema:

	False	IMAGES OF	*True*
1.	Tyrant		caring
2.	Architect	GOD	honest
3.	Santa Claus		involved
4.	Only male		source of all life
1.	Battered child		worthwhile
2.	Fitting a plan	SELF	unique
3.	Needing to be good (prove oneself)		loved
1.	Saying right things		relationship
2.	Duty	PRAYER	involving experience
3.	Make self feel good		affective, honest

Adapted from an article by John Veltri SJ

GOSPEL IMAGES OF GOD

Purpose: By sharing some aspect of our prayer during the week (and/or how it relates to daily attitudes), we desire to come to know the Trinity as scripture reveals them. This week, we will continue to reflect on gospel images of God, as well as clarify what the skills of 'review of prayer' and 'repetition' are as an aid to being more aware of how the Spirit is leading us.

Minutes

15   1. Hymn, prayer: presence, light, gratitude.

Ask to know and love the Lord as he is and to grow in sharing his mind and heart in *your* own relationships.

Reflect quietly using Luke 15:1-10.

45   2. Let us share any of our insights, awareness of our images, healing or growth in how we see God.

10   BREAK

45   3. Read any of the following passages: (Images of God)

Luke 1:45-55,77-79	God: source of joy, greatness, loves the humble, scatters the proud, is mercy, light and peace
Luke 6:31-35	The Father's compassion
Luke 7:47-49	God forgives much so that we can love much
Luke 10:21-22	Entrusts everything to the Son
Luke 11:12-13	Eager to give good gifts
Luke 12:11-12,22-32	Provider
Luke 15:1-7	Rejoicing shepherd
Luke 15:8-9	Rejoicing woman

113

Luke 15:11-32	Loving father
Luke 18:9-14	Lover of the humble
Luke 20:38	God of the living

Discuss:

a) What are some scriptural images of God?

b) How did Jesus view God?

c) What are some false images of God?

d) What implications do these have for our relationship to God (including prayer) for the way we think of ourselves and for the way we relate to others?

20   4. Preparation for prayer during the week. Include clarification of what "review of prayer' and 'repetition' are. Refer to the article.

10   5. Journal.

5   6. Conclude with a hymn and prayer.

Prayer for the Week:

Prepare as usual for prayer. Ask to know Jesus' images. Read the passage and be there with Jesus as he tells you who God is. Imagine yourself relating to God as if you have this image; imagine too how you will be with God as you relate with others.

Scripture: use a passage for as many days as it is helpful!

Luke 1:45-55

Luke 6:31-36

Luke 15:1-10 or 11-32

For further reading: Reread the article, "Review of Prayer" at the end of II-1 and then the following:

REPETITION

Repetition is an important way of disposing oneself to listen to the Lord. St. Ignatius would recommend its use frequently during a directed retreat.

What Repetition is NOT

1. Repetition is not the repeating of the material for prayer as one repeats a study assignment for more thorough understanding.

2. Nor does it mean that one returns to the same matter for prayer in order to dig for something new or different.

3. Nor does it mean that one always returns to all the material of the last prayer period.

What Repetition IS

Repetition means that you return to those points where you have experienced "greater consolation, desolation or greater spiritual appreciation" (Sp. Exx. #62). Hence, return to those points where you have experienced significant movements not to the experience itself but to the points, parts in scripture where the experience occurred.

Some Examples

1. I have prayed over the scripture account of the Last Supper. In my review I notice that I have spent much time absorbed in Jesus' breaking of the bread and sharing the cup; I also notice that I had a struggle reflecting upon the persons present at the Last Supper. In the following prayer period I return to both the action of Jesus and to the various persons present.

2. I am using my imagination in praying over the Baptism at the Jordan. In my review after the period of prayer I notice that I was with Jesus but his back was to me and I had a feeling of sadness. So in the next period of prayer I return to the place where Jesus was turned away from me and the experience of sadness occurred.

3. I am praying over the hidden life of Jesus. In the review I notice that I could not get settled; that I was filled with distractions and anxiousness. So in the next period of prayer I return to the same material.

4. I am praying over my sin history and requesting from the Lord the deeper awareness of the sin effects on my life.

This is now being given to me. In my review I have a sense that the Lord desires to show me more. So I keep on returning to the same material.

Fundamentally repetition helps us listen more carefully to God's communication.

First, repetition allows spiritual movements to take place:
Since one of our goals is to discern the interior movements in ourselves, repetition is the way we allow these movements. If we move from scripture passage to scripture passage even within the same theme we tend to cut off the interior movements.

Second, repetition is a help to NOTICE interior movements:
Since many of our interior reactions at prayer happen without our noticing them, repetition gives the time for the interior reaction to be experienced more distinctly.

Third, repetition is the way we can respect God's communication:
Just because a prayer period has ended, we should not suppose that the Lord has nothing more to say to us through the particular passage we have been using. Repetition respects God's communication for we keep on returning to the same material until we sense that the Lord wishes us to move on.

Fourth, repetition is a means by which desolation becomes consolation:
As stated above, repetition is used where there has been struggle, distraction, discomfort, ennui. Often these latter experiences indicate that the Lord is trying to communicate with us at a deeper level and we are resisting His approach. When we return to those points which were experienced 'negatively' we often discover that the Lord overcomes our barriers and desolation gives way to consolation; darkness to light; struggle to surrender.

Finally, repetition helps us to experience God's mystery more deeply:
When Ignatius writes – "I will remain quietly meditating

upon the point in which I have found what I desire without any eagerness to go on till I have been satisfied." – he
means not only within the one period of prayer, but also
over several periods of prayer, and even days of prayer.
Through repetition we allow the Lord's mystery to touch
our mystery at deeper levels of our being. Often, through
repetition a kind of simplification of our own activity
takes place as we become more and more receptive to
God's activity. Often what starts off as meditation,
through the use of repetition, subsequently becomes contemplation, stillness and union.

John Veltri SJ

GOSPEL IMAGES OF JESUS

Purpose: As we share our prayer, we hope to see how the Lord leads us (to see what 'repetition' meant for us in practice) and to continue to discover and correct our image of God. Once again we will use our imagination: to see how we picture ourselves, and how Jesus considers us. We will compare this to gospel accounts of who Jesus is.

Minutes

15   1. Hymn and prayer: gratitude, presence and light.

Ask to know Jesus personally so that you may share his mind and heart, and be more for others.

Quiet reflection on scripture: Luke 1:77-79.

45   2. Share from experience of the week.

10   BREAK

50   3. a) What images did the gospel use to tell us who Jesus is in telling about his mission, suffering, death and resurrection? The following are some examples from Mark's gospel:

Title	Number of Times Used	A Few References
Master or Teacher	16	4:38; 5:35; 9:38; 10:35; 12:14; 14:14
Son of Man	15	2:10,27; 8:31,38; 9:9,12,31; 10:33; 13:26,29; 14:21
Prophet	4	6:4; 8:28
King of the Jews	5	15:2,9,12,18,26
Son of God	3	3:11; 15:40
Well beloved Son	3	1:11; 9:7
Messiah	4	14:62

The Christ	3	1:1; 8:29; 9:41
Lord	4	16:19,20
Bridegroom	3	2:19-20
Carpenter	1	6:3

Note the article at the end of this week, "A Gospel Image of Jesus: Son of Man".

b) Lead the following exercise:

"Close your eyes and relax. Let your consciousness gradually move deep within you where God dwells. Let images of how you see yourself emerge. (Pause) How do others see you? (Pause) What image of yourself do you have in relation to Jesus? Let that surface too. (Pause)."

"Ask Jesus to show you his image of you, how he considers you. (Leave about 5 minutes quiet.) Share any of this that you choose."

"How does your image of Jesus' way of relating to you compare with the gospel accounts of who Jesus is?"

10   4. Prepare for prayer during the week by recalling the meaning and purpose of repetition. Most of all, it provides time to become at ease or open to the scene, to let one's imagination and hidden responses emerge and to discover how the Lord is leading the person within his/her own experience. With extra time, the individual can relax to let intuition and feelings surface, to become aware of the simplicity and interrelatedness of experience, and to respond with the new life of healing, creativity, inner wholeness, compassion. Each day's prayer and life itself can be a continuation of the previous encounter. Gradually we come 'to know' and relate to our God in the vibrant drama of life.

5   5. Journal.

10   6. Conclude with singing/praying.

119

Prayer for the Week:

Mark 5:35-43
Mark 6:1-6
Mark 8:31-38
Mark 9:2-9
Mark 15:16-20,26

For further reading:

GOSPEL IMAGE OF JESUS: SON OF MAN

The gospels assume that we clearly understand the fact that Jesus Christ was a concrete human being, born, growing up, knowing hunger, thirst, weariness, sorrow, joy, anger, work, love, pain, feeling rejected and abandoned, and dying. The title 'Son of Man', for example, includes the fact that he shared the fate of all human beings, but also that he was sent by God, given the Spirit of God, is the sign that kingdom of God is with us; yet he is rejected. This title 'Son of Man' expresses the tension that is found in Jesus' whole message; namely, the fullness of the kingdom of heaven becomes real for us in and through a despised, persecuted and finally executed wandering preacher. The cause of God and people is decided in and through this suffering servant. Each person's decision for or against this man is the basis of his/her salvation. Obviously, this is to the extent that they know him. His message is clearly that his way is one of love, and that what we do to others he takes as done to himself. In choosing the good according to the law of love written in our hearts where the Trinity is drawing every person to themselves, people will come to know and recognize Jesus himself . . . even though the full recognition happens when they see him face to face.

Opting for or against Jesus is the paradox of christian reality; because God became this particular man, Jesus of Nazareth, Jesus has become the criteria for what is great, significant and reputable. The incarnation has made God's revelation and viewpoint clear.

EMOTIONS: GIFT OF GOD

Purpose: Through our sharing, we desire once again to come to know Jesus better and to see how the Spirit is leading us. We will focus on how all emotions are a gift of God for us and do a few exercises to help us become more aware of our experience of them; this is a first step toward interpreting and guiding them. From now on, we are encouraging members to take time to reflect on their experience each day, as well as time to pray with scripture. An article is included for extra background.

Minutes

15   1. Hymn, prayer: presence, thanksgiving, light.

Ask to experience how all emotions are God's gift to us and a good part of our being human.

Quiet prayer on Luke 10:20-21.

45   2. Share an interior awareness you experienced in the last week.

10   BREAK

55   3. a) For a few of the following emotions, list many other words we use to name each: anger, jealousy, love, fear, guilt, sexual desire, powerlessness, courage, compassion.
b) Complete the following:
   i) When I think of anger, I think of . . . .
   ii) When I'm in an irritating situation, I tend to . . . .
   iii) At this point in my life I get annoyed especially at . . . .
   iv) When I feel angry I would like to . . . .
   v) A characteristic response of mine to anger is . . . .
*(No. b) is an exercise of the Institute on Emotional Development, Loyola House, Guelph.

121

c) Share typical and preferred ways of dealing with anger.
d) What possible feelings may have been present in the following hypothetical cases? What emotions or attitudes could be under the surface? There may be a mixture of feelings in any given example, and of course a wide variety of responses. Your responses may also give you some insight regarding your own reactions. In what ways could the Lord be with someone in this situation, revealing, healing, calling?

Use any of the following (or your own) examples:
   i) A co-worker is abruptly rude to Beth for no apparent reason. Beth is reflecting on it later.
  ii) Dan and Deb simply enjoy holding and looking at their new-born child.
 iii) A neighbour has cancer. Both Theresa and Bob want to visit but are hesitant.
  iv) Rosemary has been ill for half a year but doctors can't find the cause. She hears that Mike was taken in for emergency surgery, that all were very worried about him and praying for him, and soon she heard that all was okay for him.
   v) When the Brickers see broadcasts of hardships in third world countries, they turn the television off.
  vi) Francis enjoyed watching a sunset.
 vii) Judy and Pat were happy with their choice of Christmas gifts for their children but overheard a niece telling their daughter about the very expensive gifts she received.
viii) Marg realizes she has been very critical of her neighbour, her daughter's teacher and the pastor, all in one day.

ix) Tim realized he had co-operated well with a group and had helped to include people whose opinions were sometimes ignored.

x) After Gina upset someone unintentionally, she was extremely quiet for the rest of the day.

xi) Henry sees that the floor supervisor is unfair to a worker.

xii) Jean feels a lot of pain concerning the tensions and arguments in her home.

xiii) Bernard and Joann have received guidance from another couple and are now starting to use a natural method of family planning. Bernard has become quiet in the last week.

xiv) Carla has been caring for her elderly mother for about seven years. Lately, a real variety of feelings is mounting in her.

xv) Pierre is a miner facing dangerous circumstances at work. He hesitates to share his concerns with Elizabeth because he doesn't want to cause her to worry.

xvi) Paul is happily married but now feels attracted to another woman.

xvii) John says, "I feel that I haven't read 'enough' of anything and that I know so little."

10   4. Prepare for prayer during the week by reading it now and raising necessary questions.

10   5. Journal: (or sharing).

Did you really listen to the others?
Did you share what you wanted to?
Did you allow others and yourself enough time?
How do you feel about the process during this meeting?

5   6. Conclude with prayer/singing.

Prayer for the Week:

(A) Each day, remember something you felt that day. Let the experience surface and be with the Lord in it, pouring it out, savouring it, gently wondering what it might mean for you, whatever is relevant.

(B) At another time of the day, imagine yourself with Jesus in one of the following scenes (use each passage at least two days). (If you are not able to make time for this on some days, end your reflection time by reading one of these.)

        Mark 3:1-6
        Mark 5:35-43
        Mark 6:30-34

For further reading:

EMOTIONS: GIFT OF GOD

Since the next weeks focus on understanding and appreciating how emotions are a gift of God that lead us to greater wholeness, awareness, and better decision-making, this overview is included as a collection of some relevant points on emotions. Although some feelings for example, hunger and fatigue are not emotions, emotions and feelings will be used interchangeably. As driving powers, sources of energy that are all created by God and therefore gifts to us, they act like fuses or indicators of what is of value to us and what is happening within us, as well as energizers to enable us to respond well. Like natural organs of the body, they are all good and to be guided by reason.

1. All energy (including emotional energy) is mobile. It can be expressed in ways that build or destroy relationships, for sexual intimacy, for service, for mysticism.

2. Denying and repressing emotions requires more energy than letting them surface and redirecting their energies.

3. If we repress one emotion, we gradually repress our ability to feel. It is one ability. Repression causes

physical harm and continues to affect us until it is dealt with. When emotion is ignored or repressed, there is often a tendency to focus on less important issues, to blame, defend and evade. This taking the focus off the relevant emotion means we surrender our guidance of it; tension builds and is shown in a variety of ways, for example, in explosions that are inappropriate to the cause, in depression or in ulcers, headaches, arthritic pain, etc. We tend to overreact when we have not dealt with something. Naming an emotion that disturbs us can take the 'bite' or fear out of it.

4. Expression of emotion does *not* mean that we simply say and do what we feel when we feel like it. Expression involves honest naming of our feeling at least to ourselves and a choice regarding how we need to direct the energy involved in a way that is guided by reason, by respect for others, ourselves, and the circumstances of the moment.

We are responsible for how and when we express our emotions, whether we choose to let them have constructive or destructive impact for self, others, and material reality. Likewise, being 'open' does not require sharing all we feel, think, experience with everyone. We describe our feelings to the extent it is helpful, clarify them for others so that they are not left guessing in awkward situations. We may feel support for another but neglect to say this clearly! How important it is to check out our interpretations of another, asking for feedback, trying to listen to what the other is experiencing. It may be also helpful to imagine flashing lights when we hear generalizations so that we don't take them too seriously.

We can choose to react in such a way that we perpetuate a dehumanizing chain of influence; for example, it is easy to let another's anger or fear dominate us and therefore pass it on especially to those who seem weaker than ourselves in some way, and we may not be aware that we're doing it. Redirecting energies stirred up in a dehumanizing contact can break its power and move us to humanizing encounters. This may still require honest speaking up, action, service, etc. but the tone will be different!

When Jesus encourages us to love our enemies and do good to those who hate us, he is not talking about repression and not admitting the pain; he does challenge us to redirect our energies and to choose what leads to life rather than death. Then we can respond according to our deepest desire for good using our energy with a sense of compassion.

Also, there are times and seasons; for example, a time to pour out our emotions such as anger, disappointment, or fear and a time to let go of it. Otherwise, we may lock ourselves into resentment, self-pity or paralysis.

5. While respecting the strength of emotions, we need not be afraid of them; for example, we may need to redirect the energy in our anger until we can look at what it indicates for us. Has someone come too close to a sensitive, threatening area in our life? Or are we aware of an injustice? Is it something we need to be aware of within ourselves and 'befriend' (gently learn from it), or something we need courage and confidence to speak up about? The energy of anger can be redirected for this gentle, firm courage!

Fear of an emotion is a greater problem than recognizing and admitting the emotion whether it be sexual desire, jealousy, love or anger. In feeling sexual desire for a person other than a spouse; for example, we can become fearful and obsessed by the images that come to us, we can run after another lustfully or we can thank God that we are healthy persons and that the other is created as attractive. The latter attitude allows us to appreciate God's gifts but also to choose in a way that is guided by our deepest desire to follow Christ and whatever life commitments we have made.

6. Like any images or dreams, emotions can indicate some source of energy, power or wisdom for us. On all levels of nature, including our own subconscious, there is amazing inner thrust toward wholeness. It seems important, therefore, to allow time for intuition to shed its wisdom and light on our experience. Our concern here is not to figure out what meaning images, dreams or emotions have for us but to let the insight emerge gradually. We remember the wisdom of Mary who, ". . . pondered all these things in her heart" (Lk. 2:19), or of mothers who say, "Sleep on it and things will look different in the morning."

Sharing what emerges with a friend or director, especially if it is threatening for us, is one way of seeing it in perspective, of discovering its emotional content for us and of 'befriending' it; that is, gradually seeing what good it holds for us.

7. We tend to project our emotions and attitudes on others. The strength of the emotion in the attraction for or rejection of another's behaviour or qualities is probably indicating the extent to which the particular feeling is a projection of some aspect of ourself which we may not be able to accept. If, however, we see some real human weakness but can respond in freedom, with compassion and gentleness, we are not caught in a projection. Being aware of projections can enable us to love with greater freedom, without dependent clinging, intolerant anger or condemnation. We can then feel with others but not be smothered by them; furthermore, using our imagination with empathy can help us to discover the significance of others, be in tune with their shifting emotions without being dominated by them, and gradually to understand the meaning of the other, possibly enough to reflect it to him/her in words or images that will be recognized as clarification.

This same ability to feel joy and pain deeply with another can draw us closer to the Lord. As gratitude and wonder and joy grow, they can bond us to the Lord who finds his creation good and people very good. We may also feel pain at sinful situations, injustice, stifling conflicts and be sharing the Lord's way of seeing them. Our experience becomes a way of knowing and following the Lord; we can bring all to him to see how he faced similar experiences and how the Father responds.

> "The joys and the hopes, the griefs and the anxieties of the people of this age, especially those who are poor or in any way afflicted, these too are the joys and hopes, the griefs and anxieties of the followers of Christ. Indeed, nothing genuinely human fails to raise an echo in their hearts."

> ("Pastoral Constitution on the Church in the Modern World" #1)

8. We may have a mixture of feelings at the same time; we can cherish a person even as we feel angry about something by him/her. Both the other and ourselves are always greater than any individual feeling.

9. Thoughts and attitudes give rise to feelings which in turn shape and/or reinforce our attitudes. Our feelings may indicate what our operative view is, or possibly some area that needs further healing; for example, we may say that we do not need to be accepted by everyone but if we 'collapse' when one rejects something we say, then our operative view may be that all must accept not only us but also everything we say or do. Or we may say "Nobody is perfect", but in practice not be able to admit particular personal imperfection or sin. Or if we do face our fear that another will be uneasy with us, our tension may easily cause the situation we fear. It can be helpful to let fears and objections surface but then imagine ourselves relating to the other(s) in a positive way.

The Lord's abundant, free gift of grace far outweighs any amount of evil and sin with all its ramifications! (Rom. 5:15-21)

10. Dangers of two extremes: the one of over-emphasizing feelings so that they become the only world and criteria for a person (feelings not guided by wisdom), and the other of not being in touch with feelings, or leaving them underdeveloped.

11. Both the intuitive and the rational, discursive intellect work with emotions to give heart and mind their full potential in life. Those who claim to be more intellectual may come to appreciate these non-rational gifts as they savour insights, relish the delights of working with concepts, harmony, comparisons and analysis, and let these blossom into wonder, gratitude, relationships of ideas and people that spark a humour with perspective that is greater than our usual narrow limits.

12. Aware of society's desire for immediate gratification, for seeking pleasure and avoiding pain, for instant results, we also remember that human growth in awareness, understanding, new vision, attitudes and forming new habits takes *time* and *patience*. Watch a tree grow someday! Look in the mirror and see yourself grow!

ATTITUDES SHAPE AND ARE SHAPED BY OUR EMOTIONS

Purpose: As we share from our experience of our own and Jesus' emotions, we also go a little further to see how our attitudes and thoughts both shape our feelings and are reinforced by them. By discovering underlying attitudes we may gain freedom to change, to be grateful and compassionate.

Minutes

15   1. Hymn and prayer: presence, thanksgiving and light.

Ask for the gift of becoming aware (in touch with) your affective, non-rational side and be amazed at the depth, wonder and harmony of our being.

50   2. Share any awareness from the week.

10   BREAK

10   3. Give large papers and crayons (one or two each is sufficient). Play different moods of classical music and ask members simply to let themselves move with the music (abstractly). Use different paper for each selection so that large arm movements can be made.

10   4. Read Psalm 104:30-35.

Silent reflection: What did you feel during this time (with music, colouring, scripture)?

Is there any other feeling, value or attitude behind this? (It may be better not to read the example aloud at this point.) Example: Resistance to this may stem from:

> a need to be in control and always understand the reasons before following,
> or simply a hesitation to try something new,
> or possibly a willingness to risk,

130

a need to be successful,
a previous stifling of creativity and play-
fulness
or fears
. . . or . . . ?
Can we laugh at ourselves?

40   5. Share from this silent reflection.

Discuss any of the following as to what feelings, attitudes, ways of thinking might be involved, as well as what need or needs might be present: Ask, also, what it would mean in the light of the gospel or in relation to the Lord.

    i) Jack notices that he has made comments lately about having so many different tasks to do. He also finds that he has said more often how tired he is.

   ii) Beverly had company over the holidays and some illness in the family. It wasn't serious but now that the children have re-turned to school, she expected every-thing to be fine; now however she is somewhat depressed.

  iii) Ted finds that he is no longer very inter-ested in some of the conversations at work.

  iv) Bill goes to visit his son who is living with a girlfriend and is starting to drink heavi-ly. Although he had intended to stay longer, he leaves rather soon.

   v) Sue is impatient with her son who left for school in a rush; he took two different mitts, one of which had a hole in it.

  vi) Jane was helping her three year old to swim. She delighted in the child's trust and encouraged him when he was fearful.

 vii) Mark exploded when his son asked him for money for a movie.

viii) Fred hears a comment that capitalism is a sinful structure and starts defending it with a fair amount of anger.

ix) Elaine gets irritated when anyone even mentions "God's will".

x) Mike realizes that he often seems to be attempting to prove himself, striving to have others accept him.

xi) When Mary was angry she complained to a 'third person' about the relationship that was troubling her.

xii) Sally and Dick's two month old baby has colic trouble. Sally reflects on what she felt during the night.

xiii) Kathy becomes very angry and withdraws whenever she hears any mention of nuclear threat.

xiv) John has a headache and wonders about the cause of it.

5   6. Prepare for prayer by reviewing approach from last week.

5   7. Journal: Briefly note what you experienced interiorly this evening. What was the group spirit like?

5   8. Conclude with a hymn/prayer.

Prayer for the Week:

(A) Each day, reflect on your interior experience; for example,

DAY 1 Remember an actual moment of joy or delight in your life (preferably a recent experience). Let the Lord show you how he is with you and leading you through this kind of experience.

DAY 2 Continue yesterday's encounter with the Lord, beginning with anything you felt during the time of prayer.

DAY 3 Ponder with the Lord: How have my other experiences of the last two days affected or been affected by my prayer?

DAY 4 Remember an experience of being challenged or disturbed. Let the Lord show you what meaning this has in your life. Respond in your own way.

DAYS 5-6

Remember a moment of gratitude, joy, pain or challenge of and 6 today. Come to the Lord and talk it over or respond in whatever way is appropriate for you.

(B) At another time of the day, be with the Lord using one of the following passages. Use each at least 2 days. (If on an occasional day you cannot make time for scriptural prayer, at least read a passage):

Mark 10:13-14
Mark 10:21
Mark 14:34

INTERIOR EXPERIENCE

Purpose: Our growth in naming both emotions and their underlying attitudes now leads us to consider how we might direct our impulses according to faith values in order to recognize, be with and serve God and others through them. We will use the term "affective experiences" to include all sensitivity to emotion, as well as any disposition, tendency or impulse that is a factor in behaviour.

Minutes

15   1. Begin with a hymn, prayer of remembering the Lord's presence with us, asking for his light in our darkness and hesitation, and thanking him wholeheartedly for his abundant goodness.

Reflect quietly on the experience of the past week in the light of Romans 8:28 (for about 10 minutes).

50   2. Share any insight you have regarding any awareness of the past week; no awareness or realization is too ordinary!

10   BREAK

20   3. Read the article "Interior Experience". It is included at the end of the week.

30   4. Discuss what these different points of the article mean in terms of your experience and our meetings over the last three weeks. How can this understanding help us to make better decisions?

15   5. Journal: What seemed to happen in the group this evening? What does this mean for you? Share this briefly.

5   6. Prepare for Prayer of the Week and conclude with a hymn and/or prayer.

134

Prayer for the Week:

(A)Daily time for exercise in awareness:

Begin each time of remembering by considering the gift of the Lord's presence and personal love for you and asking him to give you his light. Take time to be grateful for the obvious, for surprises and for whatever you tend to take for granted. Remember any moment of the day when you enjoyed something, were grateful, satisfied, irritated, fearful, jealous, desirous (whatever!). Let it surface now as you remember it with the Lord. Respond in your own way.

(B) Scripture prayer, using a passage at least two days if it is meaningful for you:

>   Mark 11:15-19
>   Mark   1:35
>   Mark   8:33-37

For further reading:

INTERIOR EXPERIENCE

The Trinity is involved in every inner experience, ready to draw us to themselves through it. Their love makes no exceptions to this. There is, therefore, no need to fear any impulse, desire, emotion or thought . . . only to bring all to the Lord for wisdom, direction, healing, courage and gratitude.

How can we direct our impulses according to faith values in order to recognize, be with and serve God through them?

1. Foundation: consciously clarify for ourselves that our identity is in Jesus Christ and look for growing evidence of this in our life; for example, Jesus is first in our life, more and more replacing self as number one. Daily we desire to be radically open to the Father, trusting him totally as Jesus did. (II Cor. 1:18-19) With Jesus, it was always YES to the Father. (Look at the gospels in light of this.) We desire our normal stance in life to be YES before the Father and others with our arms wide open to them instead of closed as we hug ourselves.

2. Gradually become more in touch with ourselves on the affective, non-rational side. Let images and feelings surface. Come to recognize body signs. God dwells deeply within and anything that is not of the Lord (whether it originates in our own thoughts and impulses or whether we accept it from outside ourselves) will often register first in our bodies, emotionally and physically before we are aware of it, as in headaches, stiff neck, any tension, irritation, raw nerves.

   Similarly, what is of the Lord rests in harmony with our inner self.

3. Interpret affective experiences in the light of faith. It is not enough to be generous and sincere; even with these virtues, we may be misguided and in error. Interpretation requires wisdom of the christian mystery of the passion, death and rising of Jesus. There is counter-cultural challenge in the deep inner conviction that there is life in suffering and dying.

   Death and life *have* met and become integrated in Jesus' calvary experience. This wisdom of the cross, of believing in Jesus' victory over suffering and death and finding life *in* it is essential for interpreting if particular impulses are leading us to God or not. Society's principle of choosing pleasure and avoiding pain is totally inadequate here. Yet both are in us:

Christian paschal wisdom	faith
Pleasure/pain principle	unbelief

   On the other hand, since it is definitely *not* christian wisdom simply to choose the difficult and harder just because it is painful, wisdom is needed always to discern what is the Lord's way and for our good in particular situations.

The following signs can help us know:

What the Lord's Way is Like

- Listen with the heart and mind of Jesus: Have we chosen to act out those experiences which correspond to his way? If not where do we need freedom?
- Willingness to be with Christ.
- Suffering and humiliated or courageous before injustice.
- Socially: synergy is energizing for ministry.
- Ready for self-sacrifice.
- Freeing; openness.
- Creative, trust with Christ.
- We desire good.
- Our experience is expansive and hopeful; co-operative, self-transcending, helping us to widen our horizons, feel compassion, be generous even in painful circumstances, loving others.
- Leads us to renew openness and surrender to God.
- We desire the opposite of the 7 capital sins.
- Listen with deeper faith perception.

Are we in consolation? One or other of the following phrases can help me determine this:

- the experience is moving towards the Lord.
- leading to an interior acceptance of others.
- delicate and gentle.
- leading to a realistic knowledge of self.
- a sense of God's presence with a deeper faith perspective.
- if painful or dry or sad it is because of the Lord (for example, my/our sins have put him on the cross).
- meaningfulness and a sense of hope.
- tension may still exist but underneath there is a sense of faith, hope or love.
- not turned in on self.

Build on these experiences!

If we are in consolation we can let gratitude be our stance and strengthen us.

What is Not the Lord's Way

Are we in desolation?

– turned in on self.
– God is not part of our consciousness in our activities.
– the experience is moving towards the sensual and material.
– we feel alone and separated while at the same time desiring to be with God.
– we feel sad, separated from the Lord.
– lack of caring, everything seems hard and difficult.
– we feel hyper and happy but there is a lack of delicacy, a fanatical quality to it with our disordered tendencies influencing our actions; it is a coverup for seeking ourselves
– the experience is moving us away from the Lord.
– we cannot see things clearly in perspective.
– our affectivity is 'on the prowl' for any of the 7 capital sins.
– self-centered, restricted, turning in on self, bored, that is: without Christ.
– enslaving.
– discouragement.
– our version of desolation, of sinful impulses (and of 7 capital sins) links with others and is expressed socially in our structures, in international systems.

If we are in desolation we should begin to examine ourselves with the Lord, waiting patiently until his presence returns. The following questions may help to identify the causes.

If we are in desolation

– Is our sinfulness getting in the way again?
– Have we been negligent in our dealings with the Lord? Taking him for granted?
– Is the Lord helping us to grow in spiritual maturity?
– Is there something we do not want to face? Are we being challenged to something that we are resisting? Are we refusing to grow?
– Are we being taught that all is gift and that we should not take consolation as our making? Were we being de-

pendent on the consolation of the Lord rather than the Lord of consolation?

– Perhaps we are being invited to carry the cross or to be rejected with Jesus.

Spend Some Time Talking Over These Things With the Lord

If in consolation, we should thank Him and acknowledge that it is His work. If in desolation, we should express sorrow if we are the cause, and ask His forgiveness; ask Him for help and patience so that our desolation does not influence our daily decisions and responses to ongoing situations.

Our moods can shift within moments; these experiences of consolation and desolation are signs of a healthy affective life and, as such, become valuable indicators for us. Being gently aware of them and interpreting them in faith leads to life!

4. This discernment can help us make choices; namely, if we desire to follow Jesus, we will choose or 'go with' what leads to life and show signs of being formed according to his way. We will strive to 'go against' whatever destroys, whatever feeds the desolate, false self; basically, we go against the sinful impulses. All of this requires generosity and courage; it is also the basic discipline needed for followers of Jesus. Example: at some point we need to ponder what a potentially sinful impulse means for us. In moments when it is dominating us, however, we must give ourselves to some other positive, absorbing experience such as exercise, service of others, listening to favourite music. We may need to make ourselves do it until the initial impulse gives way to the new experience. When we can reflect on it with the Lord, we try to come to the source of the experience by asking what attitudes, needs or desires are leading to this, or simply ask what it means for us.

Note that all of this can apply to both individual and group experience and decisions!

5. In light of the above, it is worth noting the importance of praying for the gifts of a sense of humour, wisdom and wonder in order that we may be converted to the Lord's way:

– Humour to appreciate a broader perspective of life and the meaning God can give to all our experiences; humour to dare to appreciate our gifts and not take seeming failure too seriously.

– Wisdom to see, choose, love and act God's way.

– Wonder to be amazed at the Trinity's greatness, their infinite patience and care for us, the marvels of their creation.

– All of these to let God be Lord for us, to rejoice in the privilege of co-operating with God in being responsible for the human community and the world, and in the freedom of being human, and only human, with all the inherent limitations this implies.

– It is God's work. We are totally dependent on God who is totally dependable. We always have reason to stay within the Trinity's healing, loving, forgiving empowering embrace.

Based on points given by G. Aschenbrenner SJ, J. English SJ and J. Veltri SJ

SIGNS OF THE PRESENCE OF THE HOLY SPIRIT

Purpose: We will begin this meeting (as well as subsequent ones) with the prayer of thanksgiving, remembering the Lord's light and asking to see ourselves and others as he does. Our sharing then becomes a communal awareness exercise and we can respond in whatever way is appropriate for the community. We will then consider Pauline descriptions of how the Spirit leads as a further aid for discovering what in our experience is of the Lord and what is not. An approach for a daily awareness exercise will also be introduced.

Minutes

15   1. Begin with hymn and prayer.

Thanksgiving

"Remember how God, Father, Son and Spirit always look on me and others with love, what their desire is for me and others, how they actually accompany us on our journey whether we recognize their presence or not. Come in gratitude . . ."

Prayer for Light

"Ask to see myself, my inner experiences and relationships, my hopes, love, desires, disappointments, weaknesses, sin, fears, concerns, disorders, all I am with the light and love of the Father, Son and Spirit so that I may recognize more fully their desire to give me life, healing, forgiveness, guidance and direction. Thus, I ask for the guidance of the Spirit to see any inner experiences, desires impulses, urges of my life today and how the Spirit is leading me through them."

141

Reflect quietly for about ten minutes using James 3:13-14:3 and your experience of the past week.

50   2. Share any reflection on this.

Response: As the group is ready, express wonder, sorrow, hope, joy to him in spontaneous shared prayer or song.

10   BREAK

50   3. Do the following together:

    a) List some indications that help you to know that something is:
       i) going well for yourself and others;
      ii) not right for yourself and others.

    b) Read: I Corinthians 13: 4-7
                Galatians   5:16-26
                Romans   12: 3-21
     and list for each (i) further insights regarding how the Spirit leads us; and,
                    (ii) signs in our life that some attitude, decision or relationship is not of the Lord.

    c) Review the meaning of consolation and desolation. (Refer to article of III-8.)

    d) Introduce the awareness exercise, possibly in the format that follows at the end of this week's format. We have been doing different aspects of this for several weeks already.

    e) After explaining it and giving time for observations or questions, allow quiet reflection time to do it for that day.

    Share some of this.

15   4. Prepare Prayer for the Week.

10   5. Conclude with a hymn.

Prayer for the Week:

(Use the format to become acquainted with it, or for as long as it is helpful. Don't let structure prevent the heart of it from happening; namely, discerning our experience with the Lord.)

(A) Daily awareness exercise. See the following article.

(B) Scripture prayer:

Ask for the grace to appreciate how the Lord draws us to himself and to see our interior experiences in the light of faith.

1 Corinthians 13: 4-7
Galatians 5:16-26
Romans 12: 3-21

DAILY AWARENESS EXERCISE

Thanksgiving

Remember how God, Father, Son and Spirit always look on me and others with love, what their desire is for me and others, how they actually accompany us on our journey whether we recognize their presence or not. Come in gratitude and trust.

Prayer for Light

Ask to see myself, my inner experiences and relationships, my hopes, love, desires, disappointments, weaknesses, sin, fears, concerns, disorders, all I am with the light and love of the Father, Son and Spirit so that I may recognize more fully their desire to give me life, healing, forgiveness, guidance and direction. Thus, I ask for the guidance of the Spirit to see any inner experiences, desires impulses, urges of my life today and how the Spirit is leading me through them.

Reflecting on the Day

1. I remember various moments of the day. On what one experience do I want to focus; for example, enjoying, being repulsed by or drawn to some person, event or thing? Or, I could focus on a tendency I've experienced over the last

day(s) such as, my increased sensitivity, gratitude, irritability, joy, jealousy, sexual desire.

2. a) What did I feel as the incident happened? What was my urge, tendency or desire? There may have been a mixture of feelings or a noticeable lack of feeling.

   b) Was I aware of what I felt as it happened or later?

3. How did I respond to these feelings? (Suppress them, laugh, cry, take them out on others . . . ?)

4. What does this indicate for me (about my own and others' needs, fears, gifts)? I will talk this over with the Father, Son and Spirit who are *with* me and love me profoundly IN the midst of this reality.

5. How is the Spirit of God present for me in this? Are there any signs or gifts of the Spirit that I recognize here? Or some way that I am coming to know the Lord better through this?

   Are there any destructive signs, indications that at least some part of this is not of of the Spirit of the Lord?

   Can I name the attitudes (gifts and/or disorders) that underlie these particular desires and emotions actually causing and shaping them? What is at work?

6. What response in the form of attitude and/or action am I drawn to make at this time?

   What is the Lord's call to me now?

7. How was this experience life-giving for me?

   OR

   If I don't see it as life-giving for me, what do I need to ask for? Talk this over with the Lord!

8. Read a passage of scripture to let the Word shed His light on my experience.

Expression of Response

As I am led to it, I will express my wonder, sorrow, hope, joy to the Lord.

I will also talk over with the Father, Son, Spirit my desires and attitudes for the coming day.

INTERPRETING WHAT HAPPENS WITHIN US

Purpose: We are approaching the same basic question of awareness and discernment in our lives from a slightly different angle; namely, whether an affective experience is rooted in love or in fear (whether it is humanizing or dehumanizing). This can be a further aid in discernment and living as a follower of Jesus' way. We will also review the awareness exercise but focus on the 'response'.

Minutes

15   1. Hymn, prayer. (Presence, thanksgiving, light, as for communal awareness exercise.)

Ask for the grace to experience what it means to be rooted in love and for the courage and generosity and compassion to let this love give direction and order to your life.

Remember an experience of the past week and reflect quietly on Ephesians 3:16-21. Be with God who is love!

50   2. Share: What did you experience in the prayer this week?

How was it related to your daily life?

10   BREAK

50   3. Discuss:
   a) i) What does an experience of fear do to you? How does it feel?
      ii) What are some ways that fear manifests itself in our daily relationships?
   b) If a person is basically fearful, how might s/he react to an experience of weakness, one in which strength is needed, a situation that causes interior anger or a moment of love?
   c) How might a person who is rooted in love respond to experiences named in #b)?

145

d) Consider the following, looking at the behaviour only as an indication of something deeper; that is, is it the result or fruit of love and trust, or fear?

Rooted in Love and Trust

i   We can be weak, accepting and admitting humbly what we experience (both good and weakness); being vulnerable, empathetic, open, compassionate.

ii Love's strength is manifested in co-operation, contributing, ability to praise others and be social.

iii With love and trust, the energy generated through anger can become courage to express and assert ourselves, to dialogue (that is, to listen and speak with courage and willingness to change and grow), to be flexible.

iv Expressions of love that are rooted in love and trust include affirming, caring, respect for persons, generosity and readiness to call forth the best in others.

v   Allow the Lord's love to discipline us; that is, make us disciples, his followers. Let love of God shape our inner affective life. This love gives direction and order to our lives because it gives us daring freedom and deep priorities.

Rooted in Fear

i   When we are rooted in fear andfeeling weak, we may avoid persons and/or issues, withdraw, hide personal and group sin in protective, defensive ways and take refuge in some form of isolation.

ii If we are basically fearful, but desire to appear strong, we may strive to prove ourselves and direct our energies into achieving, competition and rugged individualism.

iii When our foundation is fear, our anger can easily turn to attacking, blaming, explosive reactions, rigid following of 'rules' and resentful (though often subtle) punishing.

iv Similarly, attempts to love that are rooted in fear become acts of placating, pleasing the other; there can be much jealousy because of our insecurity.

v   Go against what is dehumanizing. We need to let the feelings surface, to hear their story, and then act against them, not feeding fears that cripple. Starve a fear today!

15   4. Review the awareness exercise:
     a) by recalling the meaning of consolation and desolation (III-8) and signs of life according to the Spirit (III-9, #3 b) in view of this chart on love and fear.
     b) by focusing on the response; for example, you might discuss:
       i) What is the difference between sorrow and discouragement?
      ii) Why haven't you committed more sin today?

In the 'response' of the awareness exercise, we express what arises from the awareness of gratitude, light, affective experiences within us; for example, we may express sorrow when we recognize selfishness and then humbly and confidently seek pardon, or joy in the amazement of how God's saving grace has protected and strengthened us that day.

15   5. Reflect on what you experienced within yourself and the community this evening. Pray together in any appropriate way to end the evening.

Prayer for the Week:

(A) Daily awareness exercise (see the article at the end of III-9).

(B) Scripture prayer: Ask for the grace to experience what it means to be rooted in love and trust. Use each passage as long as it is helpful.
     Ephesians 3:17-31
     Luke   7:36-50
     Luke   6:43-49

HOW JESUS FACED HIS EMOTIONS

Purpose: To appreciate Jesus' responses and emotional life so that we may love him more and be with him for others. Taking an extra week on this topic simply gives us more of the time needed to grow into this understanding of emotions, awareness and discernment. A review of the purpose of the awareness exercise and an alternate format will be part of this.

Minutes

15 1. Begin with a hymn and prayer (presence, thanksgiving and light). Ask for the gift of wisdom and discernment to appreciate how the Trinity is drawing us individually and as a community to themselves.

Reflect on the past week's experience of prayer and daily events in the light of Mark 8:14-21.

45 2. Share some awareness and possibly what it means for you. Community members may find it helpful to give some reflection or observation of encouragement, invitation or challenge as it seems appropriate.

10 BREAK

40 3. Discuss:
a) Consider what Jesus felt and discuss what you think it means:

Mark 3:5 ". . . grieved to see them so obstinate, he looked angrily around at them . . ."

Mark 5:40 "But they laughed at him. So he turned them all out."

Mark 6:4,6 "A prophet is despised in his own country . . . he was amazed at their lack of faith."

Mark 6:34 ". . . he took pity on them because they were like sheep without a shepherd."

Mark 8:33 ". . . he rebuked Peter."
Mark 10:14-16 ". . . he was indignant (with the disciples . . . he put his arms around (the children), laid his hands on them and gave them his blessing."
Mark 10:21 "Jesus looked steadily at him and loved him . . ." (the rich man).
Mark 14:34 ". . . a sudden fear came over him, and a great distress . . ." (as he faced his own death).
Mark 15:34 ". . . he cried out in a loud voice."

b) How did Jesus relate to others during the time of his suffering and death? in the midst of the joy of his resurrection?

c) i) Can God have feelings? What kind of feelings?

ii) Can God love you personally and have compassion for you?

iii) What are ways that you experience God's love for you or apparent abandonment of you?

20   4. Read some of the following article, "Awareness Exercise" quietly.

10   5. Conclude with prayer and/or a hymn.

Prayer for the Week:

NOTE: The formats for this exercise might be used to develop the skill. They are meant to be an aid and can be set aside. What is important is reflecting on experience with the Lord.

(A) Daily awareness exercise.

(B) Daily scripture prayer. Ask for the gift of wisdom and discernment for yourself and others . . . that you may hear and perceive God's way.

Mark 8:14-21 "Are you still without perception?"

149

Mark 7:1-7 ". . . their hearts are far from me . . ."

Mark 7:14-23 ". . . on clean and unclean . . ."

Mark 7:31-37 ". . . healing of the deaf man . . ."

AWARENESS EXERCISE

The Father Draws Us

We are aware that the Father is constantly drawing each human heart to union with Himself in and through Christ.

"No one can come to Me unless the Father who sent Me draws him." (John 6:44)

This drawing registers within us. We feel it in our hearts. It registers in our feelings, moods, impulses, desires, urges. This is happening to everyone, the good and the bad. Even the most malicious sinner is being drawn. Whether s/he is aware of it or not, or whether s/he has deadened his heart against it, is another matter, but it is happening.

It may surprise us to learn this, but it is a fact that the Trinity reveal themselves more in our interior feelings and moods than in clear and distinct ideas. This does not mean that the Trinity do not reveal themselves in our intellects. But we are all aware that much of what we do is by subconscious motivation without stopping to reflect on the feeling that is moving us.

If we want to find God most intimately, then, we must let the Lord draw us at the core of our being and we must become aware of the feeling operating there. It is only by doing this that we will come to know who we really are and who we are intended to be when we fully become all that God is giving us to be.

The goal of our life is holiness — wholeness — complete union with the Lord. We attain to this union only if we listen to him and respond to his constant invitations to draw nearer. We said earlier that he draws each of us in a unique way, that he makes his presence known in the level of our being where our feelings, impulses, urges and desires register. There is an-

150

other side to this however. Our sinful nature also registers at the same level in our hearts, in our feelings, moods, impulses, desires, urges. This leaves us with a problem:

> If I am in touch with myself at that level of my being, then I am conscious of these other feelings as well. Which ones are leading me to the Lord and which are not?

> I have to sort them out.

We may even find it hard to get in touch with our feelings. Perhaps our training almost urged us to the opposite, to pay no attention to our feelings.

But How You Feel Is Important

We are not talking here about superficial sentiments but about the movements at the core of our being, deep in our heart where God dwells.

If we stay away from this area, our real selves, we will be missing much of what the Spirit is saying to us and we will not become our true selves, because it is from this level of our being that we make our decisions, that we discover our real relationship with God, our true identity.

We discover what has to be:
– faced
– interpreted
– decided
– acted upon
> in the light of this identity.

And there is a time in the faith-life of each person when s/he has to face such basic questions as these:

> Is God real?
> Does Jesus, Risen and alive, mean anything to me?

If this person can gather together all the strands of faith-experiences s/he has had and then says:

> "Yes, He is real!
> I have experience to back it up!"

Then his/her faith becomes mature and s/he has a clearer grasp of his/her identity and relationship with God.

The experience that gives this conviction is called a core faith experience that opened a person to God, that basic total surrender to God that we have all experienced or we wouldn't be here.

This may not have been a dramatic thing; it could have been a moment of quiet conviction when for the first time in our life we consciously surrendered totally to the Lord perhaps in fear, because we didn't know where he was taking us, but finally in joy and peace, because we had somehow experienced in the depths of our being what it was to be at one with God, at home with God.

We have to learn to take each present interior experience and drop it down inside ourselves at that level when we are still trying to live out our total surrender, our "Yes, Father," and if it fits into that stance before God, then this will be a sign to us that it is right and good and from God.

There will be a sense of rightness, peace and joy. But if we take our present interior experience and drop it down to that level of our being to test it against our core experience of God, but find it pops up again and all our efforts to make it fit simply cause disruption, disturbance and anxiety, then it is a temptation; it does not make us feel at home with God. It is not from God.

This is how important it is for us to be in touch with our feelings: so we can sort them out and not be blown about by them or allow them to be operating in our subconscious and coming out in harmful ways.

One of the best instruments to keep us in touch with our true self is the AWARENESS EXERCISE. It is very important that we understand it correctly. Next to the Eucharist, this exercise should provide the occasion for the most intimate encounter of the day with Jesus.

Awareness Exercise: Its Real Goal, A Discerning Heart

Its real goal is to help us to keep the faith dimension in our life, to put us in touch with our real self before the Lord. He is constantly drawing each of us to himself in an intimate and unique way.

If we live from day to day simply reacting spontaneously

to all that comes to us, we may be failing to hear the Lord's gentle and quiet invitation, because there are two spontaneities at work in us:
  – one good, from God
  – the other evil and not from God.

This is a daily prayerful exercise in discernment, helping us to respond to God's loving invitations, not just during the time of the exercise, but in all of our daily living. It is to help us find God in everything.

So it is primarily concerned not with good and bad actions, but with what occurs in us prior to action,
  – our deep inner feelings
  – how we are experiencing the drawing of the Father
  – how our sinful nature is quietly tempting and alluring us away from our Father in subtle dispositions within us.

So it is an exercise in awareness: awareness of our present relationship with a loving Father whose invitations to draw nearer to him are presenting themselves in new forms at every moment.

It is not possible for us to do this kind of exercise without confronting our own identity in Christ before the Father.

We are individual persons with particular vocations and ministries. All this is part of our identity, our second name of grace.

BUT MORE THAN THIS: over the years we have come to know God's special ways of drawing us and are aware of our past responses and how our life has been shaped because of this. We answer to a name that no one else answers to; namely, our first name of grace.

And daily the Lord is inviting us to deepen and develop this identity. Each day we should do this exercise, not just as any christian, but as the CHRISTIAN we are (individually), with as close a grasp of our identity as it is possible for us to have at this moment.

Awareness Exercise and Prayer

It is in our prayer that the Trinity gradually reveal themselves to us and the mystery of their plan for all of reality in

Christ. It is in prayer that we experience their invitations and challenges to us personally. This is why it is prayer and is related to our daily, personal, contemplative prayer. Our prayer would be empty if we did not order our life to respond to God. It is this daily exercise that helps us to sense and recognize those interior invitations of the Lord that guide and deepen this ordering. To be prayerful means to find God in all things, not just in the time of formal prayer.

Another Format Of The Exercise
(alternate to the article in III-9)

We must keep in mind the goal of the exercise: to develop a heart with a discerning vision that will be operating not just for this ten or fifteen minutes but throughout our whole day. Let us recall the five steps we need to make and see how they were intended to lead to this goal:

        1. Thanksgiving
        2. Prayer for Light
        3. Examination
        4. Contrition and Sorrow
        5. Resolution

I. Thanksgiving

If we see the exercise as related to our prayer, we will readily understand why it is good to begin with thanksgiving. In our prayer life we have come to realize that we are poor. We possess nothing, not even ourselves. We come before the Lord as people who have been gifted by Him. We owe Him everything. The deeper our faith becomes, the more truly we become aware of our utter poverty and the more we are struck by God's great goodness to us. This sense of thankfulness should become an attitude that abides with us and remains a part of our constant awareness. So we use the time to bring GRATITUDE into our conscious awareness so that we can learn to have an abiding consciousness of who God is and how good God is. Gradually we will experience what it is to believe that ALL IS GIFT and this awareness alone could change our lives.

As we make this part of the exercise we should THANK

THE TRINITY SPECIFICALLY for their gifts in the part of the day just completed. Expressing our gratitude will help us to discover gifts from God as they are given to us in the future so that we can be more spontaneously grateful as they are given.

- What has happened today that we should be thankful for?
- Do we take God's gifts for granted?
- Is our whole life becoming "Thank you" response to God?
- What do we find most difficult to be grateful for?

II. Prayer For The Light Of The Spirit

No doubt we have made enough mistakes in life to realize that seeing clearly in spiritual matters is not simply a matter of using our reason and common sense. Since only God knows us fully and knows who we will be when we become all we are capable of becoming, it is clear that only God can give us the needed insights into our life. It is important, then, that we ask for HIS SPIRIT to give us a growing insight into the mystery which we are.

We also need to ask ourselves:

Am I becoming more and more Spirit directed?

Am I open to ALL the channels by which God speaks to me?

Did I allow God to direct me in the events of this morning? this day?

Do I experience his gifts anew?

peace	patience
love	joy
kindness	fidelity
gentleness	self-control

III. Examination

This is the part of the exercise that we are most familiar with. It consists in examining ourselves. But on what should we examine ourselves? In the past many of us at this point reviewed our actions of the part of the day just finished and looked at our failures and/or victories.

THIS IS JUST WHAT WE SHOULD NOT DO!

Our real concern here is FAITH and what has been happening TO US and IN US since the last exercise. So the questions we ask ourselves could be similar to the following:

1. Did I feel drawn by the Lord any time today through:
   - a companion
   - a good book
   - an event
   - nature

   To what was He drawing me?

2. What have I learned today about Him and His ways?
   - the ordinary occasions?
   - in stray moments?

3. How did I meet Him in:
   - fears
   - misunderstandings
   - joys
   - suffering
   - work
   - celebration

4. How did His word come ALIVE to me today in:
   - my prayer time
   - other readings
   - scripture
   - liturgy
   - some community experience

5. In what ways have I encountered Christ through the members of the community or family?

   Have I brought Christ to them?

6. In what ways have I been the sign of God's presence and love:
   - to my friends
   - to the people with whom I live and/or work
   - to the people I've met today

7. Have I felt moved to go out of myself in concern for the:
   - lonely
   - sad
   - discouraged
   - needy
   - oppressed

8. How am I becoming more and more conscious of God's work:
   – in the larger church
   – in my country
   – in other countries of the world

   How does it affect me?

9. Have I experienced a growing awareness of:
   – my being loved
   – my sinfulness
   – a desire to reciprocate
   – my dependence, interdependence
   – the impact of society's values on me

10. Of what area of my being is Jesus not yet
    Lord?

Only secondarily are we concerned about our ACTIONS,
insofar as they are RESPONSES to God's calling. Too often,
we are so concerned with action that we become self-moved
and motivated rather than moved and motivated by the Spirit.
It is likely that the Lord is calling us to CONVERSION in
some area of our life. This is what we should be responding to
instead of being busy in the area we choose to work on. Only
God can reveal our sinfulness to us and God does so only out
of love.

IV. Contrition And Sorrow

A growing awareness of our sinfulness (our lack of response to love) should arouse in us:
   – sorrow and wonder at being constantly brought to new-
     ness
   – a sense of deep joy and gratitude because we have been
     guaranteed the victory through Jesus
   – a growing mistrust of self and firm trust in God
   – a humble awareness of our weakness
   – a strong faith that we are gradually being converted
     from sinner to daughter or son of God.

Here we can express sorrow over specific actions that
were inadequate to God's love at work in our hearts.

V. Hopeful Resolution For The Future

What we do in this part of the exercise should flow naturally from all that has preceded. Therefore it will be different each day.

HOW DO I LOOK TOWARD THE FUTURE? Are we:
– despondent   – fearful   – discouraged
If so, why?
– We must be honest and not repress our true feelings.

There should be a great desire to face the future with renewed vision and a sensitivity as we pray:
    – to recognize the ways in which the Lord calls us in each situation of the future
and
    – to respond to the Lord's call with more:
        faith,   humility,   and   courage
especially as we experience Him calling for PAINFUL CONVERSION IN SOME AREA OF OUR HEART.

We SHOULD BE FILLED WITH HOPE, founded not on our own powers but in our Father whose glorious victory in Jesus Christ we share through the life of Their Spirit in our hearts.

The more we trust the Lord and allow him to lead our life, the more we will experience true hope in him, in and through, but beyond our weakness, pain and poverty. And this experience brings JOY!

"I LEAVE THE PAST BEHIND
AND WITH HANDS OUTSTRETCHED
TO WHATEVER LIES AHEAD
I GO STRAIGHT FOR THE GOAL."
(Phil. 3:13)

This Awareness Exercise is an abbreviated presentation of G. Aschenbrenner's article, "Consciousness Examen" from the Review for Religious, Volume 31, 1971/72. The present format is the work of a retreat team under the direction of John English, SJ.

HAPPINESS ACCORDING TO SOCIETY (1)

Purpose: Over the last weeks we have seen how, as followers
of Jesus, our attitudes are influenced by our imagination and emotions; all this is part of the continuous circle of factors that determine our response to
events for our thinking and views also shape our
emotions.

The vision of life and reality as proposed by others also
has an impact on our attitudes. Society has an active impact on
us even as it is in fact a reflection of our collective imagination
and emotions. In the same way that we have personally
needed to be healed of our hurts, we have to look at society
and see how it needs to be healed.

Our intent in these next few weeks, therefore, is to become
more aware of what society's vision of life and reality is, what
its imagination is, and where these are to be found. How are
they both concealed and expressed? What are our myths?
There are myths filled with truths, explaining our realities with
insight into human foibles, psychology, communication and
faith. There are also deceptive myths that contain some truth
but are twisted with deceptive dehumanizing attitudes. They
tend to capture, create, reflect and reinforce our collective
imagination and emotions in destructive ways. During the next
three weeks we will focus on several of these deceptive myths
of our society so that we may be freed of their spell. Becoming
more aware of ourselves, our society, and the gospel can help
us to choose more freely to follow Jesus within very practical
issues of our daily lives.

Minutes

15   1. Begin with a hymn and prayer (as for the awareness exercise). Ask for the wisdom and understanding to see society as the Trinity does and
respond with them to particular needs of our
time.

Reflect on your prayer and experience of the
last week in light of John 3:16.

45   2. Share any of this reflection.

5   Has any clear awareness or insight emerged for the community in today's sharing?

10   **BREAK**

50   3. Discuss:
- a) What do we mean by myth in our society?
- b) One myth today is that of efficiency: "We are what we do."
  - i) What are some of the indications in our lives that we have let 'efficiency' take over?
  - ii) Who are the 'inefficient' people around us? What can they teach us?
  - iii) What are the values and kind of happiness this myth promises? (What is its vision?)
  - iv) Who proposes it?
  - v) Who benefits?
  - vi) What does the gospel say about the attitudes that are part of this myth?
  - vii) What would change in our faith/in our religion if we were rather 'out' looking 'in'? If we were 'inefficient' looking at the 'efficient'?
  - viii) How does this apply concretely in our own lives? Is there anything we need to ponder, search out and change?

15   4. Journal: What happened in you and in the group this evening? What does it mean for you/us?

10   5. Conclude with prayer and a hymn.

Prayer for the Week:

(A) Daily awareness exercise. Be alert to slogans and general attitudes in society too.

(B) Scripture prayer:

Luke   1:46-55
Luke   2:26-35
Luke 10:29-37
Luke 13:20-30

For further reading:

A CASE OF 'MYTH – TAKEN' IDENTITY

"The emperor has no clothes on!", blurted out the child.
But the adults quickly hushed it up, whispering that kids don't
know much about life anyway.

We so often look at reality with the eyes others tell us to
have, lacking the sense of innate truth or analysis that children
so often (even embarrassingly) come out with. It takes new
eyes to look at our everyday symbols and "catch phrases",
new "glimpses" to seek truth critically as it really is.

People's thinking about themselves and the world is often
summarized in proverbs ('A fish in the pan is worth two in the
stream') or in myths. A myth is a statement that tries to por-
tray or explain imaginatively that which some people believe;
for example, "Blondes have more fun" or "Nuclear energy is
clean". Some people would emphatically agree with both
statements but just as many people might categorically oppose
them. These statements are clearly not neutral. They both express a particular world vision, which gives meaning and identity to certain persons. Myth then might be seen as an attempt
to show the world as it is, or as some would like it to be. It is
the projection of truths, fantasies and/or terrors of one's existence into words and images that others can relate to, identify
with and even build upon. It is an attempt to organize one's
life into understandable coherent packages in order to make
sense of one's experience. It is using an image that gives meaning to the facts and problems of ordinary life, to the multiple
forms of stimuli that bombard us each day. It tries to express a
view on our own situation and on that of our culture.

As a mirror and a model, a myth can be very positive. In
fact, many of the original bible stories (creation, the garden of
Eden, the tower of Babel) are widely accepted today as not

having any actual historical base (being snapshots of what really happened). These stories are rather myths, illustrations that tell humans something about themselves; for example, the greatness of humans and yet their limitations. The truth is in the attitude or the message, not in the "props" used to transmit it. Aesop's fables, Jesus' parables and many of our present day fairy tales all have in common the use of myth. It can be used to give direction to people's lives, to motivate them and to help them become more human. Because of its basic simplicity, people from all walks of life see themselves in the myth and attempt to become that which is conveyed. We actually need myths to survive in our societies.

Since myths are so powerful, it is important to recognize their existence, to determine their source and the extent of their use. Myths are not a thing of the past. New myths are constantly being created. As a snapshot possibly of a very complex social/political/economic/psychological reality frozen in time, a myth can become similar to an instant picture that proposes to capture the richness of a whole process. The picture is true; but someone may construe a whole new story around the snapshot to make a new point that benefits him/-herself. Over time the "new" story told about the snapshot becomes more 'truthful' than the snapshot itself. Thus a person with a child's eyes or with another experience could call the previous story "naked", a "myth-taken" story, a warped story.

We have many such "naked" stories going around in society's bosom, myths built on a kernel of truth but rendered cancerous through dehumanizing attitudes. Lacking significant humanizing events in our lives and even good myths that could bond us together better, we remain very vulnerable. We all too often grab onto societal slogans, images and ideas in their totality without discerning the values they carry within them. All these myths need to be looked at. Some are leftovers from a very distant past ('whites are better', 'the poor are lazy') but some new forms are kept very active, even today, in order to justify the *status quo* and the games some people play. Most of these myths definitely reveal themselves as anti-gospel statements, especially when they are closely scrutinized with the child-like eyes of faith.

The Myth of Efficiency: we are what we make and do.

A person's worth is equated only to what s/he can produce within the economic system. Production becomes the goal of life because it gives people identity: "Hi, what do you *do* in life?" People become controlled by 'measurable' time and space: in work, in health, in education, in shopping, in television programming. Because production is increased through standardization of products and ever more rapidly producing machines, quantity becomes the primary goal (with its side-effect: profits). Quantity even replaces quality in relationships: I *am* more because I *have* more. Even 'quality of life' is measured by 'quantity' standards (more goods) that can always be improved, made more efficient; this leaves people dissatisfied with themselves, others, and more open to feeling inferior and inadequate. Advertising creates this deception and offers the solution "Buy more!". Inventions are viewed for their marketability. Creativity and artistic production become the possession of the elite, whose status is 'enhanced' by the acquisition of others' ideas and imagination. Only a few specialized managers and technocrats create, but always in view of greater and improved production. Efficiency has even narrowed down our capacity to celebrate: there is rarely any real spontaneity other than "open up a bottle". Within this myth also, there are those who are part of the efficiency group/set and those who are out of it. If you are no longer efficient, then you are disposed of . . .

The seniors, the handicapped, the poor, the natives, the children, the Third World, are often labelled as those who aren't "productive, profitable, or efficient" (maybe even lazy) and, therefore, have little place or no value within society.

Even a certain Church theology encouraged part of this myth. We were saved if we produced merits and good works. The Church itself is viewed as an organization, a machine whose purpose is to produce christian life, to bring those 'out there' into 'our' fold: there are those who are 'in' and those who are 'out'. Worth is given according to the power and efficiency of the person in the hierarchical scale, be they lay or ordained: "they did *so* much." Unfortunately, there is little left for the gift of grace, for the work of God. We have become

God's producers. Jesus did not start his ministry with those who were *in* existing religious structures, so as to be more efficient, using a respected 'network' so as to produce more conversions. Actually Jesus' efficiency seemed absolutely non-existent since he ended up his life alone on a cross, dying, with all his 'friends' scattered and hiding. Humanly, that was no way to affect structural change. Instead he went out of his way to touch the misfits, the outcasts of society, the 'inefficient', accepting them as they were, as children and images of God, calling forth from within them the faith of the Creator Spirit which itself alone can change, in depth, the hearts of people and the structures they give themselves. All true 'efficiency' comes from God alone.

HAPPINESS ACCORDING TO SOCIETY (2)

Purpose: By sharing our reflections and experience of the last week, especially as it relates to the myth of efficiency, we can sort out better what is helpful and harmful. We will continue the same process focusing on the myths of progress.

Minutes

15   1. Begin with a hymn and prayer.

Ask for wisdom and discernment to see our society's values in the light of the gospel.
Remember your experience and prayer of the week with the Lord in the light of Luke 2:33-35.

45   2. Share any of this awareness.

5   Is our awareness of myth and society's way of thinking increasing?

10   BREAK

50   3. Discuss the following:

Regarding the myth of progress: "if we can make it, we must; if it's new, it's better."

    i) What does the average person on the street understand by 'progress' today?

    ii) Is it progress for some more than others? Why the 'some' more than others?

    iii) What values and kind of happiness does the myth of progress promise?

    iv) Who proposes it?

    v) Who benefits?

    vi) What would christian progress look like (Romans 8:21-23)? What should it take into account?

    vii) What kind of consequences would this new understanding of "progress" have on our life-styles?

165

viii) What forms do the seven capital sins (greed, ambition, pride, envy, lust, gluttony, and sloth) take today?

15   4. Journal: What happened in you and in the group?

What does this mean for you/us?

5   5. Prepare together the prayer for this week.

5   6. Conclude with prayer.

Prayer for the Week:

(A) Scripture: Luke 4:1-3, 3:10-16.

(B) Daily awareness exercise, remembering myths of efficiency and progress, or other slogans as they affect us.

On each day, read and ponder one of the following myths, considering what values and kind of happiness it promises, who proposes it, who benefits and how it relates to gospel values. Talk it over with the Lord! What does this mean for you/us?

For further reading:

SOME CHERISHED MYTHS

1. THE MYTH OF PROGRESS: IF WE CAN MAKE IT, WE MUST; IF IT'S NEW, IT'S BETTER

The earth is ours and all that's in it. Our purpose on earth is to make life easier for ourselves and for everybody by multiplying time-saving gadgets. Progress is needed to make sure everybody has a fair share of the goods. Progress is good for the economy, it makes the system go on. Progress affects the quality of life.

Unfortunately, personal ease and leisure as well as multiplication of goods become goals in themselves. Trying to quench this greed with more goods is like trying to extinguish a fire with grease (Hindu proverb). These can never be sufficiently satisfied. So "progress" becomes the property of some against others. Progress is even used to prevent others from participating in development (computers, psychological warfare, armaments, etc.). Change becomes an end in itself: change for change's sake. It's the only way to keep the industry producing. The sky is the limit. We become intoxicated by our 'creative' power without sufficiently examining all the consequences. People do not sufficiently take into account the fact that goods are limited in this world; it is as if there were still an unlimited golden frontier to discover out there, there for the taking. Some feel that the earth is more theirs than it is anybody else's: they can do what they want with it on a short-term basis even if it means disturbing or destroying the delicate balance of life on the planet. We seem to forget that humanity is part of a continuum, that there has to be a faithfulness to the present on our part as there was one by those who preceeded us. Will we be leaving anything for our offsprings, as our ancestors left goods for us? Can we act without consideration for the future generations? At what cost 'progress'?

The Trinity acted "progressively". God's word was revealed progressively: in a people, in a tradition, and finally in the Son. But God the Revealer is also God the Creator: creation carries seeds of redemption and as such is treated with care. It is a living being (Gen. 1:28-31) lent to us by God. At times, we are like sorcerers' apprentices who have found some 'magical forces' which lead us to believe we are independent gods on our own. It is when 'progress' gets out of hand that we are compelled to turn humbly back to the Creator.

2. THE MYTH OF KNOWLEDGE

Those who know are superior to those who do not. If someone is competent in one field, then they must be competent in all fields. Information is power: "I have a resource that you don't have." If you don't know, then all you can do is trust the one who seems to know. This is where the "credibility gap" sets in: Watergate, Three Mile Island, Viet Nam, your doctor, your repairman, etc. Anyway science is neutral, non-political, non-moral.

The more it is complicated then the more it must be true. Technology becomes the god that can solve everything (even

167

meaning) and the scientists become the high-priests. Our lack of understanding in one field becomes a faith in those who control it. Then, of course, there are those who are able to understand and those who can't . . . so don't try; that way the power stays in the hands of those who hold the mystique of knowledge, and you feel ever more powerless.

Jesus never hoarded his knowledge: he came to let the world know the Father. "You have heard it said . . . ; I tell you . . .."; he spoke in parables so that all could understand. Knowledge is not ours; it either belongs to the world, or is caught in sin.

3. THE MYTH OF THE BIONIC MAN/WOMAN

Humans are able to conquer all. We have our sport athletes, our engineers, our space heroes. Just a little drug here, a little transplant there, or a little more cunning, and we can all hope to become a race of the fittest, driving out death and evil, sin and limitations.

Jesus chose agony and powerlessness by death on a cross. It was through and because of Jesus' emptying of himself that God was able to take up all the space and to raise Jesus high with resurrection-life (Phil. 2:7-9).

4. THE MYTH OF REALITY

What is real today, what is truly important to each one of us? The media attempt to trivialize our reality by highlighting other events that create mass anesthesia and de-possess us of the true fabric of our lives. Be it through sports, T.V. soap operas, the evening news with (at times) its gore, the T.V. violence (13 murders per night), instant replays of the most "action-packed" scenes, all this makes us lose track that our everyday life is just as important, if not more so, than all the sensation-oriented stimuli that we are subjected to.

We are invited to share passively in all these media events, be they artistic, cultural, social or political. Powerlessness, paralysis, grows: we can't do anything. There is not true communication: it is all one way. No one can have any impact on the decision-making process nor offer any real challenge to it; because the masses are to think alike, or if not all exactly alike, then sufficiently alike so as not to rock the boat. Though pluralism is tolerated and even (falsely) encouraged (i.e., be different, like everybody else!), any strong contrary opinions will be persecuted and eventually eliminated. Persecution takes many forms.

Faith in the Father and compassion for the outcasts were the two poles of reality for Jesus. He dared to be different, and this brought him to confront the religious powers of his time. It ultimately led to his death.

HAPPINESS ACCORDING TO SOCIETY (3)

Purpose: We will share our insights from praying on the myths of knowledge, bionic people and reality and then reflect on how these affect us. Finally we will consider the myth that everybody is born equal.

Minutes

20   1. Begin with a hymn and prayer.
Ask for the gift of listening well to others, for humility to hear the good news in our lives and see how it relates to our attitudes in society.

Reflect on your prayer and experience of the week (possibly rereading the 3 myths) in the light of Philippians 3:4-16.

50   2. Share awareness, especially of what is happening within you regarding awareness of society's vision.

10   BREAK

50   3. Discuss the myth that everyone is born equal:
   a) What do we really mean by equality? Are some more equal than others?
   b) What values and kind of happiness does this myth promise?
   c) Who proposes it?
   d) Who benefits?
   e) Does private enterprise really exist? How far should private property exist?
   f) Is Acts 4:32-35 just a pipe dream? Could our equality be one of sharing rather than hoarding?

15   4. Journal: What did you/we experience?
                What does it mean for us?

5   5. Conclude with whatever response is appropriate.

Prayer for the Week:

(A) Daily awareness exercise.

(B) Daily scripture prayer asking to know the Lord and see his way of looking at attitudes that are part of our myths.

         Luke   3:1-6
         Luke   4:16-19
         Philippians 3:4-16

THE MYTH OF EQUALITY: EVERYBODY IS BORN EQUAL

Everybody who comes into this world has the same chances for development. Determination, stamina and at times good luck are what it takes to pull yourself up and to succeed. But it all depends on you. You are number one and nobody will do things for you. You are your first enemy and your best resource. You deserve what you have because you worked hard to get it. Free enterprise is the only way because it gives everybody the same chance at reaching the top.

Unfortunately, chances are not equal for everyone: most people start life affected by malnourishment, disease, handicaps, or negative social environments. The myth of equality justifies those who have reached the top by making everyone believe that they have earned that position through natural selection. If everyone was truly equal then everyone should equally be 'on the top': but the social ladder or pyramid only allows for a few on the top. Free enterprise ends up disappearing in favour of the big groups buying out the little ones. The rich become richer and the poor poorer, not only on an international level with sinful disparities of affluence and starvation, but also within countries even of the "first world". Success, competition and being one-up become the predominant values, all in the name of equality! Equality also breeds individualism and self-centredness.

God made us equal in nature and humanity, but not in circumstances. The world is not for some, it is for all. When some are hurt, diminished or victimized, then the Body of Christ is affected. The models proposed in the Acts of the Apostles are: sharing, collaboration, caring, not: having, competition, or "each one out for themselves". This myth of equality also promotes "private" property, "private" religion "between me and my God". There is no room for a deeper understanding of the theology of creation (the air is for all, the water is for all, why not the land? So believe the North American Indians), nor of a theology of the People of God, where we are all part of each other's journey to the Father. Common good has always been the antidote to the myth of equality.

REFLECTING ON VARIOUS WAYS TO HAPPINESS

Purpose: As a way of drawing together and reflecting on society's values and what we have experienced over the last months and in the light of the beatitudes, we will consider various ways to happiness that they propose. We will ask ourselves about our choice to be a follower of Jesus and what this involves, then plan a celebration of gratitude for the following week.

Minutes

20   1. Begin with a hymn and brief reflection on the last week's awareness.

Also, write out:
a) Ways to happiness according to society. What are the goals and means?
b) Ways to happiness according to what you have experienced and concluded in the last months.
c) Ways to happiness according to the beatitudes. Luke 6:20-26.

50   2. Share the above and any awareness.

10   BREAK

15   3. Reflect quietly: how does this exercise (before the break) affirm and challenge my views? Whom do you desire and choose to follow?

20   4. Discuss:
a) As followers of Jesus, how do we implement his vision? What difficult choices and discipline does this involve?
b) How can we help heal society's vision?

20   5. Prepare a celebration: discuss how we can celebrate among ourselves elements of personal, group or societal healing (for 2 weeks from tonight).

173

5   6. Prepare Prayer for the Week. Note together: as part of prayer for the week, read and reflect on the article about Deirdre and Dermot McLoughlin.

10   7. Conclude with prayer.

Prayer for the Week:

(A) Daily awareness exercise.

(B) Read and ponder the article "A Long Night of the Soul Leads to a New Vocation", and Luke 6:20-26 (all week!).

A LONG NIGHT OF THE SOUL LEADS TO A NEW VOCATION

> I said to the man who stood at the
>   gate of the year
> Give me a light
> That I might tread safely into the
>   unknown
> And he replied:
> Go out into the darkness
> And put your hand into the hand of
>   God
> That shall be to you better than light
> And safer than a known way
>   [By M.L. Haskins]

It was night. Dr. Dermot McLoughlin stood in the bay window of his century old house perched high on a hill overlooking Kempenfeldt Bay. As he watched the stars flicker over the waters below his mind turned once again to the long long thoughts of the past ten years.

By North American standards, at 38 years of age, he had won by his own sweat, all the trappings of success that were supposed to bring peace, comfort, happiness.

There was the house, built by a Wexford sea captain in the 1880's. A beautiful wife, four healthy sons, the cars, the cottage, the antiques, the shelves groaning with the weight of Waterford crystal. As the head of Georgian Radiology Consultants he had the esteem of his peers. He was active in his church, a member of the school board. His wife Deirdre was president of a guild devoted to the promotion of arts and culture. She was also president of St. Mary's Catholic Women's League. They were the definitive picture book family, comfortable, secure, affluent. Not bad for a kid from Tipperary, schooled by the monks near the Rock of Cashel where St. Patrick first used the Shamrock to explain the doctrine of the Trinity, and where poverty and sharing were priority values.

Like the waves at the foot of the bay beneath his exquisite house McLoughlin's thoughts tumbled and fell in a torment of spiritual searching. He had seen the lepers of Nigeria and worked among them. He had lived in a Glasgow slum and watched his young wife Deirdre stuff the floorboards with newspapers to keep the drafts away from their two baby sons. They had promised themselves if they ever got out of this at least ten years of stability for the sake of their children.

Well, he'd got the security for them. But where was the contentment it was supposed to bring?

"I talked to God out that window," Dr. McLoughlin said recently. "I felt he was saying to me: I showed you Nigeria. I showed you Glasgow, now look where you're at."

That long night of the soul by the window took place more than seven years ago. Now all the status symbols have gone.

175

The house, the crystal, the antiques, Deirdre's mink coat. Only the house and the kids remain.

Instead there is Ashling House, a common house, in a common neighbourhood, on a street in Toronto's east end, where multi-coloured children play ball in the streets on a Sunday afternoon, forcing cars to inch their way through the throngs of humanity endlessly waiting for signs of spring.

Inside Ashling House, Dermot and Deirdre and their sons live in service to God and humanity, along with anyone else who happens to have dropped in for a few days, or weeks, on the road to their own particular spiritual journey.

It's a hospitality house, reaching out to wrap its arms around people seeking surcease from life's storms. It was founded by Dermot and Deirdre six years ago. They are lay members of the Order of Spiritans, formed in 1975 as a direct response of the Congregation of the Holy Ghost to Vatican II, when the council advocated a much fuller participation by the laity in the Church. It was the same order which had shaped Dermot's future as a boy in a boarding school in Tipperary, the order which had sent him as a young doctor to the mission fields of Nigeria, and which had reached across an ocean, in some infinitesimal way, to claim its own. But wait. Let's let Dermot tell the story.

As a boy I attended a boarding school run by the Spiritan Fathers in Tipperary. Their mission fields were in west and east Africa. Priests taught me, and somewhere along the line I decided to become a doctor. After graduation from medical school at Dublin's University College I applied to the Medical Missionaries of Mary, an Irish Order, the first in the world whose nuns were doctors. I was sent to Abakaliki in eastern Nigeria, known as Biafra during the civil war, now eastern Nigeria again. There were three doctors for a quarter of a million people and one of those doctors was fully engaged in public health administration. That left two of us to do everything.

My specific role was the charge of a 100 bed hospital, providing the general medical, surgical, and obstetrical needs of 8,000 people with leprosy in the province of Abakaliki, and as well as that, to treat their leprosy. The United Nations provided drugs for leprosy and we were also assisted by the government of Nigeria, the British Leprosy relief association, the Medical Missionaries of Mary, and a small Irish group of priests known as the Kiltegan Fathers, Ireland's equivalent to the Scarborough Fathers.

Tropical Medicine

I was then only a general practioner with a five week crash course in tropical medicine and surgery, but it's amazing what you can do when you are the only person to do it. Deirdre, a physiotherapist, came out six months later to join me. We were married in Nigeria, in a village of lepers, in their church, and the chief of the village was delighted to comply with our wishes. We stayed for two years. I began every day by seeing 100 people in a clinic, then to the hospital for two hours, then on to a tour of the rural patients. I saw up to 300 people each day. We were, one doctor, two nurses, and 13 paramedics. I received $2,400 a year, paid by the Kiltegan Fathers who also provided a house for us.

Our son John was born in Nigeria. He nearly died of malaria and an obscure viral illness seven weeks after his birth, forcing Deirdre to fly with him to Sick Children's hospital in Dublin where he recovered. I followed two months later, my tour of service over. Our plans had been to return to Nigeria for a second tour of duty but the child's illness prevented this.

Back in Dublin Dermot took six months of study in paediatrics and spent another six months as a casualty officer in charge of emergency services at a small Dublin teaching hospital.

After that the McLoughlins moved to Glasgow where Dermot spent three and a half years specializing in radiology. He was still at the $2,400 level. They had another son, Barry, and about three quarters of the way through the course it became apparent that they'd have to give up the course or move to cheaper quarters.

They moved to the basement of a condemned tenement building. For a year the family lived in the same style as the poor of Glasgow. It was here that Deirdre learned to stuff her floorboards with newspapers and not to wear high heels because the floors were full of holes.

"My neighbour across the corridor had seven children in two bedrooms," said Deirdre. "She had a very stressful existence. Yet she taught us a lot about caring. One morning we came in from a visit to Ireland about six o'clock. We found our fire lit and the breakfast set out for us. That woman knew a lot about reaching out to others."

It was in this basement apartment that Deirdre learned to bathe her children with water heated in pots on a gas range, the chimney for the hot water tank having collapsed and the landlord having refused to repair it.

In the mid 1960's Ontario was experiencing a doctor shortage. Dermot had completed his course in radiology and was persuaded to come to Toronto General Hospital by a colleague seeking United Kingdom trained doctors for work in Canada. The McLoughlin's lived in a rental apartment for six weeks before finding a house in Don Mills.

Relief Service

Dermot's duties as a radiologist involved working at the hospital three days a week, and in the field at Midland and Penetanguishene two days a week. Soon he was also providing relief service to a radiologist in Barrie. Spotting a need in the Georgian Bay region for a more comprehensive radiology service Dr. McLoughlin moved the family to Barrie in 1967, taking up duties at the Royal Victoria hospital as resident radiologist. He later founded Georgian Radiology Consultants, serving a broad area.

Two more sons had been born. Deirdre and Dermot were now parents of John, Barry, Dermot-Paul, and Mark. It was here that the family experienced the comfortable lifestyle for ten years that they were later to give up.

"It was very pleasant, but I began to feel twinges of guilt," Dermot said. "I felt that I was losing my idealism. I didn't want to spend the next 30 or 40 years doing just this."

Deirdre, however was content to continue in the comfortable suburban role of wife, mother, and community volunteer worker, knowing at last that her children were secure and well provided for. On her holidays, one year, she went back to Ireland to visit relatives and friends.

Dermot says: "While she was away, and unknown to her, I booked us into Combermere for a week's family retreat. On her return she agreed, reluctantly, to accompany me. The retreat consisted of a challenge to people's lifestyle," he recalls. "It was for comfortable, well off people, comparing our lifestyle to the average person's in the world. All of us, as families, defended our lifestyles. As there was only one priest, and 10 families, obviously we won the debate. At the end of the week we felt we had justified our lives and went away not intending to change. That was in 1973."

But the retreat did have the effect of getting Deirdre and I talking. After a great deal of discussion we concluded that the leader, Father Bob Wild, had been right and that we only won the debate because we were numerically stronger. So now Deirdre and I were on the same wave length. Six months late we went back to Father Wild and said: "You were right. We were wrong. Now what should we do?"

Father Wild laughed and said: "I can't tell you what to do. But I can teach you how to pray. Usually, if we ask, God shows us what he wants us to do."

We kept in touch with Father Wild by letter and by tape. Long distance phone calls were too costly and not satisfactory for our discussions.

Nothing happened. Deirdre joked: "Nothing is changing so God must be happy with us just as we are."

She joined the Toronto Youth Core Team, a "think tank" catalytic group of two priests, two sisters, a family and a couple of teenagers, responsible for initiating youth and adult programs in the diocese of Toronto. They were the group who brought Mother Theresa and Jean Vanier to Toronto for speaking engagements.

Deirdre's commitments to christian outreach now equalled Dermot's. By sheer chance she had been driving by St. Monica's school one morning and noticed a number of cars in the school yard. It was July of 1974 and she remembered hearing something about a religious education course for teachers that was taking place. Curious as to what they would be teaching her children she walked up to the door and was greeted by John Prokopich, religious education consultant for the Simcoe County RCSS board, who invited her to audit the course as an interested parent.

"They were talking about building a christian community and I thought to myself – it's all fine talk but what about the practicalities of this," she recalled. "Soon I began to see the beauty of what they were about and I wanted to be part of that growth."

Time passed. As Deirdre's involvement with the Youth Core continued, Father Tom McKillop invited Deirdre and Dermot to join the team as a family resource people. The program they were involved in took place at Regine Mundi farm, run by the Sisters of the Good Shepherd at Sharon, near Newmarket. Through their contacts here the possibility of working with the Bazilian Fathers in Niger was explored and accepted.

Soul Searching

Deirdre and Dermot will never forget the deeply disturbing soul searching which preceded their total commitment as a family to this project. For guidance, they turned to prayer and the scriptures. They found their answer in Acts II, through the words of the apostle Peter: "And all who believed were together and had all things in common. And they sold their possessions and goods, and distributed them to all, as any had need."

Pulling up roots in Barrie, the family sold all but the most essential of their worldly goods and returned to Toronto, where Dermot went back to the Toronto General Hospital, as a resident in the tropical diseases unit, to refresh his skills in general practice and tropical diseases.

On completion of the preparation program the medical component of the Niger program was scrapped by the government of Niger.

"Naturally, I was frustrated and disappointed," Dermot recalls, "My income had been reduced by one third as I was studying part-time and working part-time. I returned to radiology."

Dermot obtained a position as Director of Radiology, Chedoke Division, McMaster Hospital in Hamilton. As well, he is on the faculty of radiology at McMaster University. He commuted from the house in Toronto to his job daily.

Then, one Pentecost Sunday, Dermot's reunion with the Spiritan Fathers took place. At a social occasion, Deirdre found herself standing beside the Provincial of the Order, Father Michael Doyle. In conversation, she told him of the desire she and Dermot shared to work in a christian ministry.

Father Doyle said that the order had been seeking lay people to work with them for some time and that their work was no longer just for nuns and priests. He thought the McLoughlins would be an ideal couple.

Founded in France in 1703, the Spiritans are an international family of 4,000 missionaries, serving people in over 40 countries of the world, in Africa, Latin America, Asia, Canada and the United States.

Service brought to people by the Spiritans include regular pastoral work, educational and vocational training, and socioeconomic development projects ranging from credit unions to construction programs.

Talks between the McLoughlins and the Spiritans continued. Eventually, Deirdre and Dermot agreed to open a house of hospitality. Vague in concept at first, it was agreed that the house would serve principally for lay missionaries coming back to Canada who were in need of transitional accommodation.

That's not the way it worked out. In turn, the house became a haven for: the abused teenager, the battered wife and her children, the theology student struggling to study without adequate funding, the alcoholic trying to dry out, the kid on parole looking for a job, the poor and the outcast.

It's a communal style accommodation with everyone doing his/her share towards meals and maintenance, a community of christians reaching out to help each other. Tucked away in the basement is a study area where the group meets for prayer each evening. Living in the house at the present time are Dermot and Deirdre, their four sons, Margaret Laffey, another lay Spiritan who is a counsellor with Manpower, and who is involved also in an Ontario housing high rise ministry, and a young nurse.

Across the road, there is an apartment, housing a young family. The father is working toward his master's degree in theology before resuming work in Kingston.

Ashling House is financed totally by the McLoughlins, out of Dermot's salary. Those who are given shelter there help if they can. The apartment is partially subsidized, with Dermot and Deirdre taking up the slack. Dermot, Deirdre, and Margaret Laffey are the only three lay Spiritans in English-speaking Canada. Everyone in the community is expected to have some outreach, but there is a welcome there for those who are just searching and who hope someday to be able to do something for others.

The McLoughlins' four children are also deeply committed to living their faith. All are supportive of their parents and do their share in maintaining the property and contributing their time and talents where need exists.

Retreat Teams

But the family's involvement with christian outreach does not stop with the running of Ashley House. Deirdre, who has studied at the Toronto School of Theology, works on spiritual retreat teams as director. Currently she is involved with the Jesuit lay institute program at Ignatius College, Guelph, and acts as a resource person at christian conferences.

Then there is their work with Canadian Indians. This grew out of a conversation with Father Doyle, the Spiritan's provincial, who said to Dermot: "You were looking for something at the other side of the world. Why don't you look at Ontario? There is great need in northern Ontario, both in radiology and in general practice."

Accepting the challenge, Dermot was sent back to Dr. Bernard Reilly, former chief of radiology for the Hospital for Sick Children, the same man who had recruited him in Glasgow for service at Toronto General.

He put Dermot on the roster of radiologists at Sioux Lookout hospital for two weeks each year. Doctors there told Dermot of the great need for a general practioner at the New Osnaburgh Indian Reserve, 400 miles north of Thunder Bay.

Leave of Absence

There was no difficulty in getting time off from his job at

Hamilton for this work as one of the conditions of employment secured by Dermot before accepting the post at the hospital and university was that he required three months leave of absence each year for his own Christian outreach work.

Now, he spends two weeks of each year at Sioux Lookout Zone hospital doing radiology and the other 10 weeks he serves as coordinator of radiological services, Moosefactory Zone, northeastern Ontario.

"Most problems on the reserve are not medical, but social," he said. "The biggest problem I discovered was with the boredom and apathy of the young people. I wanted to help in this regard but had no idea of where to begin. Also, when I went to the reserve I was in the hypocritical position of living in federal luxury, (hot water and plumbing) amidst native poverty."

He and Deirdre decided that to get to know the native people of Canada they would have to live among them. Not as city people, come to observe and study them, but sharing their way of life. Not to preach at them, or judge, just to listen and be their friends.

They talked to Chief Roy Kaminawaish about their proposal and he replied: "We are glad you have no program for us, and we have none for you. Come here and live with us and do what the white person seldom does. Listen to us. When you have been here a while, and if the people trust you, they will ask you to do things for them – and these are the things you are meant to do."

Fifty-percent of the Indians on the reserve are christian. Only a small percent are Catholic. Many still worship in their native religion.

"We don't go as evangelists. We go only to be a friend," says Deirdre, knowing that when she and her two youngest children move into the abandoned church which will be their home this summer, that they will be tested over and over again. The church is without electricity or running water or toilets, but they will live as the Indians do and try to get to know them.

"I would like to be able to build you a house," the chief told the McLoughlins. "But white people have come and gone before."

Dermot says that the social problems of the Indians are the result of apathy, brought on by the violation of native rights and land settlements.

"In the English Wabigoon river system, pollution by mercury from the Dryden Pulp and Paper Mill has made the fish unsuitable for consumption for the next 70 years. This has stripped the Indians of employment. Where there is no fishing, there is no fishing, there is no tourism, or no call for guides, the Indian's chief source of employment."

"I was shocked to learn that the average life expectancy of the Canadian Indian male today is 46 years", says Dermot. "Strangely, we do not have available figures for the woman's life expectancy."

"The medical people are saying: Let's quit putting money into increased medical service. Instead, let us provide for each community, piped, clean running water, proper sanitation, community baths, showers, toilets, laundry facilities."

"We've got to educate them about nutrition too," he believes. "The junk food has moved in. Chips and coke are the big thing."

It's been a long life in a few years for the McLoughlins. From Nigeria to Glasgow to Toronto and now to the isolation of an Indian reserve in the far north. But isolation is the wrong word. They are never alone. Guided by the Holy Spirit they move around the world carrying the message of Christ, for living by his rules, and spiritually supported by his message of love and concern for the least of these, my brothers and sisters.

By Sheila Coo, *The Reporter.* May/June, 1981. Vol. 6, Nos. 8 & 9. (A magazine for the Ontario English Catholic Teachers' Association.)

GOD'S VISION OF SIN, MERCY AND FORGIVENESS

Purpose: As we discover God's feelings, we realize that the Trinity has great desires for us, for our good. Yet we live in a society in which there is little or no sense of sin (except the sin of "getting caught') even as we suffer the widespread effects of sin and the need for healing. Our purpose is to remember the Lord's way of seeing sin, mercy and forgiveness so that we may experience his gift individually and collectively. We will take time to discuss some questions on sin, forgiveness and healing; we will also symbolize our call to be a healing community in a mutual anointing with oil.

Minutes

15   1. Begin with a hymn, prayer (presence, thanksgiving, light). Ask for the gift to desire reconciliation and unity as God does, to experience it in our lives.

Lead the following:

"Let us remember that God has already forgiven us; because of this, we are able to go beyond ourselves with compassion. The Trinity is the sacred source of our lives and of all others who journey."

"Imagine yourself with any person you need to forgive . . . recognize the Trinity's love for him/-her . . . reach out and offer forgiveness; see the other's peace and imagine how you can now relate together in a new way . . . (Pause)"

"Imagine yourself with someone whom you have hurt; see yourself asking pardon and receiving forgiveness. Imagine the new life and hope filling both of you so that the Lord's grace will far outweigh any evil. How do you show or celebrate this?" (Pause)

"Imagine forgiving yourself and accepting it; throw away the burden of guilt! Come before the Lord and let him forgive you. Celebrate this! (Pause)"

"Imagine representing a nation. Come before another "people", ask for and receive forgiveness . . . offer forgiveness. How can you celebrate this? Imagine relating well together now." (Pause)

"Society needs healing. Embrace it in a healing way . . . (Pause) We also need to find healing between ourselves and the earth. We have wounded and destroyed it for selfish purposes; what we have done to the earth, air and water, we have done to ourselves and others. Pour healing waters over it; treasure it in gratitude." (Pause)

Read Luke 1:76-79.

45 2. Share any of this.

10 BREAK

45 3. Use your imagination to picture each of the following and then discuss some of them:
   a) How did Jesus relate to sinners? (Mark 2:5-10,10-17, 3:28, 14:41, 7:6, 12:15,24)
   b) What keeps me from forgiving myself?
   c) How is sin one of the hurts that needs to be healed in community?
   d) What group, institutional or societal sin are we reluctant to admit today? Why?
   e) How can we be a healing society? How can we be a healing church?

15 4. Read the article on sin, mercy and forgiveness. (Refer to the end of this week.) Comment on it as desired.

15 5. Continue to plan next week's celebration so that it integrates elements of personal, group and/or societal healing.

Recall how oil can be soothing, healing, strengthening; as such it can be a symbol of our desire and promise to be a healing community. Stand in a circle; let one person pray aloud for the next and anoint his/her forehead with oil. Continue this around the group. Join hands and remember all those for whom you want to be a healing community. End this celebration with song and/or prayer and any final preparations for next week's celebration.

5 6. Prepare Prayer for the Week.

Prayer for the Week:

(A) Daily awareness exercise. Include one of the following each day:

a) Remember some hurt you have experienced. Imagine it happening again and invite Jesus to be with you and any other(s) involved to heal you.

b) Remember yesterday's prayer and continue with any moment of it.

c) What is needed for you "to get over" past hurts? What are you willing to do about them? Invite Jesus to share your concerns and to heal you.

d) In what ways have you felt and expressed any discouragement or depression over a past hurt or loss; e.g., "I don't care", feeling more tired, generally irritable, being more sensitive, or closed and critical. Let the feelings surface and bring them to the Lord. Ask him how he feels about you!

(B) Daily scripture prayer:
> Luke 5:1-11
> Luke 5:17-26
> Luke 6:36-38
> Luke 7:36-50
> Luke 15:1-10
> Luke 15:11-32

187

For further reading:

SIN, MERCY AND FORGIVENESS

God is the loving creator and redeemer. The Trinity brought us into existence and relates to us personally, thereby, making us persons. As Father, Son and Spirit relate with us, their loving gift of themselves continues to be creative for us. Sin is basically an unwillingness to carry on this relationship and communion with God, preventing God from letting their love take root in us. Ungrateful pride and self- sufficiency isolate us, saying, "Leave me alone." It is non-sense and anti-social. It cuts off relationship with God and the people of God. It is individualistic, a non-response to love offered. We cannot love alone. Only God initiates love; we get in tune with it. But sin cuts us off from the source of love; it is self-destruction and leaves us helpless. Cut off from loved ones and unable to communicate or even ask forgiveness, our self becomes fragmented.

Only as the Trinity forgives and takes the initiative in giving themselves to us can we be recreated, redeemed and given salvation or wholeness (within ourselves and with others).

The story of the old testament is a history of a people's relationship with God. Although people are continually breaking the covenant relationship, God is always faithful. The image of God is one of a loving mother, or of a persistent husband, loving his adulterous wife and bringing her home. In the new testament, the image of God is one of a loving father desiring the return of his son and of a shepherd seeking out the lost. Focusing on ourselves, we find it difficult to admit sin; it is a sign of grace and relationship that we consider ourselves sinners. It is because the woman (Lk. 7:36-50) was forgiven much that she can love much! Forgiveness precedes her loving. It is natural, spontaneous and freeing for her to go to Jesus and pour out her tears of love. It became a way of celebrating the forgiveness! We are body-persons and celebrate externally what is real within. Also just as sin is anti-social (and affects others deeply), the gift of relating with the Trinity makes us more social, more loving.

Our christian community is a communion of sinners with the Lord. We need not be surprised by the presence of selfishness, betrayals, misunderstandings and all other violations of the ideal. We do not need to pretend they do not exist or defend them. We are all sinners who are loved by the Lord. Whenever we come together for a eucharistic celebration, we begin by admitting our common bond of weakness; we receive forgiveness and forgive others. It becomes obvious that it is the Lord's power that is at work in us!

CELEBRATION OF CHRIST, THE HEALER, AND IN HIM HOW WE ARE A HEALING COMMUNITY FOR EACH OTHER AND FOR SOCIETY

Refer back to III-16, #5.

The following article may be helpful at any point along the way. It seems particularly important in Units III and IV to reflect on experience in depth.

COMPANIONING ANOTHER ALONG THE WAY

PURPOSE: to walk with others in attaining freedom re: God, others, self, to read my/our own religious experience of God transforming me/us into Jesus Christ. This can apply to individual and group interaction.

GOD: How do I feel about God? How do I imagine Trinity? How does God feel about me? Does God love me? like me? Really? How has God treated me in the past? What are the significant experiences of God in my past? How do I experience the person of the risen Christ?

What has the Lord/Spirit been saying to me during the past week/month?

OTHERS: immediate relationships

How do I feel about various other people? What is my relationship with them? Am I free? Where I am not free, how do I respond—run? try to dominate? Do I leave people free; do I manipulate? Do I foster fraternal or sisterly union? What is my relationship with authority? What is my contribution to family/community life? Am I loved by my family/community? Do I share with them? Where do I find my affective support? Where are my loyalties?

The quality of presence in my immediate life will be the quality of presence in larger issues. Adding world view to the spiritual conversation is valid and bridges the gap between others and self-knowledge. Self-knowledge and self-acceptance are important for a free response to God. Self-knowledge, if it is to be true and not false, includes not only knowledge of my relatedness to God, self, and others (those in my immediate relationships) but knowledge of my relatedness to:

- my sisters and brothers across the world
- the culture as it influences me positively and negatively
- the balances and imbalances in the physical universe
- the present socio-economic-political structures of the country in which I live.

The pivotal areas relating the above dimensions are:

- Union with God:
  Where do I find God in all of this? How do I experience union with God in the here and now of prayer? of life? of the interpenetration of the two?

- Conversion of heart:
  What area(s) of my heart is God asking me to open up NOW in order to allow Jesus to free me, to heal me, to integrate within me a life of faith and justice in service to others as was his own?

- Sacrament of the present:
  Can I see that living in the moment or centering in the present: am, and that God is, and that I am not God? Can I see that living the present moment is an entry into relatedness and awareness? Living the justice of the present moment interpenetrates the larger issues of justice in the world.

WORLD VIEW: JUSTICE IS CONSTITUTIVE OF THE GOSPEL MESSAGE

We are striving for a oneness that finds the action of God in those we meet in our experience of human development, in all dimensions of the human community, AS WELL AS in solitude and formal prayer. The spiritual life involves participation in the salvation history of a whole people, AS WELL AS, a uniquely personal relationship with the Lord.

How wide is my vision . . . Do I realize that we do not have private ownership of God but that God is working to bring about justice and liberation for the poor and oppressed peoples of all nations?

What are the implications here?

for me? for the way I live?

for us? . . . community/family . . . for the way we live?

What do I know of social structures, power-relationships and social institutions that are oppressive in the neighborhood and city in which I live? What about the power-relationships and oppression in my own heart?

Is it important to me at all to be aware of this?

How is God present to me in this awareness?

Do I ever feel moved to action in behalf of justice?

Do I ever feel moved to action in behalf of justice especially when it means being misunderstood and rejected?

What does it mean concretely in my life to reverence the created things with which he has surrounded us . . . ?

What method do I use for examining the simplicity in my manner of living and my responsible stewardship of resources?

THE WORD JUDGES ALL CULTURES AND VALUE SYSTEMS . . . IT IS THE CRITERIA AGAINST WHICH ALL ELSE IS MEASURED

I need to discover, if I don't already sense it, that the graced-positive things of our culture are under attack; that is, the human family, a high sense of equality, the dignity of the human person as an irreplaceable and unique being capable of commitment, the beauty of the land, the sense of the poor.

You could name more I am sure. There are some wonderful and precious aspects of reality—

>eager search for spiritual meaning
>high value placed on freedom
>growing aspirations for justice and human rights
>longing for genuine human community.

Yet there is a DARK SIDE

Where do I stand with regard to society's idolatry which worships:

root	root	virtue	counsels
Individualism Self-reliance	Pride	Faith	Humility

Technology
Growth and progress
Hard work and
    productivity
Consumerism
Saving and planning
    ahead
	Avarice	Hope	Poverty

Instant gratification of the senses	Gluttony	Temperance	Discipline
Competition	Envy	Justice	Generosity
Sex and violence	Lust	Charity	Chastity
	Anger	Prudence	Peace
	Sloth	Courage	Zeal

Not only where do I stand—but do I find myself seeking my self-worth in any of these areas?

Have I so identified with one or other cultural stance that I find myself defining who I am out of that false God?

Can I see that these things close me off from my basic poverty and vulnerability and dependence upon God?

Am I willing to face the false god(s) and see the possibilities of graced movement involved in a transformation into the heart and mind of Christ?

What do I hope in? believe in? trust in? love . . .

Why do I get up every morning?

What are my cultural idols and addictions?

Discernment is needed to sort out what is authentic from what is inauthentic in all that claims to be of God's Spirit. We are seeking to read the signs of God's action and to attain the conversion of heart, inner freedom and fidelity necessary for every genuine prophetic voice.

What does the phrase "signs of the times" mean to me? Currently, what are they? How do you perceive God speaking in all of this?

What do I think are the great world issues/crises? Where is the Trinity in all of this? What do I think are the elements of evil present in the nation?

Can I and do I critique the society in which I live?

Do I see any points of controversy and conflict between the Word of God and the dominant attitudes and values prevailing in society's way of life today? Where is God in all of this? Where is my heart? What does this say to my life-style?

Am I aware of racism, sexism, paternalism and authoritarianism, and indifference to human life? How do I address myself to these evils?

THE TRINITY MANIFESTS THEMSELVES TO US IN SIGNS AND SYMBOLS—AND THE FINEST SYMBOL AND SACRAMENT OF GOD UPON EARTH IS THE HUMAN PERSON.

Incarnational spirituality is a way of meeting and responding to the Trinity in daily life. It is the spirituality where we find contact with God in contact with human beings.

"The joys and the hopes, the griefs and the anxieties of the people of this age, especially those who are poor or in any way afflicted, these too are the joys and hopes, the griefs and anxieties of the followers of Christ." *Gaudium et Spes* #1.

The Trinity's saving action becomes especially evident to us when we encounter the poor and the marginalized. What is marginal to our society is central to God. Our conversion toward solidarity with them is part of our move to a deeper union with God.

What has been my experience of God in the people I encounter?

Do these experiences of relationship enter into prayer in any way for me.

Among the others I encounter in day to day life, what is the extent and depth of my direct contact with the materially poor and dispossessed?

Do I have any friends among the economically poor, the handicapped, the alienated, the broken people who always live on the edge of things? What is my attitude to these people the Bible calls "the anawim'? Have I ever prayed the gospel standing in the shoes of a poor person?

How many hours a week do I spend watching TV?

How is the nuclear arms race a part of my life with God? Does the possibility of a global holocaust have anything to say to my life of hope? Where do I find the "Tridents" in my own heart? Is there violence in my interrelatedness with people?

What the securities, the non-negotiables of my life? How tightly do I hold on to power? Am I learning to give without power and receive gratefully without resentment?

These questions like all the rest are but a help to get in touch with my life with God. They are multiple in order to over-emphasize a point. In no way would anyone try to cover all of these in a short time, but perhaps over the years, some of these questions would be helpful to growth in the spirit.

Genevieve Cassani SSND

UNIT IV
INTEGRATING FAITH AND JUSTICE:
HEALING OUR COLLECTIVE EXPERIENCE

Thrust: Healing is a process that involves more than our personal imagination, awareness and emotions. Just as it requires personal understanding of myths that dominate our society (and that we tend to maintain) so also does it require healing in the collective (societal, corporate or public) realm. This necessarily involves a search for truth: the truth of God's vision and dream for us, the truth of how we destroy the vision and each other, the truth of our call and human potential in union with the Lord. Yet even as we search, we know that God is truth and life and that he expresses this reality fully in Jesus. We know the Lord and ourselves; we experience the truth of our existence as we are united with him and open to others.

As we continue to meet the Lord, we gradually become more aware that the place and time of our meeting is now; that is, he is really present with us here and now in the reality of our lives, individually and socially. In fact, the Lord communicates with us not only by sharing his Spirit with us and through his word in scripture, but also in a special way through his body; that is, through all humanity and creation. Openness to the 'mystical body of Christ', God's people, leads us to union with the Lord himself and we are healed anew. The more our interior attitudes inform and are expressed in our external social realities, the more we will experience simplicity, oneness, wholeness. Inner integrity and being true to our consciences requires that we act on the truth that we discover.

Our personal healing is thereby strengthened; it is expressed and expanded in healing the collective. In turn, the societal impact on us is then not only less devastating, but actually life-giving and energizing for us. In this unit, therefore, we desire to face our collective reality and do whatever is required for its healing and wholeness.

Process: In these next weeks, we will 'walk through' some experiences in our faith history (in both old and new testament times) to discover the Trinity's vision and ways more clearly. In the last unit we came to know the Jesus of the gospels better through sensing his presence imaginatively in prayer. Now we will bring the place of meeting him to greater fullness. To meet the risen Lord and know him today, our imagery changes to meeting the body of Christ. We therefore expand our prayer to include social contemplation. To help us with this and to integrate it with our daily lives, we will learn from others' experiences and walk through our streets to meet the Lord. In bringing justice, we see the need for analysis and being informed on some current issue(s). This naturally leads us to face guilt, powerlessness and the challenge of encountering those who oppose; we look to our source of hope and conclude with a celebration.

Our prayer each week will still be the daily awareness exercise and scripture prayer. The focus, however, shifts to one of social consciousness; that is, to bring ourselves as social or relating persons to the Lord, to broaden our image of Jesus to be attentive to the 'body of Christ' today in all people and creation and to confirm or root what we experience in prayer, in community truth and action. For extra reading, we suggest the Book of Wisdom and the letter of James. We have used some excerpts here.

198

Discernment is needed in a special way in these weeks. Since this material touches on attitudes and customs that are not main-stream thinking in society, people may find themselves particularly sensitive, vulnerable or angry and hardly know the reason for it. It is important to keep in touch with the Trinity's vision, profound love for us and promise to be with us (basic consolation) and to pray for heart-felt trust and wisdom in the way the Lord leads us, gently, one step at a time. It is understandable if we tend to hide in fight or flight in any of the many forms these defense tactics can take: directly in prayer, avoiding prayer, or projecting the fight or flight in ways that influence relationships within the community or with others. We will need to be both sensitive and respectful of the movements within individuals and groups but not be afraid of them. We will stay with or return at a later time to the source of challenge, 'befriending it', that is, letting the Lord reveal any need for healing, change, reassurance. Instead of pushing or forcing an issue with an individual, we will be extra supportive. Little by little, the Lord corrects us so that we may trust him! (Widsom 12:1)

Week 1 Learning From History: The Trinity Sides With The Poor

Week 2 Learning From History: The Trinity's Hope Is Justice For All

Week 3 Learning From Others' Experience (1)

Week 4 Learning From Others' Experience (2)

Week 5 For Jesus Or Against Him?

Week 6 Walking With Jesus In Our Streets

Week 7 Learning From Jesus' Mother, Mary: Woman Of Faith And Model Of Discipleship

Goals:
- to discover more clearly God's vision, pref-
erence for the poor and hope of justice for all
- to learn from resource persons (the marginalized, anyone who is unemployed because of unavailability, handicap, lack of jobs, responsibility at home, and/or someone who is terminally
ill) in order to learn compassion, what impact
society (ourselves) have had on them, how they
react to their situation ... and what this means
for us
- to meet the Lord as he communicates through
his body today, as he is present among us. To
reflect on, articulate and interpret this experience in the light of faith, probing to understand
our social realities better so that we may act
more effectively to set things right
- to become more aware of how social structures
affect our lives

- to realize that social consciousness and working for justice is intrinsic to the gospels and church teaching

- to realize that any feelings of guilt and power-lessness which paralyze us are deceptive; to trust Jesus more as Lord of history and Lord of our lives

- to experience that dialogue with another is a form of communion and must be based on love and respect for the other. To develop readiness to encounter others even in disagreements with willingness and ability to listen openly and speak honestly, humbly and simply so that both participants may discover the good that is greater than their individual insights

- to celebrate our discipleship in community

LEARNING FROM HISTORY: THE TRINITY SIDES WITH THE POOR

Purpose: The Lord has a vision for his people and he sets up a covenant with them. We see how it worked and how it didn't work. Because the vision was being destroyed, the Lord intervenes and takes sides with his people to set the vision straight; that is, to correct the two basic sins of idolatry and injustice. We will do an overview of this in the old testatment and then new testament: in compassion, God sides with the poor to correct the vision, build the kingdom and save all.

We will also prepare for weeks 3 and 4 by deciding on resource people and clarifying reasons for having them.

Minutes

15   1. Begin with a hymn and prayer, taking a few moments to remember quietly a Genesis account of creation, how God found people very good and walked in the garden with them. Imagine ourselves being with God for others in the same way. Read aloud Wisdom 9.

   Reflect quietly for about ten minutes.

5   2. Give an overview of the unit (refer to the initial Thrust and Process) and of this evening.

50   3. In partners, read and share some experiences in our faith history to discover God's vision and ways more clearly. Read them with an attitude of trust that God will lead you in the path of wisdom:

   a) Genesis 15:5-6, Exodus 3:7-11, 19:3-8, Deuteronomy 15:1-11, 24:10-21, 26:5-10 Amos 5:24, 8:4-6, Jeremiah 5:26-29.

   b) The article 'God's Preferential Option for the Poor' (It is included after the Prayer for the Week.)

10   BREAK

45   4. Come together, reflect quietly on the following
      questions and share your conclusions to the to-
      tal process:
      a) How did God take sides?
      b) What does this mean for you?
      c) How are we then to love the rich (including
         ourselves if we are)?

15   5. Prepare for Weeks 3 and 4 by deciding whom
      you will invite as a resource person, for Week 3,
      someone who cannot find work because of unavail-
      ability, handicap, lack of jobs or responsibility at
      home; for Week 4, someone who is terminally ill,
      widowed, a single parent on welfare, or unem-
      ployed and on welfare.

      Purpose: our community would appreciate hearing
      what you're going through. It could happen to us
      and we want to know how your're coping with it so
      that we can learn from you.

      Decide who will invite the person, give her/him an
      outline for the meeting and arrange transportation.
      (For further clarification of our purpose, refer to
      IV-3.)

10   6. Journal: What happened in you and the com-
         munity this evening?

      Prepare for the Prayer of the Week by noting
      the focus.

5   7. Conclude with singing/praying as it is appro-
      priate.

Prayer for the Week:

(A) Daily awareness prayer, being particularly aware of atti-
    tudes toward others and subtle prejudices and preferences
    within ourselves.

(B) Daily scripture prayer:
Ask to appreciate the Trinity's vision and covenant with us, and how they invite us to share it in our daily lives.

DAY 1 Deuteronomy 15:1-11.

DAY 2 James 1:27. Who are the widows, strangers and orphans in your life?

DAY 3 Wisdom 6:7-8.

DAY 4 James 2:1-4. Do you set up 'we' and 'they' categories?

DAY 5 What image of God have you seen over the past week? Exodus 3:7-12.

DAY 6 Whose side are you on? How? How do you love the rich and poor in your life? Talk this over with the Lord and read Wisdom 7:27-8:1.

For further reading:

THE TRINITY'S PREFERENTIAL OPTION FOR THE POOR

Does the Trinity really have a preferential option for the poor? If God's views are already slanted in favour of the poor, how can the Lord claim to be just for all? Where does that put those of us who are maybe not all that poor?

In the beginning it is not at all clear that God sided with the poor. Rather he sided with Abraham and Sarah, concluding a covenant with them and with all their offspring (Gen. 15:5-6, 17:15-18 and Hebrews 11:8-13). The Lord would never go back on his promise. So when he heard the cry of his people coming up to him from Egypt, he took measures (through Moses) to free them (Ex. 3:7-10). This, of course, is the story of the Exodus (Dt. 26:5-10), an experience of liberation so strong that it became the founding event for the people of Israel and the occasion of a new alliance (Ex. 19:5-8). The Lord had not willed poverty and oppression for his people; he had wanted prosperity. He saw that the poverty of his people did not just happen; it was deliberately made by human beings. Overcome by the power of others, the people had no other recourse but to God. But the Trinity used the experience of that pain to install among their own a more humane treatment not only of the members of the people but even of the strangers in their midst (Dt. 15:1-11, 24:10-21). The Lord presented himself as the defender of the needy, the protector of human rights when the powerful abused their privileges. God had willed creation for responsible use by all. Poverty caused by injustice made God a liar; God could not stand by idly. So when some Israelites became greedy and started to enslave their brothers and sisters, hoarding what was meant for all (Am. 8:4-6), the Lord sent the prophets to remind them that if they did not repent of their injustice, the Lord himself would side with the poor, so that justice would be upheld (Jer. 5:26-29). Neither the Lord nor his promise would be mocked: he would set things as the covenant had set them. God took sides, not because the poor were morally better, not because God hated those who were better off, but simply out of fidelity to the original plan of liberation for all God's people: after all God had brought them to the land where milk and honey would flow for everyone. God sided with the poor because, since they were the ones being made poor by the rich, they hurt more and called more readily on the Lord to administer justice. The rich on their side preferred to call on the local fertility gods (Ba'al) with their promises of flocks and crops. When the powerful became too arrogant and rich however, God chastized the whole people, purifying them through upheavals and exiles, yet remaining forever faithful to the little poor remnant who upheld his covenant.

It is in this last tradition that Jesus traces his spiritual roots, for he came from a family which recognized God's original project (Lk. 1:46-55). Yet in Jesus a new covenant is struck. The people of God no longer represent only Israel, but every human being in the universe: God's image was not only in Abraham and Sarah's posterity but in each of Adam and Eve's descendants. By his attitudes, Jesus shows that every person, no matter what his/her condition, is a child of the Father, worthy of his love. Jesus sides with the outcasts for they, more than anybody, are the ones who need the doctor (Mk. 2:16-17). Jesus sides with the poor in his own behaviour, opting for utter powerlessness (Mk. 15:31-32) against those who would prefer riches (Mk. 10:17-23), prestige (Mk. 10:35-40) and power (Mk. 10:41-45), be it civil (Mk. 12:17) or religious (Mk. 7:6-8, 11:27-33). Children especially, the most vulnerable and powerless segment of the Jewish culture, are presented by Jesus as models of discipleship (Mk. 9:37, 10:14-15, 10:24). The poor, like the children, were less full of themselves and of material goods, and therefore more ready to respond in faith to the call of the kingdom (Mk. 10:25-27).

Jesus' message and his compassion led him to be fully on the side of those who were suffering, rather than stand with those who were in power. It was not enough to have his head and heart with the poor; he expressed this love by walking with them, by putting his feet there too! This conscious choice by Jesus necessarily strongly influenced what he had to say about himself (Lk. 4:18-21) and about the kingdom of God (Lk. 6:20). Maybe Jesus sided with the poor because he knew that the message, if given first to the poor would trickle up to the rich, but the reverse might not have been true. Surprisingly, history bore fruitful witness to the process Jesus used in making sure the message got around. As christians ourselves, with whom are our alliances? Where do our feet stand?

LEARNING FROM HISTORY: THE TRINITY'S HOPE IS JUSTICE FOR ALL

Purpose: We will reflect on the scriptural view of kingdom and what it means for us, particularly in our attitudes and encounters with the marginalized. The focus for Prayer of the Week is on this awareness and on letting the mystery of Jesus' presence and kingdom take shape in our immediate and global milieu; this means that we will need to take a little more time to introduce the approach to prayer this week.

Minutes

15   1. Begin with singing and prayer (similar to the prayer for the awareness exercise since the first part of the meeting is a shared awareness exercise). Refer to III-9: presence, thanksgiving, light or wisdom.

Ask to appreciate and share Jesus' understanding of kingdom. Read Mark 2:15-17, imagining yourself with Jesus and his companions.

50   2. Share any aspects of prayer and awareness of the past week.

10   BREAK

45   3. Read, reflect and share the following with a partner:
   a) What does kingdom mean to you?
   b) What does kingdom mean to the Trinity?
      i) Refer to 3 or 4 of the following gospel passages: Mark 4:26-34; 10:17-23,35-45; 12:17; 15:31-32.
      Luke 6:20; 13:18-21; 14:15-24; 16:19-31.
      ii) Read or refer to the article, 'Your Kingdom Come....?', which is included after the Prayer for the week.
   c) Compare a) and b).
   d) Who are in the kingdom?

207

      e) What feelings and images come to you when you think of the unemployed or people on welfare.

How does this fit with the Trinity's vision of the marginalized? What does this mean for you?

10   4. Prepare for the Prayer of the Week.

15   5. Journal and sharing: What happened in you and in the community this evening?

What does this mean for us?

5   6. Conclude with prayer and/or a hymn.

Reminder: resource persons will be with us next week.

Prayer for the Week:

(A) Awareness and prayer. When you go to work, shopping, church (anywhere) notice people and remember, 'This is the body of Christ'.

(B) Scripture prayer using our imagination to broaden our understanding of who Christ is. Therefore, be with Jesus in the gospel scene. The next day, use the same gospel passage but picture yourself with people in your immediate range of contacts, especially those whom you consider the least. Look at them and remember, 'This is the body of Christ'. You may want to do the same picturing destitute people in oppressed areas.

This is our way of encountering Christ today; he communicates with us, meets us through his body; namely, all people and creation. The 'place' of meeting the Lord is expanded as we sense the shape of the mystery today.

DAYS 1-4

Mark 9:37 and Mark 2:15-17.

DAY 5 When have you felt unwanted, useless or rejected? What did it do to you? What temptations and problems developed for you? Remember this with Jesus; talk with him about it. Let him heal you and give you understanding compassion for others.

DAY 6 When did you disregard, ignore or reject another? How did you deal with it? Do you still have some reconciling to do? Remember this with Jesus. Let him show you the moments and the way. Ask for the ability to make good decisions. Pray the 'Our Father'.

For further reading:

YOUR KINGDOM COME....?

These words of Jesus have been uttered thousands of times by people in prayer as a salve for the wounded world. Yet how many people are aware of the radical if not revolutionary effect the coming kingdom would have on their lives? For many, 'kingdom' simply evokes a series of fantasies around kings and queens, around courts and fairy tales. 'Kingdom of God' on the other hand, probably conjures up images of heaven or paradise lost, a place where bliss eliminates all pain. But is this truly what the 'Kingdom of God' is all about?

For many years after the great Exodus from Egypt, the Lord intervened directly among his people through chosen persons called judges. But there came a time when the people grumbled saying: 'We want a king, so that we in turn can be like other nations; our king shall rule us, and be our leader and fight our battles.' (1 Sam. 8:20). The purpose of the king, and the reason power was given to him, was to keep the people of God together as a holy people. More than any army chief, his role was to rule over the people, to administer justice (1 Kings 3:9), to behave as God would in the midst of his people (Wis. 6:1-9). The king was God's presence on earth: this is why, more than anyone, the king was to follow God's plan for his people and respect God's covenant. He was to be as accessible to any member of the people as God was. (This mentality still exists in many Arab countries where the kings, the sheiks and the ayatollahs receive people each day asking them to solve local disputes). Thus any Israelite could go right to the top to get a fair hearing, if s/he felt that justice was not granted him/her by a magistrate at the door of the city (the judges, often rich landowners, would hear cases at the gates of the city, where the elders also often congregated). Sometimes the judges would be bribed by the rich or there were conflicts of interest (Amos 5:7-12, Is. 10:1-3). The people were always to be able to count on the king as on God (Ps. 72). But some kings themselves became corrupt giving themselves over to greed or to idols. This could not be God's kingdom; therefore, God needed to intervene to set justice back on its right path (Is. 51:4-8). Unfortunately, the years of the kings, the years in exile and even the years of reinstallation in Palestine (Neh. 5:1-9) did little to improve the basic rift between the people's behaviour and God's hopes for them. Something(one?) special was needed.

In presenting himself to the public, Jesus' first words concern the kingdom: 'The Kingdom of God is close at hand. Repent and believe the Good News.' (Mk. 1:15). This word will be used no less than 162 times in the four gospels, indicating its major importance in Jesus' preaching. An essential turning point has been reached in the history of the People of God: through Jesus, God is taking over again.

What is this kingdom all about? Paul puts it very clearly: 'The Kingdom of God does not mean eating or drinking this or that. It means righteousness and peace and joy brought by the Holy Spirit.' (Rm. 14:17). It is a mysterious kingdom (Lk. 8:10) not at all like the other sovereignties of the world. Righteousness means justice for all. Peace means a balanced social order, and joy is the result of the blessing brought by justice and peace. This is not a 'pie in the sky' spiritualistic paradise. It is very much a 'this world' reality. The kingdom is no less than God's hope for humanity come true. It is however paradoxical, symbolized at its height by the powerlessness and the love of Jesus, suffering and dying on a cross while an inscription says: 'Jesus, King of the Jews'. Putting things in a divine perspective means turning society's values upside-down. Loving service, not success, is what counts in the kingdom. Those who are called to the kingdom are certainly not those one would expect: sinners and tax-collectors (Mt. 21:31), people who are hurt by life (Lk. 10:10) or outcasts (Lk. 14:21-24), people who are not blinded by riches (Mk. 10:23), who are like children (Mk. 10:15), coming from everywhere (Lk. 13:29-30) who either follow Jesus consciously (Lk. 12:32) or unknowingly (Mt. 25:31-46). One who submits to the sovereignty of God must be willing in faith to submit to the disturbances and revolutions this choice imposes on one's life. Calling forth the presence of the kingdom in our lives is calling forth no less than the struggle against selfishness, be it individual or collective. It challenges our many false securities, the little 'idols' we keep around, 'just in case ... '. It shatters our narrow vision of things in order to thrust us into the perplexing world of God's vision where 'death' is life and birth. It disturbs all our laws of logic and plunges them into the truthfulness of love and hope. The kingdom is gift, beyond all our possibilities (Mk. 10:27). But it is offered (Mk. 9:47) to all those who hasten its coming through prayer and action.

Kingdom anyone?

LEARNING FROM OTHERS' EXPERIENCE (1)

Purpose: A resource person (previously invited and someone who cannot find work because of unavailability, lack of jobs, or responsibility at home), will share with the community:

   a) The community can learn compassion as others share the story of their efforts to fit into society; seeing that they are not naturally outcasts, we also see how they are often pushed aside by others. James 2:19

   b) In the context of the 'humanizing process', we can ask how they are reacting to the situation they are in, how they feel part of society, how they feel excluded, what all this means to us as a community and individually. We reflect on what is humanizing/dehumanizing, and the effect it has on all of us.

   c) By seeing that 'it could happen to me', denial is stripped away.

   d) By seeing that our collaboration in allowing poverty to exist necessarily involves us in responsibility for the consequences of it; for example, we are part of any theft, abuse, prostitution; we can understand more compassionately without judgment on them; we can ask forgiveness. St. Basil: 'Their sin is our sin'. James 2:16

   e) Hopefully this experience will be affirming for the guest resource person (you value me enough to hear what influence society has on my life).

Minutes

10   1. Welcome the guest(s); give the format of the evening.

10   2. Hymn and prayer: presence, thanksgiving, light. Reflect quietly for a few minutes using Mark 4:26-34 to shed light on the experience of the past week.

45   3. Tell the guest what the topics for prayer were the past week and then continue with the sharing as usual.

10   **BREAK**

50   4. Invite the resource person to share re: her/his present situation. Possibly ask questions for clarification; such as, how s/he is responding to the situation, how s/he feels part of society and/or excluded from it, what is most difficult in this situation and what has helped up to this time.

20   5. Each of the community writes: 'If I were this resource person, I would .... '.

Check with the speaker about how s/he does feel.

10   6. Group reflection on the meeting, in the form of prayer; for example, thanksgiving for the particular ways the resource person has touched their lives.

5   7. Conclude with singing.

Prayer for the Week:

(A) Awareness prayer.

(B) Scripture prayer:

Ask to realize what impact society has on us and how the life of each affects others.

DAY 1   Remember what was shared at the meeting and talk with the Lord re: how it touched you. What did the community experience? Luke 6:20

DAY 2   Pray on any event in the news. How is it affecting those involved, their families, society and you? Ask the Lord to be with you in this. This is the Body of Christ.

DAY 3   Recall the suggestion for prayer in IV-2. Mark 7:6-8.

DAY 4   What is one thing you felt at work today. Let it surface again and ask the Lord to be with you in it.

DAYS 5-6
        Luke 8:1-3.

LEARNING FROM OTHERS' EXPERIENCE (2)

Purpose: Refer to Week 3 of this Unit.

Repeat the process of Week 3 with another resource person who is either terminally ill, widowed, on disability pension, a single parent on welfare (needed at home because of children), or unemployed and on welfare.

Prayer for the Week:

(A) Daily awareness prayer.

(B) Daily scripture prayer:

DAYS 1-3

Luke 9:36-38.

OTHER DAYS

Read Bishop M. Gervais' article, 'It's As Simple As That', and be with Jesus in any part that strikes you.

'IT'S AS SIMPLE AS THAT'

Concern about social justice issues, issues having to do with poverty and the slavery that results from poverty, is not a new thing in our day. On the contrary, it is part and parcel of the whole heritage of the people of God from the beginning.

The concern to struggle against poverty, misery and injustice goes back thousands of years to the Old Testament and is continued throughout the New Testament. So if there is what seems to some people to be a new thrust towards social justice, it is only because we are not aware of our roots. Social justice concerns are an integral part of what we are, of what our history is and of what God calls us to as his people.

When Our Lord came and began to teach, he accepted as part of his own teaching the goals and the objectives of the Law and the Prophets of the Old Testament. This is made very clear in the story of Lazarus and the rich man. (Luke 16:19-31) The rich man goes to hell where he calls up for help and Lazarus, the poor man, is in the bosom of Abraham enjoying the Kingdom of God. The rich man out of his torment asks that he be rescued and, of course, he is told that the gulf is unbridgeable. Then he says, 'Send Lazarus back to my brothers for if someone comes from the dead, they will listen to him.' Abraham then says, 'If they would not listen to Moses and the Prophets, they will not listen even to someone raised from the dead.' It is very simple. The issue of social justice ignored by the rich man is an issue on which people are tried and on which eternal life depends. So Jesus accepts the objectives, the goals of social justice of the Old Testament.

We see this acceptance also in the behaviour of the first christians. One of the great signs that they have entered into the life of the Spirit was that they struggled to eliminate poverty among themselves; this struggle was seen as one of the proofs of the Holy Spirit among them. (Acts 2:43-47; 4:32-37) (One of the things that always bothers me because I teach scripture, is a saying of the Lord's about scripture scholars. He said that they lay burdens on people's backs and never lift a finger to help! Well that is a terrible thing to try to avoid. Some of the things that our Lord said are in fact very hard things, very difficult, very harsh. So, it is with a bit of trepidation that I continue and if I blush it is because I feel accused by my own words more often than you suspect.)

I have said one thing about the continuity in our Lord's teaching with the Old Testament. Now I would like to say a few things about what makes our Lord's teaching different from the Old Testament.

First of all, Our Lord begins his teaching by saying that he has come to bring good news to the poor. In the Old Testament, among the prophets especially, it was taken for granted that if social injustice were present then those benefitting from the injustice were to blame. The prophets made no bones about this; it was clear to them that the rich were to blame. But most of the prophets went a step further and said if the rich were to blame for social injustices then the correction of social injustices depended on the conversion of the rich; so prophets like Amos, Isaiah, Jeremiah, Ezekiel addressed the rich in particular. When it came to solving the problems of social injustice, the rich were roundly condemned and this was done precisely to bring about the conversion of the rich. The idea was that if the rich were converted then possibly social injustice could be corrected and the poor could have their rights respected. The startling and very upsetting newness in the teaching of Our Lord is that, unlike so many of the prophets in the Old Testament, he does not hope in the conversion of the rich. In fact he says that the conversion of the rich is practically impossible and any plan for the construction of the Kingdom of God that bases itself on the possibility of the conversion of the rich is hopeless; it cannot be done. The building, the proclamation of the Kingdom of God is not going to depend on possible conversion of the wealthy in the land.

When he said it is as impossible for the rich to enter the Kingdom as it is for a camel to go through the eye of a needle (Matt. 19:24; Mark 10:25; Luke 18:25) it was a very upsetting thing, a thing that nobody understood. Peter replied, 'Who can be saved then?' implying that if the rich can't be saved, nobody can. Our Lord did not back down at all on this statement. He didn't say it was absolutely impossible for the rich to be saved, but that if they were saved or converted it would be a sign that God is omnipotent. God does convert a few rich people but when they are converted they cease being rich. You can't have both. Zaccheus is saved and proves his salvation by stating his intention to give up half his goods and repay fourfold anyone against whom he has committed injustice (Luke 19:1-10). He wouldn't have very much left after that. Jesus' hope in the poor is something quite new and quite upsetting. It is the poor themselves he banks on for the upbuilding of the Kingdom of God. He does not place his hope in the rich but in the poor.

This leads to a second newness in our Lord's teaching and that is his model of what is human. Traditionally, particularly among those who are religious and economically comfortable, the ideal model of humanity is the strong person, the intelligent person, the industrious person, the self-sufficient person, the one who is independent, the one who has a certain maturity and adulthood about him/her, the one who can generously help the poor. But the image of humanity that Our Lord presents is practically the opposite. He says it is the weak, it is humanity in its weakness that has in itself the potential for God and that coming to terms with our weakness is what opens us to the Kingdom. It is not in our strength, it is not in our sense of fullness and completeness, but in our weakness that we can hear the gospel and build the Kingdom. It is in our acknowledgement of our incompleteness that we become people capable of receiving the gospel. It is not in our strength and our maturity and our adulthood, but in our helplessness, our childhood that we become recipients of the gospel. It is not in the clarity of our understanding that we become proper subjects of the Kingdom of God, but in admitting our inadequacy, admitting and submitting to this mystery of the Kingdom of God, admitting that we are not in control and that we do not understand everything. We like to think of the ideal human being as one who knows that s/he is virtuous, who knows that s/he is doing the will of God, who knows what the right way is, who can do it, and who can be assured of being acceptable to God. But our Lord tells us on the contrary that unless we admit that we are all in need of forgiveness, we cannot enter the Kingdom of God.

The situation is something like this. The attitudes of the traditional model of humanity, the attitudes described as strength, self-sufficiency, independence, virtue, certainty, knowledge, all of these are supported economically by wealth. Wealth supports all of these attitudes which foster a false image of human nature.

218

On the other hand, economic poverty actually supports the opposite; it actually supports the admission of weakness, of incompleteness and helplessness; it also supports incompleteness by making the admission of sinfulness more possible. So when our Lord says he hopes, he plans, to build the Kingdom ON the poor, IN the poor, it is simply because the poor are more likely to want to change, are more likely to have the dispositions which he describes as apt for receiving good news.

It is not, therefore, a question of the gospel saying 'go and help the poor', or 'go hope for the poor' or 'go and be generous to the poor'. It is much more radical than that. It is saying that OUR HOPE IS IN THE POOR and that if we want to enter into the hope of the Kingdom then, in some strange way, we have to become poor; we have to be willing to admit our sinfulness, our inadequacy, our incompleteness; we have to come to terms with the fact that we are sinners in need of forgiveness; we have to become poor ourselves.

To push the matter even further, our Lord does not just talk about poverty, he doesn't just talk about hoping in the poor, but he himself identifies with the poor and becomes poor. This is not just economic poverty. He becomes everything that the poor are: empty, abandoned, helpless, accused of being a sinner and rejected as a criminal. All those things which are embodied in the poor he becomes, and certainly he becomes them perfectly on the cross. So we have to remind ourselves just who we are, what we are called to do and who we are called to follow.

We are called to follow a crucified leader; we are called to follow one who incarnated not simply humanity, but POOR humanity, EMPTY humanity, HELPLESS humanity, SINFUL humanity. If we are called to be Jesus' disciples, then we are called to be one with him in his poverty and his emptiness. Coming to terms with this and becoming one with our Lord in his emptiness has to be expressed on earth by being one with those who are like our Lord. There is no abstract or direct line of union with a crucified Lord that can bypass our crucified brothers and sisters. THERE IS NO WAY THAT WE CAN BE UNITED TO OUR LORD ON THE CROSS UNLESS WE ARE, HISTORICALLY, UNITED WITH OUR

BROTHERS AND SISTERS ON THE CROSS ON EARTH. It is as simple as that.

Another point which our Lord makes which is quite different from the Old Testament is that this hope in the poor, this call to identify with himself and with the poor, is a call on which our very salvation depends. It is not something on which only a temporal reordering of life depends. It is not a call to rearrange social structures on earth only for the sake of some earthly utopia. There is an absolute in our Lord's preaching. Read passages like Luke 12 and 16 and you will see that what is at issue is eternal life: money and eternal life; wealth and eternal life; poverty and eternal life; justice and eternal life. Remember the man with the good crop, in chapter 12 of Luke. He didn't really work for it; he just happened to have a good crop, a bumper crop. The thought of sharing it doesn't even cross his mind. The only thought he has is how to build bigger barns. That's the only thought that comes to his mind and the passage ends, 'You fool, tonight God will ask an account from your soul.' There are so many passages on this subject you could fill pages with them.

We are not just talking about an earthly kingdom but about eternity and there is an intimate connection, as our Lord says, between our attitude toward people who are here and our being accepted into eternal life. 'Make friends now so you will be received into the tents of eternity.' (Luke 16:9) So it is hardly an optional thing; it is hardly just something that is nice to do as a work of surplus grace. It is an issue that is essential; it is not something that is optional. It is an integral part of our faith.

Another point which our Lord makes, which is an addition, a refinement on the Old Testament, is that he speaks of his community, of the people of God as he renews it, as being a prophetic presence in the world. It is to be prophetic as a community: it is to be leaven, salt, a light in the world, a city on the hilltop, which means a guiding city, a city that is lifted high so that people can find their way by it. In the Sermon on the Mount, the key to all the beatitudes is prophecy. A community that accepts its prophetic role is a community that will accept and identify itself with the poor. 'Blessed are the poor in spirit' means blessed are those who are poor, not just intellectually, but poor through and through, who are willing to identify with the poor. And the last line is that if you are persecuted, if you suffer, it is only because you are like the prophets before you (Luke 6:22). The true prophets are persecuted, false prophets are accepted. It's as simple as that. The prophetic presence is a presence that does many things, among which is that it insists that the hope we have and indeed the hope for the world is to be found in the poor. This is a very harsh and insulting thing for the rich to hear; it is very difficult to accept such a thing.

Another of the new things in the teaching of our Lord and which adds to the depth and the mysteries of the gospel is that our Lord makes it absolutely clear that God loves everyone, including the rich. God hates no one, neither the wealthy, nor the poor, nor the sinner. He loves all, even his enemies and he asks his prophetic community, which is us, to behave in exactly the same way. Too often when we get active in justice issues, we end up at best with the worst attitudes found in the Old Testament. These can border on hatred: hatred of sinners; hatred of those whom we label as ememies; hatred, if not envy, of the rich. (Too often social justice can become simply one way of expressing frustration with the fact of personal economic failure.) Our Lord makes it absolutely clear that God does not hate anyone. If he is harsh towards the rich, it is because he wants to make it absolutely clear that he loves everyone. In order to do this, the Lord must make it clear that he loves the least, because if he does not love the least, you can doubt whether he loves anyone else. And so it must be made clear in the prophetic function of the church that we too have this love of the poorest, the love of the least significant, the love of the most powerless. This should be a witness that is clear because it is in this way that we reveal who God is, the lover of all, including, and especially, the weakest of all.

Another aspect of this question that our Lord adopts, which is not entirely new but which is reshaped and reformed in his hands, is that the calling of his people is not a calling simply to wait for an instantaneous and complete establishment of the Kingdom of God. In his day there were many people who

221

hoped that the Kingdom of God would simply be established at some given moment, that it would sort of fall out of heaven as an immediate, sudden and total solution to all human problems.

There were a lot of people who thought like that. And all of us, of course, would like to see that utopia take flesh sometime or other. It will come, but it will only come to those who work at it now. I think many of us, particularly those of us who have been involved in social justice issues and have heard the stinging accusations of the Marxists that we preach pie in the sky, are almost afraid to say anything about eternal life, about the Kingdom of God, about life forever with God, which is the goal of humanity, indeed, the only goal worthy of humanity. We shy away from the notion of speaking of the notion of eternal life. And perhaps we should be more cautious in this because there is some truth in the accusation that we have preached a kind of pie in the sky. What I say is that if the christian message involves pie in the sky we at least have to pick our apples now. But there is more than that. There was something about the teaching and preaching of our Lord that was very disappointing to all those who expected the Messiah to change everything in a flash. He disappointed them terribly when he started saying such things as, 'Well, the Kingdom of God is like the little mustard seed that doesn't look like a lot, in fact, you can hardly see it'; or 'the kingdom of God is like a bit of leaven, disturbing the existing state of things' (see Matt. 13:31-33). What he is calling us to do is to be involved in a process, to begin something, to stick with it and to leave the final results to God because he assures us there will be a harvest. What we are called to do is to be sowers, to be tenders of the garden and to be harvesters eventually, but we don't have to worry about the harvest. We're on a winning thing; we can't lose. So we must begin, even if it seems very small, very insignificant, very trivial. Our Lord, in fact, does not expect us to eradicate poverty completely because, if we understand poverty as being basically the truest expression of the universal human condition, it will always be here. (Matt. 26:11) It is poverty itself, human poverty in all its aspects that is the result of the sinfulness, the inadequacy of the whole race. We will always have that with us as long as we have humanity.

So what are we called to do? We are not called to say, in an ideological way, that we are going to solve all the social problems tomorrow as long as we put all our money into it. This is not what we are called to do. Rather, we are called to work, to do the things our Lord asks us to do: to be identified with the poor; to let it be known that we identify with the poor; to preach a gospel that is good news to the poor; to invite all people, including the rich, to join us, and to make sure everyone understands that our prophetic movement is not motivated by hatred of anyone, not by hatred of the unjust, not by hatred of the rich, not by hatred of anyone, but by a love which comes from God and which articulates the love of God here on earth. It is not necessary for us to solve all the problems but it is necessary to work at them always and to work at them as intelligently as possible. Again, the Lord says in chapter 16 of St. Luke: The children of the world use their heads much better than my disciples do when it comes to money (16:8).

Finally, let us look at ourselves: Who are we when we look at the gospels; where do we stand? This is something which we must ask of ourselves and which all of us must answer for ourselves. In Our Lord's time the social situation was not very complicated. There were a few extremely rich people. These were the Romans and their officials, the priests, the elders, the officials in Jerusalem, and some of the merchants. Then there was the vast majority who were very, very poor and, in between, a very small group we might today call middle-class, represented largely by the Pharisees. It is very clear in the teaching of Our Lord that the extremely wealthy are just on the brink of damnation. It is an act of God's omnipotence if they hear the gospel. In his day, the extremely wealthy were obviously manipulators; they were obviously in control of the situation, obviously causing oppression, poverty, misery. There is no question that to save one of these oppressors would require a miracle of God.

I have stated already the Lord's attitude towards the poor. What was his attitude toward the middle group? This group is represented, symbolically at least, by the Pharisees.

They were not extremely wealthy by and large, but as Our Lord points out in the gospel, they loved money (Luke 16:14). I think, and this is a personal judgment, that the majority of us are with the Pharisees.

We're kind of an auxiliary class that can move in either direction. We can move in the direction towards which we are naturally inclined, that is, to join forces with the rich. Or we can opt, as a large number of Pharisees did in Our Lord's day, for Our Lord, which means opting for the poor. Many of the first disciples came from the Pharisees, but this demanded a real conversion, a conversion of heart from their righteousness, their self-sufficiency and conviction of their personal virtue. They had to be converted to an acknowledgement of sinfulness, of inadequacy, the need for forgiveness, of their own emptiness. They became some of the very best of the disciples, some of the greatest saints in early Christian history. And they were the Pharisees. They were, as many of us are, a kind of auxiliary class.

I think however, we have certain problems which are a little more special. Many of us have gone within one lifetime from poverty to relative wealth. For centuries we, especially French Canadian Catholics, were given the virtues of the poor, living a simple life and having lots of children. But it seems to me we have never really come to terms with our newly-acquired power. In fact, most of us don't want to admit that we have power. We do have it, and whether we want to admit it or not, we exercise it. We are part of those people who tell other people all over the world what to grow, what to sell, what to market. If I want to drink more coffee, I expect that somebody will grow that coffee for me. Whatever I want, because I have economic power, I can make it happen by the very fact that I am a member of this society and I wield this economic power along with the rest of my society. I have this power.

Our Lord said: 'From those to whom more is given, more is expected' (Luke 12:48). There is not one standard for everyone in the gospels. More is expected of us, much more, and one of the most difficult things expected of us is the will to relinquish power and to give it to those who have none. It is not a question of just giving up money but of willing to restructure society in certain ways, ways which all of us together can do and which a lot of people with good will and no faith will help us to do. We have to relinquish power; we do not necessarily have to give it all up, but we do have to give up a great deal of it. This means, in fact, that we have to lower our standard of living; we have to stop telling people to give us coffee. (I love it. I was just using that as an example.) We have to decide how we are going to share this power. I know that if all the people in this room sold everything they had and we put it in a big cheque and sent it someplace where everybody was starving, then everyone would eat for a week and everyone would be hungry thereafter, including us. Nothing will be solved by a simple transfer of gold. It is the transfer of power that is much more important, even though it is a much more difficult and complicated thing to do. Those of us who are involved in social justice issues and political issues must ask ourselves how we can willingly transfer power so that we might truly become a community of good news to the poor. That is the challenge of social justice.

I have in conclusion two questions for discussion: One is on justice and love. There is still confusion and there probably will be for a long time as to the difference between justice and love. There is a relationship between justice and charity. There really is. Very briefly, true charity begins where justice becomes inadequate. You cannot cover up injustice with charity. Impossible. Because charity is justice plus. I would like you to discuss that particularly in terms of the differences between justice and love. What is the relationship between justice and love? The second one is: Could you describe the various features of a prophetic community today?

Bishop Marcel Gervais
Auxiliary Bishop of London, Ontario

Reference for this article:

Leaders' Study   Action Guide to the Work Issue
Ten Days for World Development 1980
MAKING A LIVING (pages 4-9)

FOR OR AGAINST JESUS

Purpose: After sharing our reflections on our experience of meeting with resource persons and our responses to Bishop Gervais' article, we will read Mark's gospel to see who was for Jesus, against him or undecided. We do this so that we may appreciate the gift of our freedom and use it well.

Minutes

15   1. Begin with singing and prayer (presence, thanksgiving and light). Ask to be open to hear the Lord's invitation and generous in following it.

Reflect on Mark 2:13-14.

50   2. Share any awareness of prayer or from the week. How are we supportive of each other as we share?

10   BREAK

50   3. Mark's gospel.

a) Have each person read one or two chapters of the gospel and write down the names of those who were for Jesus, undecided or against him, and some word from the gospel or symbol to describe how.

b) List these on chart paper; note any who changed from one position to another and why they did so.

FOR JESUS	UNDECIDED (According to Mark)	AGAINST JESUS

c) Discuss: If you lived in Jesus' time, with which group would you be? Why?

d) Who are those today who would be against Jesus? his family? the disciples? the leaders? Refer to the article, 'Jerusalem...A One Company Town'.

10   4. Note the prayer for the week and especially the grace. Recall the benefit of review of prayer and continuing to use the same passage for as long as it can be helpful.

10   5. Journal: What happened in you and in the group this evening? What does it mean for us?

5   6. Conclude with praying together in whatever way is appropriate.

Prayer for the Week:

(A) Awareness prayer: Who are your friends? Why?

(B) Scripture prayer:

        Mark 8:29-33

        Mark 3:8, 11:9, and 15:13-14

        Mark 15:39

Refer to the chart of the drama of being for, undecided or against Jesus as it is portrayed in Mark's gospel.

THE DRAMA OF 'FOR OR AGAINST' JESUS IN MARK'S GOSPEL

This chart gives a visual impression of the stands various persons took in regard to Jesus during his ministry; it is based on their acceptance, indecision, or refusal of the faith option.

On this chart, Mark's gospel is divided into the 16 chapters. The numbers in the columns represent the verses of the respective chapters.

1	2	3	4	5	6	7	8	9	10	11	12	13	14	15	16
1	5	7		7	1	36	29	7	28	9				39	
7	14	8		18				24	47					41	
11	16	11		20					52						
18		13		24	FOR JESUS										8
20		35		28					13	17				43	
24				34					17	34			1		
40		UNDECIDED			18	17	15	26	18				10		
45				22	2	25	21	32	47				11		
				28	55	32	22				12		46		
		10	13	41	56	37				18	13		50		
22	12		41	42					18		15		51	3	
27						11	19	22					55	13	
40		2			6	29							56	14	
		5		40	2	33							64	20	
	7	6	40		6								65	24	
		19			52								68	29	
		21											70	31	
		30			AGAINST JESUS								71	32	

For further reading:

JERUSALEM: A ONE-COMPANY TOWN

Finally after so many years ... a chance to go to Jerusalem to celebrate Passover. The Sons of Israel at the synagogue in Alexandria were so happy for me. With Roman peace on the Mediterranean sea, it took only a month to make it to the Holy City. And here I was, a true pilgrim, at the gates of Jerusalem.

The first thing I noticed as I entered was the noise of the crowd. During these times of the Passover Festival, it was said that some 60 to 100 thousand pilgrims came to swell up the normal population of some 25 thousand residents. The city looks like it is ready to explode: the fires, the smell, the need for water, food and housing, the different languages, the chaotic organization. No wonder the Roman Governor, Pilate, came up from the coast with his troops to bolster the garrison of 1,000 soldiers here. They don't want any riots in this out-of-the-way city lost up in the Palestinian hills.

And there it was, the temple! What beauty! Tears came to my eyes. Each year I had been faithful to send two days wages as a tax to allow the priests to maintain upkeep of the temple. And there were six million of us, 10% of the Roman empire who did the same. Oh, but how the temple stood out, how rich were its decorations. Everyone, it seemed, was polarized by it, drawn to it. It was so unlike anything I saw back home. I became progressively aware that all activity gravitated around the temple: Jerusalem was the city of one industry. Craftsmen took care of the building's upkeep, furnished blocks of stone and wood, precious jewels and fine clothes. The fields around provided the food and animals for the temple, the priests and the guards, not to mention the 18,000 lambs required just for this Passover. Merchants and tradespeople also were very tied into the temple operations.

As I look around I do not see very many rich people though. Most people here are poor and 90% of the locals live on agriculture. Even the craftsmen aren't that well off. Those who seem to have made it here are the priests, the elders, and the scribes, the ones who control the Sanhedrin, the Great Council. There are 70 of them. They have decided to accept the Roman presence, though the Romans are not believers, as long as the councillors can enjoy a certain power at their level. In this city, they are the ruling class in every aspect: religious, economic and political.

For example, the priests wield great religious and economic power. They are Sadducees (fundamentalists) and they interpret the Law in everyday life. Four or five families of chief priests are mainly the ones who control the temple empire: they decide about the captain of the guards (who are responsible for security and order in the temple), about the overseers (supervisors of liturgy) and about the treasurers (who kept accounts, but also lent money out). They live off our taxes from abroad, the 10% of all produce and breeding, the choicest portions of the various sacrifices (including the hides) the first-fruits of the harvest, the renting of space in the outer courts to money changers and animal sellers, and gifts people make to the temple. No wonder they are so well off. And they have land, too.

The elders, or senators, equally of the Sadduceen tradition are respectable men from the leading land-owning families, many for whom the temple offers a great market outlet. The scribes on the other hand are for the most part of the Pharisee (or 'separated') tradition. They are devout laymen, experts of the Law who, contrary to the Sadducees have added a separate tradition to the written Law. They have great authority over the people because of their knowledge. Their three main concerns are respect for the Sabbath, keeping away from unclean people and reacting to any acts of blasphemy against God.

The Romans have basically given over all the internal administrative power to the Council. They only retain responsibility over direct taxation, capital punishment and national order.

People in the crowd have been mentioning more and more now the name of a certain Jesus, an out-of-towner from

Galilee who went into the temple a few days ago and became so mad at what was going on that he started throwing out the money changers and the animal sellers. He accused them of turning the temple into a robber's den. I must admit that I was short-changed when I bought the necessary temple currency: my money was quite devaluated. And I had to accept the very steep prices the animal sellers asked, for there was nowhere else to buy the lamb except here. But I think this Jesus was getting at something deeper. Anyway, this disruption got to the ears of the chief priests and the scribes. They, probably more than anybody else, understood clearly what this Jesus was up to, or at least what the consequences of this event could mean for their financial network. Jesus was threatening the whole temple structure: he was challenging the authority of the priests and endangering the meticulous empire that had so benefitted those in power. An action like this could promote civil disobedience among the crowds. And what would the Romans do to the leaders then? No, it was too risky to let this Jesus, this religious purist, this self-styled activist, walk around freely preaching subversion. He had to go. But word was out that the priests and leaders were playing this one out cautiously because of Jesus' supporters and because of the impulsive crowd that had just hailed him into Jerusalem recently.

In the crowd here there are some who really support Jesus. They truly respect the courage he had to attack the corruption of the present system. Others feel that he had no right to upset the tradition of the elders. All I know, is that the leaders are definitely afraid of him. At times, I wonder what to make of him myself.

WALKING WITH JESUS IN OUR STREETS

Purpose: After sharing our awareness of being for or against Jesus this week, we continue to expand our understanding of where we meet Christ and of how the Lord is calling us. We choose particular ways of meeting him on our streets.

Minutes

15   1. Begin with singing and praying.

Ask that we may recognize Jesus in our streets and that we may let him touch our lives.

Reflect on Mt. 25:31-36.

50   2. Share awareness of being for, against or undecided about Jesus in the last week.

10   BREAK

50   3. Discuss:

a) i) Of what have you become aware in the last five weeks?

ii) Is this changing anything in your life? What? (Re: compassion, judgments, lifestyle, prayer, friends.)

b) i) Are there particular groups of the marginalized with whom you feel special compassion?

ii) Is there any way you are called to be with them? What would that involve?

c) Can our group formulate and undertake one concrete way of being with the marginalized twice a week, weekly or as possible (individually or as a group); for example, visit with a terminally ill person, tithe time to expose oneself to our own and others' vulnerability, volunteer with the Vincent de Paul Society or a phone-in line, walk through a poor neighbourhood stopping at a corner store to buy something and chat, or walk through a

public housing project and chat with someone there, stay at the 'Y' or a rooming house
overnight, or walk the streets (use bus, res-
taurants) during the night and meet the
homeless...or? We 'walk through' the bible;
let us listen attentively and be ready to meet
the Lord as we walk through our streets.

5   4. Prepare the Prayer for the Week.

Minutes

15   5. Journal: What happened within you and the
group? How do you know this? (Possi-
bly ask for clarification.) What does
this indicate for us? Is there any gift of
the Lord for which we need to ask?

5   6. Conclude with praying and/or singing.

Prayer for the Week:

(A)Daily awareness prayer which would include the following
as it is appropriate:

1. What steps have you taken to implement what we discussed this week?

2. How did you react when you met someone on your walk?
What does this indicate for you?

3. How did that person feel about you? How do you know
that?

4. If you did not act on any of our discussion, why didn't you?
Be with the Lord in this.

(B) Scripture prayer:

Ask daily to recognize Jesus in our streets that we may let
him touch our lives.

Luke 10:17-22
Luke 10:23-24
Luke 9:57-62

LEARNING FROM JESUS' MOTHER, MARY: WOMAN OF FAITH AND MODEL OF DISCIPLESHIP

Purpose: We desire to gain insight and inspiration for living as disciples by pondering Luke's images of Jesus' mother, Mary, a woman of faith and model of discipleship.

Minutes

15   1. Begin with a hymn and prayer. Ask for the gift of deep faith to live as a follower of Jesus. Reflect on Luke 1:26-38.

50   2. Share awareness of the past week.

10   BREAK

50   3. Reflect on and discuss the following:

       a) What attitudes and actions have brought you to experiences of joy, peace, deep faith, trust and love?

       b) What is your image of Mary, Jesus' mother? Do you picture Mary as a happy person? Why/not?

       c) In what way might Mary have had interior experiences similar to those you remembered in 'a'? If so, what? What did these mean for her?

       d) Consider:

The Magnificat (Luke 1:39-56) serves almost as a prologue of themes for Luke's gospel: joy in living according to God's way, the blessedness of the poor, the contrast of fates for the proud/mighty/rich and the lowly/hungry, special compassion for those on the edge of society; for example, the downtrodden, sinners, widows, women, Samaritans. Mary is shown as the spokeswoman on a theme of

reversal that is a central part of Luke's gospel. (Consider, for example, Luke 12:16-21, 14:7-11, 16:19-31, 6:20-26.) Mary believes and accepts the word of God about Jesus (Luke 1:38, and 45). Because of her faith she is the first disciple and example of one who lives what is necessary to be part of Jesus' kingdom (Luke 8:21). Luke also associates Mary with the poor of Yahweh in the first covenant times, giving her a role in salvation history; this is evident from the infancy narrative through the ministry of Jesus, and into the early church. Consistently, Mary is portrayed as one who lives as a disciple, a woman of faith, Spirit-filled and joyful, ready to ponder the word and act on it, ready to suffer in living out her 'yes' to the Father.
Refer to Luke 1 and 2; Acts 1:14,
and to Acts 2:43-47, 4:32-35, Psalm 14:9-14.

10 4. Journal: What did we experience this evening? What does this mean for us?

5 5. Prepare the Prayer for the Week.

10 6. Conclude with prayer and singing.

Prayer for the Week:

(A) Awareness prayer.

(B) Scripture prayer.

Ask for living faith, hope and love that you may be a follower as Mary was.

Luke 1:26-38
Luke 1:39-56
Luke 2: 1-21
Luke 2:22-52
Luke 8:21

SOCIAL ANALYSIS: LOOKING FOR THE TRUTH (1)

Purpose: By sharing our reflections about our experiences and prayer of the last week, we hope to assist each other in sorting out and seeing what these situations of poverty and injustice mean for us.

Minutes

15   1. Begin with singing and prayer (presence, thanksgiving and light). Ask for the wisdom to recognize and sort out your experience of meeting the Lord in the streets during the past week. Include the following questions, they may help you to focus your reflection and sharing:

What did you see?

What has this meant for you?

Why do you think this particular situation exists?

Are we part of the solution or part of the problem?

Is there any issue which concerns you enough that you are willing to spend more time learning about it and responding to needs? In this area is there any group already working on the issue with whom you could work?

What difference does my faith in Jesus make in all this (especially about motivation and analysis)?

(Continue this week with the 'action' of IV-6, #3, c.)

50   2. Share experiences of the last week and what they meant to you. Some people may share this week and others next week if there isn't enough time.

10   BREAK

50 3. Issue analysis:
    a) Read one of the 3 articles included after the prayer outline.
    b) Use it to answer the following questions. Put a summary of results in the chart:
       i) What is the problem or issue?
      ii) Who are involved (actors or agents)?
      iii) What are their goals, motivation and values?
      iv) What is the proposed solution each offers? (What must get done?)
      v) What are the steps of action (operating strategy) each is taking?
      vi) How consistent is the effort and action with the proposed goal of each?
      vii) How successful was each?
      viii) With what position do you agree?

ISSUE: _____

ACTOR OR AGENT	GOALS, VALUES MOTIVATION	PROPOSED SOLUTION	OPERATING STRATEGY	CONSIS-TENCY	SUCCESS	AGREE-MENT

N.B.: In the next weeks, you may want to use one of the other 2 articles upon which to undertake a similar analysis, or become aware of an issue in the news for example, a strike in your town or some neighbourhood conflict.

5 4. Prepare the prayer during the week.

15 5. Journal: Note your experience this evening and what is happening in the community. Check this out; are your perceptions correct? What light does the gospel shed on this?

5 6. Conclude with praying and/or singing.

237

Prayer for the Week:

Continue 'the action' (refer to: IV-6, #3 c).

(A) Awareness prayer: Include what happens within you at work, public events, on the streets, in the news and be aware of questions; such as,

What did you see?

What does this mean for you?

Why do you think this situation exists?

What difference does your faith in Jesus make in all this?

Be with the Lord in this reality.

(B) Scripture prayer:

Ask to see the truth of situations and be willing to let this truth touch your life in both your attitudes and your actions.

Imagine the scene of the gospel as you use it the first day but meet Jesus in our time and reality on the second day (and more if it helps).

Luke 10: 5-16

Luke 11:37-54

Luke 13:22-30

1. THE INFANT FORMULA CONTROVERSY

For decades breast-feeding has been on the decline throughout the world. Extensive and aggressive promotion of infant formula has been identified as a major cause. Bottle-feeding has been seen as the 'modern way'. (The trend away from breastfeeding continues in the developing world though it has begun to turn around in developed countries.) Virtually all the research done on this subject both in economically advantaged areas of the world and economically disadvantaged areas, reveals higher levels of illness and death amongst formula-fed infants than amongst those breast-fed. The issue is particularly critical in areas of the world where families cannot afford to buy sufficient quantity of formula to prepare it at proper strength, are without the necessary sanitary conditions to keep baby bottles clean and sterilized, and have only impure water available for mixing with the powdered formula. In these situations levels of illness and death are much higher amongst formula-fed infants than breast-fed infants.

As formula promotion by the infant formula industry emerged as a major issue, four demands were made of the companies involved:

- stop all direct consumer promotion;
- stop use of 'milk nurses' who promote the product;
- stop the distribution of free samples;
- stop promotion within health institutions and to medical personnel.

As a result of the international pressure the major companies have made some changes usually in the most obvious forms of promotion. For instance, one company has agreed to halt direct consumer promotion but continues to use other types, for example, 'milk nurses' though they are now called 'medical representatives', free samples, and promotion to health institutions and personnel.

An international boycott of this company's products has developed since it:

        a) controls the largest part of the infant formula market;

        b) has been more resistant to changing their promotional practices than some of the other companies; and,

        c) as a foreign-based firm is not open to the use of shareholder resolutions as are the home companies.

The boycott is supported by many church groups.

Spokespersons for the boycott expressed cautious optimism about the announcement that the corporation would abide by the WHO (World Health Organization) code restricting promotion of infant formula. They added, however, that the boycott would continue until a number of remaining differences were resolved.

An international boycott has been in effect for five years to pressure the company to change its aggressive marketing practises in the third world. Health experts contend that such promotion has contributed to the malnutrition and death of millions of infants by persuading their mothers to bottle feed rather than breastfeed.

The corporation's announcement is a major shift of policy because the company apparently finally acknowledges its responsibility to exercise control throughout the corporation for the safe use of infant formula and to implement the WHO Code internationally.

A representative of the United Church speaking for INFACT (the Infant Formula Action Coalition) said that there remain some serious issues to be resolved prior to the boycott being lifted. In regard to advertising, free samples, 'milk nurses' and educational material, there are apparently a number of discrepancies between the WHO Code and the corporation's interpretation of it in the instructions that it is sending to their marketing personnel around the world. These issues and a system of monitoring the company's compliance with the Code must be agreed upon before the boycott can be lifted.

The International Boycott Committee has invited the corporation to meet with them to discuss these issues. In a telegram of invitation to them, the chairperson said, 'We will seriously study the proposed changes in practices. We invite you to meet with us to identify any differences that remain between us and to determine the procedure which we hope will lead to a satisfactory end to the boycott.' The corporation's willingness to negotiate will be one of the tests of their commitment to comply with the WHO Code and end the boycott. In the meantime, the boycott continues.

Boycotts can work and they may be a more effective weapon of non- violent struggle than many of us credit them to be. What better way to strike at the centre of an unjust economic system could there be, than to affect corporate monopoly in its home base.

2. TEXTILE WORKERS

At a local textile company, the workers are almost entirely women, 90% of whom are immigrant and have worked there for 10-25 years. Six years ago they were certified as a union. Most do piece work but at very low pay, working long hours at high speed with almost no break; even then, they earn only a little more than minimum wage. Two years ago, the company installed nine closed-circuit television cameras: in the parking lot, production, shipping and stock rooms and at the door of the women's washroom. The workers objected to this infringement of their rights but their protest was ignored. They also needed ventilation systems installed, rotation from highly dangerous areas, for example, from high dust levels, stronger seniority rights, protection against layoffs, grievance procedure (purses were searched), better wages and welfare benefits. When issues were raised, they were only reminded that many other people would be happy to have their jobs.

They took their concerns to their member of parliament who raised the matter with the provincial legislature; the Labour Minister expressed concern that it be dealt with expeditiously but avoided arranging for any process or assistance. Public health authorities were called in but management delayed their recommendations.

After two years of consistently fruitless proceedings, the women refused to work under these degrading conditions and tensions. They decided to take a stand for justice and go on strike, even though there was very little strike pay.

They went to the local newspaper editor to ask for publicity; at first she refused to print the story because the company advertised in the paper.

While maintaining picket lines, they wrote songs, appealed for and received private support through church-related groups, and asked people to speak to managers in stores where their products were sold. Managers were not available.

The owner came to the factory only once during the strike. The women wondered why he used the side door instead of the front in his own factory. He refused to meet with

241

the union for collective bargaining and hired a lawyer who was known for his hard-line on labour issues.

A member of the confederation of Canadian Unions assisted the women with press releases, organizing picket fliers and duties, contact with other unions, a benefit night and negotiations.

At last the Minister of Labour appointed a mediator to arrange resumption of talks, and promised to consider how best to examine the implications of electronic surveillance in the workplace as a whole; he would do this after an agreement was reached.

The strike lasted three months. The company finally agreed to give a wage increase, offer some retraining and seniority provisions, install a ventilation system, remove the camera at the washroom door, and accept an arbitrator's decision on the other eight cameras. The workers are still waiting for the ventilation system.

3. A MINING COMPANY

A mining company which had accumulated a large stockpile of refined ore decided to lay-off workers and cut wages. Over the last years, they had used profits generated by these workers to develop new mines overseas. The Canadian government had not only done nothing to discourage this overseas diversification; it had also financed the expansion with millions of dollars of loans.

This flight of corporate capital meant loss of investment and job creation at home in a time of increasing inflation and unemployment. The government had also repeatedly extended deadlines on pollution controls in spite of the company's being a major source of pollution.

Investment of this company in Central America enabled the company to rely on foreign production to wait out any strike, regardless of length; in addition, the company has favoured a third world region where wages are low and restrictions on their activities minimal. The government there has repressed workers' organizations and offered extravagant concessions to foreign capital. Excesses of the military dictatorship have been well documented by Amnesty International and the United Nations.

The company managers here are quick to blame, first of all, our workers as greedy and unproductive, and secondly, federal and provincial governments who are, according to them, stifling industrial growth through excessive taxation and other restrictions.

The workers went on a long strike which was supported by groups across the nation. Concerned researchers and citizens called

1) for increased contributions through taxes from companies rather than the current painful reduction of necessary social services;

2) for ways of preventing layoffs on short notice;

3) for the cessation of government loans which facilitate the corporation's development in maneuvering its resources around the world. (As a transnational corporation, its goal is to maximize its profits by gravitating to places where it can produce the most at the least possible cost, regardless of the human expense involved.)

They are also supporting workers from Canada and third world countries in their exchange of stories and strategies on this issue. Their organized, united aim is that governments will curb corporate power, be for the people, create labour-intensive jobs (as opposed to technology-intensive), uphold human dignity and care for the earth. They are asking why workers should have their pay cut or be laid off and why companies should be subsidized when the owners are themselves personally becoming multi-millionaires. Through their efforts and the co-operation of many educators, some of the public are beginning to be more aware that they are not powerless when they co-operate together.

Collated by Virginia Smith of the Latin American Working Group.

SOCIAL ANALYSIS: LOOKING FOR THE TRUTH (2)

Purpose: By following the same purpose and format as for Week 8 but with a different issue for analysis, we hope to become more at ease with the approach.

Use the format and questions suggested in IV-8, #1-6 with the exception of 3 a) which is the description of the issue to be used for analysis.

This week, use a local issue, one from the news, or one of the three included in IV-8.

Prayer for the Week:

(A) Daily awareness prayer: Include what happens within you and others at work, public events, on the streets and in the news. Be aware of questions, such as,

What did you see?

What were you and others experiencing?

How do you know they felt that?

What does this mean for you? for them? for the community?

Why do you think the situation exists?

What difference does your faith in Jesus make in all this (individually, collectively)?

Be with the Lord *in* this reality.

(B) Scripture prayer:

Ask daily to see the truth of situations and be willing to let this truth touch your life in both your attitudes and your actions.

Luke 13:31-33
Luke 13:34-35
Luke 17: 1-3

AWARENESS OF SOCIAL STRUCTURES THAT CAUSE INJUSTICE IN OUR LIVES (1)

Purpose: By sharing injustices in our own lives especially regarding how we are affected by social structures and how we maintain them or contribute to existing problems, we hope to deepen our compassion for others, be aware of what needs to be changed in ourselves and/or structures and be energized within the community to take necessary steps to implement this new understanding.

By sharing this with a supportive community, we can gain freedom from any destructive forms of resentment, selfishness, cowardice, disregard for individuals and whatever obstacles are within us; these tend to be expressed in unhealthy fight or flight. We desire to be rooted in love and trust, courageously responding to injustice, in our lives.

Do these exercises to the extent that the group is able, without pressure or concern for 'expert insight!' Note that the sharing changes.

Minutes

15   1. Begin with singing and prayer:

'Come, Holy Spirit, fill the hearts of your faithful and kindle in us the fire of your love. Lord, send forth your Spirit and we shall be recreated and you shall renew the face of the earth. God, you instructed the hearts of your faithful by the light of the Holy Spirit, grant us in this same Spirit, to be truly wise and always to rejoice in your consolation. We ask this in the name of Jesus, the Lord. Amen.'

30   2. Read and ponder Wisdom 1:1-8 and then maintaining this atmosphere of prayerful reflection,

245

each person considers brief answers to the following questions (or as many as you can in the time allotted).

a) Personal Involvement

    i) What is one way that you think you have been treated unjustly? (Preferably choose a situation that involves an institution or group; e.g., work, civic group (sports, volunteer services, taxes, church. The example need not be an injustice that affects only you; it may affect an entire group.)

    ii) What is the background to the unjust situation?

    iii) What is your personal involvement in this situation? (What is your relationship with the people involved?)

    iv) What is the injustice?

    v) What is the source of the injustice?
        – you?
        – individuals close to you?
        – structures?
        – systems?
        – do you know the individuals involved in maintaining these?

    vi) How have you experienced within yourself any need for justice in this? What is the faith dimension of this situation? How have you prayed about it?

    vii) What do you think is the best way for you to act in order to bring about a just resolution of the problem?

    viii) In what ways do you feel helpless to resolve the situation?

N.B.: IF there is an institution or group involved in the injustice, continue with the following questions:

b) Economic Questions
  i) How does the institution support itself (income)? How much and from where?
  ii) How does it spend its money (expenditures)?
  iii) What proportion of money is spent on what operations?
  What proportion of time is spent on what operations?
  What proportion of talent is spent on what operations?
  INCLUDE ALL SERVICES AND ATTACH MONETARY VALUE.
  iv) Who benefits from transactions? In what ways?
c) Social Questions
  i) What are the institutions, programs and operations?
  ii) To whom are they directed, mainly and secondarily?
  iii) What is the social class of the institution?
  iv) Who runs, directs and supervises these operations?
  v) What is the relationship of groups involved in this?
  With the poor and the marginalized; e.g., immigrant workers?
d) Political Questions
  i) What are the effects of above operations on the political system?
  ii) Does the institution encourage evaluation and criticism of itself?
  iii) Does it encourage participation, sharing?
  iv) How is power viewed and used within the institution, from one level to another as well as within any group?
  v) Why were these operations started?

e) Religious Questions
  i) How are the
    – operations
    – motives
    – views
    – accomplishments

        of the institution related to the gospel vision?
    ii) What image do outsiders, insiders, have of the above relationship?

Marita Carew RSHM

10   BREAK

60   3. Focus on one issue volunteered by a member, allowing plenty of time for sharing the feelings involved if s/he chooses to do that, and for clarifying what the issue is.

Continue with the same issue from others or another issue.

25   4. Journal and sharing:
    a) What happened within you this evening? Share any of this.
    b) If any members are eager to share some insight or concern from the past week, this may be an appropriate time for it.
    c) Ask if one or two are willing to share their experience of injustice next week, continuing the process used this week.

15   5. Pray and sing together as the Spirit leads you.

Prayer for the Week:

(A) Daily awareness prayer. Continue to pray on your experience of injustice as begun during the meeting.

(B) Scripture prayer:

Ask daily for the experience of knowing and loving the Lord as you meet him today and for wisdom, humility, and courage to face issues with him.

Luke 18: 1-8
Luke 19:11-27
Luke 19:41-44

AWARENESS OF SOCIAL STRUCTURES THAT CAUSE INJUSTICE IN OUR LIVES (2)

Purpose: Through further reflection in faith upon the injustices in our lives, we desire to experience healing (of ourselves and the institution), to discern what response is needed and to strengthen one another in seeking out just solutions.

Minutes

15   1. Pray and sing together. Ask for wisdom, compassion, humility, and courage in seeking out the Lord's way in the face of apparent injustices. Reflect on the experience of the last meeting as well as your prayer and awareness during the week, using Wisdom 18:3.

40   2. Share any awareness of the week, especially those relating to justice/injustice.

10   BREAK

50   3. Sharing of an individual's experience of injustice based on the questions outlined in IV-10, #2 a) to e).

20   4. Journal: What light does our faith in the Trinity shed on this situation?

Share any reflections with the community. If the community is finding this approach helpful for individual and group growth, take more weeks on it!

15   5. Pray and sing together as the Spirit leads you.

Prayer for the Week:

(A) Awareness prayer. Include some reflection on how your awareness has broadened in the last months. Let it draw you closer to the Lord!

Is there an issue about which you desire to learn more, pray for and if possible act upon? How?

(B) Scripture prayer:

Ask for the gift of desiring and being able to act justly, love tenderly and walk humbly with your God.

Micah   6: 8

Luke   20:45-47

Luke   20: 1-8

FOLLOWERS OF JESUS AND WORLD ORDER (1)

Purpose: We have been remembering our experience of injustice in a faith context. Now we move on to expand our horizons to our world view.

By remembering the Lord's presence with us as a community, we hope to be energized to face current events and issues of our time. We will share our present feelings about the world future, imagine (with Jesus) a preferred world view and finally read an article about this process.

We encourage members to choose a particular issue of need today if they have not done so already and to learn, pray and act on it as they are able; this effort can certainly increase their awareness.

Minutes

15 1. Begin with singing and praying together.

Ask to experience how the Lord is with this community, leading us in the reality of our time into the future; thank him for the confidence, courage and wisdom he will give you as a community!

Reflect on Exodus 2:23-25, 3:7-11.

50 2. Share some awareness especially of a way you have experienced the Lord's presence in his people generally or in this community.

10 BREAK

20 3. Answer the following together:

a) On a scale of 1 to 10 that represents your feelings of pessimism to optimism in terms of our world future, where would you put yourself?

    b) List both external trends and internal experiences of life that cause you to feel the way you do.

    c) If you lived in a land where the top soil is disappearing or where there is rampant oppression, what differences would you make in the above?

20   4. Imagining what the new age could be like:

    a) Lead the following reflection:

'Take a few moments to imagine yourself with Jesus....See how he fully embraces our human condition with all its joys and weakness, hopes and despairs....He brings salvation and wholeness not apart from the world but by taking it on. Jesus finds the world so good that it is worth doing this even through the pain this solidarity involves. (Pause) See him inviting you to be with him in doing the same.' (Pause)

'Together with Jesus, see how we are moving into a new age in world history....With him, see and let go of older structures such as nation, states, narrow categories, isolation, selfish individualism, grasping security beyond all reason....letting go of myths and world views that no longer fit the new age. Ask him for light and wisdom to see what can no longer be held for our time. (Pause) Imagine yourself and the community letting go of them to walk with Jesus. Now with the Lord and the support of the community imagine a new world....a global village. What would it be like? We will now take about 10 minutes simply to dream, to imagine what the world would be like ....as you prefer it, not as you anticipate it now. Imagine yourself co-operating with all people of good will to achieve it.'

b) Share what you felt and what your preferred image of the world is.

c) Read the article 'Crisis: Breakdown and Opportunity', which is included after the Prayer for the Week. At least share what questions it raises for you even if there is not time to discuss them in depth now.

20   5. Journal: What did you and the community experience this evening?

When you think of signs that the Holy Spirit is present, how does your community experience fit with this?

What does this suggest for you?

Share what you notice.

10   6. Pray and sing together.

Prayer for the Week:

(A) Awareness prayer. Does your awareness include external and internal realities, even global issues and your response to them?

(B) Scripture prayer:

Ask the Lord to open your ears so that you may listen like a disciple in our time.

Exodus 3:1-6
Exodus 3:7-15
Exodus 4:1-4, 10-17
Baruch 5:1-5, 8-9

For further reading:

CRISIS: BREAKDOWN AND OPPORTUNITY

We are in a time of major world changes and it presents a crisis for us. This involves the breakdown of old systems, structures and views such as, family breakdown, pollution, use of money for proliferation of arms instead of social needs. Disintegration of the familiar leaves us sensitive, insecure and vulnerable. This happens in individual maturing; it also happens collectively in history and therefore has a profound impact on individuals. Suicide rate has increased even among the children. It can seem overwhelming and we ask, 'Is there a God big enough to set this right?'

At the same time, crisis can bring opportunities, breakthrough, new vision, meaning and ways of relating.

We are entering a new phase of consciousness. We realize that we are responsible for the direction of our evolution, that we are not adequate to do it individually, that authentic religion requires that we embrace the real human condition with Jesus. What is life, history, asking of us at this time? How can we be living communities with and for others in our global village? In assuming the challenge of caring for the earth, how can we rediscover our dependence on and relation to it?

Being with the Lord and using our imagination to shape a preferred vision serves like a magnet, helping us to open up to new possibilities, release our creativity and actually fulfill our dreams. We need concrete vision, images, models of hope, both individually and collectively, to pull us out of the negative, downward, self-fulfilling pull of the nuclear threat. Because of the prevailing, even if unspoken, threat of collective death, a hedonism tends to trap us and our youth: with no future, lack of spiritual and community strength to deal with the depth of the crisis, we (as an entire society) appear apathetic. 'Tomorrow we die. Today we look after ourselves.' We need a spirituality that is sufficiently wholistic, energizing and communal to lift us out of despair and take us through the psychic death of letting go of old structures, to give birth to a new age. As we are in communion with a sacred center and source of life, we can journey forward alone and together. Then, with global awareness, we can find ways of loving and caring for our human community and planet. Just as we have been part of world sin and accomplices in evil, so now we can discover we have a blest world history that gives us direction for the future.

We have let our intuitive imagination prevail in our search; it is important to play with ideas that come! (The work of the critical mind follows this making judgments, assessing repercussions and deciding strategies.) As we allow ourselves to imagine and believe there are alternatives, we develop imagery with a sense of hope; it becomes a sign of faith that God can create in and through us. Because our imagination tends to set the direction of what we 'allow ourselves' to achieve, we need clarity regarding our own values and our preferred images of the future. There are, after all, various ways of moving to a new world order; namely, in response to a catastrophe, by drifting or by co-operating in our efforts to realize a preferred world order.

FOLLOWERS OF JESUS AND WORLD ORDER (2)

Purpose: By sharing our reflections on our experiences of the last week and doing so in the light of faith, we hope to gain insight and be strengthened in our way of following Jesus today. Doing an exercise on our preferred vision can help us to clarify our values and goals.

Minutes

15   1. Begin by singing and praying together.

Let us ask the Lord to open our ears so that we may listen like disciples in our time.

Reflect on Isaiah 2:1-5 letting it shed light on the past week.

50   2. Share some awareness of what happened in you this past week. Are our meetings affecting your daily awareness and prayer and vice-versa? How? (or, why not?)

10   BREAK

25   3. Quietly imagine a preferred vision of the world but this week be as specific as you can. Use your journal.

a) What values would be essential?

b) If there is greater interdependence, the possibility of conflict is great. What would be your preferred ways of dealing with conflict? Imagine yourself, your family, this community and nations resolving conflicts this way.

c) What life-style(s) would be adopted?

d) What would the social-political, economic, educational, religious aspects be like on a small scale and globally?

e) Imagine yourself and all people using the energy and resources that are now used for destruction (within families, for armaments, etc.) in positive ways. See how the Father gives you his Spirit abundantly for this.

25   4. In groups of three:
a) Share your preferred vision based on the questions above and speaking in the present tense as if it is the reality now.
b) Choose a future date (possibly about 50 years from now) when, in your imagination, this world vision is a reality. Do a time line back to the present: these are the steps we used to move toward it and the obstacles we overcame; for example,

---

1985	1995	2015	2075	2035
				preferred vision

20   5. With the whole community, share what you noticed this evening. Is it in harmony with our experience of how the Holy Spirit works in our lives? If not, what seems to be the problem?

Also, is there any issue that we have faced that needs to be brought to further public attention; e.g., through Sunday liturgy, newspapers, writing to and/or inviting a member of parliament to visit on an issue.

5   6. Sing and pray together.

Prayer of the Week:

(A) Awareness prayer: Any inner awareness whether it seems very ordinary, dull, embarrassing or insightful is a worthwhile focus; in all of these, the Lord is with us. Take time to respond wholeheartedly!

(B) Scripture prayer:
>Luke 9:23-26
>Luke 9:28-36
>Luke 12:49-50

(C) Further reading:

What is the call of the church in terms of our involvement in current issues? Read and ponder the following excerpts:

1. Action on behalf of justice and participation in the transformation of the world fully appears to us as a constructive dimension of the preaching of the gospel, or, in other words of the Church's mission for the redemption of the human race and its liberation from every oppressive situation.

   The Third Synod on Justice in the World (Rome) emphasized that acting for justice is not an optional activity for Christians. It is integral to the proclamation of the gospel and the practice of the Christian faith. Indeed, the struggle for justice and liberation is a major theme running through the scriptures. (Justice in the World, Synod of Bishops, 1971.)

2. It is up to each Christian community to analyze with objectivity the situation which is proper to their own country, to shed on it the light of the gospel's inalterable words and to draw principles of reflection, norms of judgment and directions for action from the social teachings of the Church. (Paul VI, Octogesima Adveniens, no. 4, 1971).

3. The present economic order is characterized by the maldistribution of wealth and the control of resources by a small minority. In the Third World this order emerges from a history of colonialism. In Canada, in the words of the Senate Committee on Poverty, 'the economic system in which most Canadians prosper is the same system which creates poverty'. In both Canada and the Third World powerful corporations are

planning the use of natural resources without the participation of the people who are most directly affected. Governments in the First, Second and Third Worlds often do not exercise their responsibility to protect people from these abuses of power. The human consequences of the present order are dependency, loss of human dignity, poverty and even starvation. (Canadian Church Leaders, Justice Demands Action, 1976.)

4. In many such ways, our country is still profoundly marked by the founders of liberal capitalism....The theory of the survival of the fittest leads many to accept widespread poverty and the concentration of wealth and power in the hands of a few. Industrial strategies are designed specifically to produce maximum gratification and profit, so that wasteful consumption is systematically promoted....The result is clear: many are kept from achieving certain basic necessities while others, trapped in their wealth, find great difficulty in meeting God, in knowing the person of Jesus and living his message. Succeeding generations are drawn into a culture, into ways of thinking and behaving, alien to God's purpose. (Canadian Bishops, A Society to be Transformed, 1977.)

5. Indeed, development and underdevelopment have been two sides of the same coin in modern decisions which ultimately shape the patterns of development and underdevelopment in both Canada and the Third World. In capitalist societies, priority is placed on the maximization of profits, the goal of serving human needs and the common good becomes secondary. The social consequences of such an economic system are uneven patterns of development, inequitable distribution of wealth and power, dependency and loss of human dignity. (Canadian Bishops, Witness to Justice: A Society to be Transformed, p. 20, 1977.)

6. Across Canada today, there are some encouraging signs among Christian people who are raising these and

related ethical questions. A variety of Christian groups have been working with the poor and oppressed peoples of their communities, organizing educational events on issues of injustice, and pressing leaders of governments and industries to change policies that cause human suffering. Unfortunately, those who are committed to this Christian way of life are presently a minority in the life of the Catholic community. Yet, this minority is significant because it is challenging the whole Church to live the gospel message by serving the needs of peoples. (From Words to Action, article 7, 1976 message of the Canadian Bishops.)

7. In recent years, the bishops' messages have increasingly encouraged the formation of small Christian communities for justice. Over the past decade, several hundred small communities have been organized in Canada around a variety of social justice struggles: workers' rights, native peoples, refugees, repression of human rights in Central America, nuclear energy, disarmament, women's rights, solidarity with oppressed peoples in El Salvador, Nicaragua, South Africa, etc. Through these communities, Christians attain new levels of spiritual growth through prayer, liturgy, and gospel reflections — 'coming to know God more deeply by their efforts to overcome human suffering'. (A Society to be Transformed, article 1, 1977.)

8. In promoting small communities for justice, the bishops also suggested some pastoral guidelines in their statement, 'From Words to Action'. In addition to developing a deeper understanding of the true meaning of the gospel message of justice, these guidelines entailed: 1) modifying affluent lifestyles in order to renew our spirit and open our hearts to the poor in our midst; 2) listening to the victims of injustice and sharing in their struggles; 3) denouncing injustice and speaking the truth to those in power; 4) participating in actions to eliminate the cause of injustice by changing the policies of governments, corporations, and other institutions that generate human suffering; 5) providing di-

rect assistance to poor and oppressed groups struggling to change conditions in which they live. (From Words to Action, article 9, I-VI.)

9. Some people will choose to continue reforming our present capitalist system in the light of the gospel. Others will choose to participate in socialist movements, trying to reconcile them with the teachings of Jesus. And still others, rejecting these options, will become involved in searching for some alternative socio-economic order based on gospel principles.

   As people pursue these different strategies, there is bound to be within the Christian community tension and debate which can be a healthy process for change. But one thing is certain: No option is valid that does not unite people in efforts for the creation of a society based on justice. (A Society to be Transformed, article 18.)

10. The Canadian North is fast becoming a centre stage in a continental struggle to gain control of new energy sources. The critical issue is how these northern energy resources are to be developed — by whom and for whom. We are especially concerned that the future of the North not be determined by colonial patterns of development, wherein a powerful few end up controlling both the people and the resources. Some present examples of industrial planning give us cause for grave concern. For what we see emerging in the Canadian North are forms of exploitation which we often assume happen only in Third World countries: a serious abuse of both the Native Peoples and the energy resources of the North. Herein lies the Northern dilemma. What has been described as the 'last frontier' in the building of this nation may become our own 'Third World'.

    In the final analysis what is required is nothing less than fundamental social change. Until we as a society begin to change our own lifestyles based on wealth and comfort, until we begin to change the profit-oriented priorities of our industrial system, we will continue placing exorbitant demands on the limited supplies of energy in the North and end up exploiting the people of the North in order to get those resources. (Northern Development: At What Cost?, Message of the Canadian Bishops, 1975.)

(Above paragraphs 1-10 were taken from a presentation made by Bishop Adolphe Proulx of Hull, during a joint meeting of the Canadian Council of Churches, the Canadian Jewish Congress and the Canadian Catholic Conference of Bishops, Toronto, 1982.)

11. The current structural changes in the global economy, in turn, reveal a deepening moral crisis. Through these structural changes, "capital" is re-asserted as the dominant organizing principle of economic life. This orientation directly contradicts the ethical principle that labour, not capital, must be given priority in the development of an economy based on justice. There is, in other words, an ethical order in which human labour, the subject of production, takes precedence over capital and technology. This is the 'priority of labour' principle. By placing greater importance on the accumulation of profits and machines than on the people who work in a given economy, the value, meaning and dignity of human labour is violated. By creating conditions for permanent unemployment, an increasingly large segment of the population is threatened with the loss of human dignity. In effect, there is a tendency for people to be treated as an impersonal force having little or no significance beyond their economic purpose in the system. As long as technology and capital are not harnessed by society to serve basic human needs, they are likely to become an enemy rather than an ally in the development of peoples.

In addition, the renewed emphasis on the "survival of the fittest" as the supreme law of economics is likely to increase the domination of the weak by the strong, both at home and abroad. The "survival of the fittest" theory has often been used to rationalize the increasing concentration of wealth and power in the hands of a few. The strong survive, the weak are eliminated. Under conditions of "tough competition" in international markets for capital and trade, the poor majority of the world is especially vulnerable. With ¾ of the world's population, for example, the poor nations of the South are already expected to survive on less than ⅕th of the world's income. Within Canada itself, the top 20% of the population receive 42.5% of total personal income while the bottom 20% receive 4.1%. These patterns of domination and inequality. . .are in our view morally unacceptable as a "rule of life" for the human community. (*Ethical Reflections on the Economic Crisis*, Episcopal Commission for Social Affairs, Canadian Bishops, 1983.)

12. All of the encyclical, *On Human Work*, by Pope John Paul II, 1981.

GUILT AND POWERLESSNESS

Purpose: Since 'injustice is so big', we may let ourselves become overwhelmed by powerlessness. Our place among the privileged leaves us with feelings of guilt. This week, we 'name the monster' of dehumanization and see how it is beneficial to the system to have us be both guilty and powerless because as long as we are paralyzed by guilt and weakness, we do not challenge or threaten the system by rocking the boat. We need then to embrace and 'befriend' powerlessness and guilt; that is, face them with Jesus and see how they can become the occasion of letting his power work in us.

Minutes

15 1. Begin with singing and prayer.

Ask to experience personally how Jesus is lord for you and all people.

Remember your awareness of the past week and reflect on Luke 11:13.

50 2. Share your awareness.

10 BREAK

50 3. Discuss:
   a) How are we individually and collectively involved in and/or responsible for injustices in the world?
   What feelings does this awareness create in you?
   How do you feel about guilt? powerlessness?
   b) Feelings can be energizing (positive) or crippling/debilitating (negative). How do you see guilt and powerlessness being used by society in a crippling way?
   How do you see them being used by christians in an energizing way?

265

c) How did Jesus respond to his own powerlessness? Read Mk. 14:32-42; 15:33-37; 16:5-8.

d) How did Jesus as Christ respond to our guilt? Read Heb. 9:28; Phil. 2:6-11; 1 Pet. 2:21-25.

e) Read the article, 'About Guilt and Powerlessness' which is included after the outline for prayer. What does it mean for you now to say that Jesus is Lord of History, Lord of our lives?

f) What is the Lord's invitation for you now? How do you know this?

10   4. Journal: What happened in you and in the group this evening? How was it in harmony/disharmony with the Lord's gifts to you?

5   5. Conclude with praying/singing together.

Prayer for the Week:

(A) Awareness prayer: Being particularly conscious of your experience of guilt and powerlessness, meet the Lord in reality.

(B) Scripture prayer:

Ask daily to share Jesus' response to guilt and powerlessness so that you can trust with bold confidence, letting him be Lord of your life. What is his invitation to you now?

Luke 10:17-20
Luke 17: 4-6
Luke 15:31-32

Reflect on the following article,

ABOUT GUILT AND POWERLESSNESS

Though basically free and independent, we human beings are also bonded into solidarity and interdependence with all those other persons who inhabit this planet of ours. Beyond the evident forces of cohesion however, we soon discover and experience the limits of our finiteness as well as the divisive reality of evil keenly at work within ourselves and within our world. Because we are in communion with all living beings we may wonder to what extent we are guilty, for example, of the injustices, the suffering and the sin of this world. Why is it we feel so helpless when we read the newspapers or watch the news on TV? Why is it that major issues concerning the future of humanity, such as nuclear use, the arms race, multinational take-overs, global human rights, pollution, world hunger, and unemployment, leave us numb, in a quasi-state of shell shock?

Like it or not, we must face the question of guilt head-on: are we in fact really guilty for these? Maybe we are: if not directly by doing something wrong ourselves, then indirectly by not doing anything about the wrong done to others (Js. 1:22-27). Maybe we aren't: and in thinking we are not, we simply help the powers controlling society to maintain the status quo on injustice. Or maybe we act like those who single-handedly attempt to be saviours of the world, trying to assume all responsibility, and then feel guilty for not totally succeeding.

Guilt, no matter how true or false, real or imaginary, should never get the best of a follower of Jesus. Obsessive guilt is simply not christian. For the life of the Kingdom brought by Jesus was a gift (Lk. 12:32) which cancelled out debts (Lk. 7:41-43), healed through wholeness (I Col. 1:30) and forgave our complicities (Col. 1:13-14). The forgiveness which characterized Jesus' mission (Mk. 2:11; Lk. 7:49) was a sign of the boundless free mercy of the Trinity (Eph. 1:7) heralding in a special age of humanizing love. This love was not offered to generate guilt but rather to liberate humanity from all the dehumanizing ties that bogged it down throughout the ages: the chains of violence, of revenge, of domination and of injustice. Now, in spite of all that might have happened, we are completely forgiven (Heb. 4:15-16). Jesus gave his life for us (Mk. 10:45; 14:24; Rm. 3:4). The question may be asked: do we really believe this enough?

If we do remain in real guilt, it may be because we have refused the gift of life and pardon that has been offered us; we have not truly repented. Repenting does not mean going off somewhere and undertaking 'good deeds' for the sake of merits; repenting is simply opening ourselves up to the love of the Trinity, and letting it take over (Eph. 5:1-2). Instead of remaining self-centred and feeling sorry for ourselves, we will become more forgiving and compassionate for others, become life-givers, able to hear the cries of the weak and the hurt. Open (and vulnerable) we'll work at dismantling the bombs of prejudice and favouritism, refusing to be accomplices of the systems which foster pain and sorrow, adopting new and simpler life-styles and especially being critical of the dehumanizing values promoted by some segments of society. We will have no real reason to feel guilty, because our actions or our stands will clearly indicate our refusal to participate in the evil perpetrated around us. We will compare that which is told us 'officially' with the message of the Good News and with the degree of suffering observed. By thinking as Jesus would have thought and not necessarily as the dominant culture does, we might even end up being 'dysfunctional' in the system: not going along with everything automatically, but making our different opinions and views known to society so as to humanize it, to give it back to its real self, with the purpose it was meant to serve. Defused of its emotional impact through critique and transformed by the love of the Trinity, guilt would no longer have any hold over us, unless of course in our basic freedom we still choose to let it.

Whether we feel guilty or not about the injustices that exist around us, one thing is certain: we probably feel powerless in doing anything about them. We feel like little cogs in an otherwise very big wheel. If we work alone, we don't stand a chance. Those who stand to benefit from the system and the status quo will grind our efforts to a slow crawl. Despair and cynicism will set in. We may give up and passively condone those practices we were once so set against. So what can we do?

Probably first of all we need to acquire a sense of perspective: christians are a people of past (rememberance), present (action), and future (hope). So, we can take a long hard look down history lane and see what went on before us so as to give us some roots. We can, for example, look at how some apparently hopeless movements made headway: the abolition of slavery, women's rights, native rights, peace manifestations, ecological concerns, even the growth of the christian church itself! All these efforts started with a very small core group, humbly, before becoming realities to be reckoned with. We could reflect also on the meaning of life and on all the life-giving forces at play in our times; for example, as believers and as followers of Jesus, we cannot act as if we were alone (Lk. 10:19-20; Jn. 14:26-30). On the contrary, Jesus was sent by the Father to be with all and to bring salvation for all, even for those who, at times unknowingly, perpetrate injustices. Jesus conquered sin and confronted in his person all the destructive forces of the world (Lk. 11:20; Rm. 8:1-4). Through him the Trinity intervenes in history, but on the Lord's terms and not on ours. Thus, according to world standards: the Trinity proposes something which appears truly foolish - the power of love expressed in the powerlessness of the cross (Mk. 8:34-38; I Cor. 1:18-25). Against the choice of self-importance, self-advantage, and self-absorption, against those powers trying to destroy creation, the Trinity contrasts the example of a Suffering Servant (Is. 53:11; Mk. 10:42-45) offered in love for us (Jn. 3:16-17; Gal. 1:4; I Tim. 2:5-6).

This love of the Trinity is an individual and collective gift. It cannot be forced. It becomes life for us only when it is received, only when we, in turn, open ourselves and accept the power of this love which is meant to be passed on and not to be hoarded. This power of love, which even Jesus never kept for himself but always relinquished, is stronger than any hatred or any injustice; it is stronger than death itself. Because we pass on the gift we remove the sting of death and become life-givers (like the Lord); those however who have power in the world are often life-takers and therefore remain givers of death. Those who accept being powerless in the Lord and give of their life, get their life given back to them in freedom to continue their life of serving; whereas the life-takers (those who serve themselves) are powerless in giving life back to themselves.

Thus our feelings of powerlessness must not make us turn around and adopt the same forms of death-giving power the sources of injustice use (Tit. 2:11-13) such as intimidation, domination, violence, greed, etc.; nor should our powerlessness lead us to abandon hope or to forsake our responsibilities through escapism or inaction. Truly, the power of love, the Trinity's love, for we are not alone, is there, at work in us (Eph. 6:10-17) in an actively compassionate way, willing to commit us in many forms and forums, seeking justice for everyone, since they too are loved into being, through us, by the Lord. Faced with apparent powerlessness, the power of love from the Trinity will give us the light to recognize whatever justice requires in the diverse and changing situations of our time (2 Tim. 4:16-17). This same love will empower us so that we can act on these situations. The Lord's love in us is creative, seeks wholeness, endures whatever comes (even the feeling of powerlessness) and always maintains hope.

Maybe our guilt and our powerlessness are not fundamentally problems of relief but rather of belief: that the Lord is truly offering us a life of love which the world can never take away.

ENCOUNTERING AND/OR CONFRONTING

Purpose: Last week we focused on the paralyzing reactions of guilt and powerlessness in the face of injustices; this led us to remember that Jesus is saviour and the consequences for us as followers.

Now we will discuss the issue of confronting or encountering another in dialogue, especially when there are two sets of values that oppose each other. We define confrontation as facing an issue with another (co-front) when both have full opportunity to listen and speak so that together they may discover the greater good. It requires humility, wisdom, respect for the other and courage; it also takes practice and patience. If another is not willing to dialogue, an injustice (or apparent injustice) may still need to be brought to the light.

There is a wide range of application for this topic; it could include ways to deal with conflicts with families, communication skills, co-operation with others to face structural injustices (or apparent ones) at work, in society, the church. Because of this, you and the community may decide to spend several weeks on this topic.

This outline includes only some imagery and discussion on personal encounters, and some reflection on Jesus' confrontation of injustice. An article on the latter topic is included as an extra reference.

Minutes

15   1. Begin with singing and praying.

Ask for humility, wisdom and courage to trust the Lord; ask to live as a disciple even in moments of disagreement, conflict and injustice.

Reflect quietly on Romans 12:1-21.

271

50   2. Share any awareness of the week. How are community members supportive of each other during this sharing? Is there sufficient trust to question and respond?

10   BREAK

45   3. Discuss each of the following:
       a) When you hear the words encountering and confronting, what feelings and/or images come to you? Does love permit and/or require them?
       b) What are your real and preferred responses to others when you meet them, especially if there are disagreements between you?
       c) Remember experiences when you or another person initiated the encounter or confrontation:
          i)   one that helped you and worked for good
          ii) one that seemed destructive
          iii) what helped/hindered in the encounter?
       d) What are some of the causes of conflict within families?
       e) Was there tension and conflict between Jesus and his relatives and friends? Read Mark 3:20-21,31-35; 6:1-6; 10:29-30; 13:12-13.
       f) Was there tension between Jesus and his disciples?

       Read one or two gospel references:

       Mark 4:40-41; 7:18; 8:17-21,29-33; 9:6,18-19,32,33-34; 10:32,41; 14:27-31,37-40,50-52.

10   4. Lead the following reflection:
       a) Imagine a scene in which you are facing someone whom you consider a source of injustice to yourself or another. Imagine yourself speaking and responding to her/him with courage, clarity, conviction and gentleness. (Pause)

b) Now imagine someone coming to challenge you on an apparent or real injustice. Imagine yourself respecting that person, listening well and responding simply with honesty, humility and courage.

10   5. Journal, quiet reflection:

Are you able to speak honestly, openly, with trust, humility and courage and love within the community? Do others? What do we need? Do we have a sense of humour as a group?

10   6. Conclude with praying and singing together.

Prayer for the Week:

(A) Awareness prayer.

(B) Scripture prayer:

Ask for the gift to dialogue honestly, humbly and courageously in confrontative situations so that you may discover the greater good.

Romans   12:14-21
Mark   3:20-21
Mark   4:40-41

IMITATING JESUS IN HIS CHALLENGING OF INJUSTICE

1. Getting to Know the True Jesus
   – Jesus is for us the Way. By his life he shows us the path to the Father that we must take. His outlook, attitudes, values, must become our own.
   – So, in our reading of scripture, our prayer on it, our retreats, it is very important that we come to know the true Jesus, the complete Jesus, as gospel reveals him.
   – Not only, therefore, the Jesus, who heals, who prays, who is gentle, who is forgiving, but also the Jesus who speaks out boldly against false ideas of religion, who condemns injustice even when done by religious leaders, who challenges meaningless practices and traditions when these get in the way of justice and love.

2. Jesus, 'the Justice of God', is Very Prominent in All Four Gospels
   - In every one of the four gospels, Jesus repeatedly condemns the injustice, hypocrisy and false attitudes of the religious leaders, the 'scribes and Pharisees'.
   - In every gospel, the conflict with them begins early and builds up.
   - In every gospel, it is given as the immediate cause for his arrest and execution.
   - Chapter 23 of Matthew is a striking example (the 'woes'), though only one.

3. One Question: Are the Things Jesus Condemns Present in Our Life Today?
   - Jesus condemns not practicing what we preach.
   - He condemns interpretations of laws that are overstrict.
   - He condemns focusing on minutiae while neglecting the larger law of love.
   - He condemns stress on the outer appearance of things while neglecting the inner spirit.
   - Are the things he condemns present in any way in my own life?
   - Are the things he condemns present in any way in our own community or congregation, our own parish or school or hospital, our own diocese, our own universal church?

4. Deeper Question: How Are We Called to Imitate Jesus In His Challenging of Injustice?
   - Clearly, Jesus' challenging of injustice is an important element in his life.
   - Clearly, Jesus is for us the Way. We are called to follow him, to be like him, to imitate him in his basic outlook, attitudes, values.
   - So, somehow, in some way, we must be called to imitate his challenging of injustice.

5. False Answers That Avoid the Question
   - It is no answer to say, as some used to, that Jesus was God and it was all right for him to challenge injustice, but we mustn't do so, because we're only human beings. Such an answer refuses to take seriously the humanity of Jesus. He was God, yes, but he was also a human being.
   - It should focus on attitudes and practices and structures (wherever possible), rather than on persons.
   - It should be done without hatred or bitterness or self-justification, in fact it should be done with love. It is perfectly possible to have a deep sense of the church, a great love of the church, and yet be impelled to speak out boldly when the situation or injustice demands it. We have examples in our own day of christians like that: Karl Rahner or Teresa Kane or Archbishop Romero. They are, all of them, close followers of Jesus, who have shown us the way to do so.
   - Today, more than ever in history, the church keeps calling us to commit ourselves to the struggle for justice, as being part of our faith. More and more, christians are recognizing that our commitment to justice must also mean, challenging human rights violations and injustice. We must do so only with much prayer and great humility, aware, as Rahner put it, that 'the critic must always remember that s/he is part of what's wrong with the church'. But where it is necessary, we must do it, also within the church, the Body of Christ, of which we are part. It is simply a necessary part of our following of Jesus.
   And it was precisely as man that he combated injustice. No reputable theologian would accept this as an excuse for our inaction.
   - It is no answer to say the situation was different in his day, and that we don't have such injustices today. The injustices, the violations of human rights today, both in the world at large, and within the church, are many and serious. So, somehow, as followers of Jesus, we too are called to witness to truth. How?

6. Special Characteristics of Jesus' Challenging of Injustice
   - For one thing, Jesus distinguished sharply between the principle of authority and its valid use on the one hand; and false interpretations of law, or practices contrary to justice, ·on the other. He accepted the principal of authority and its right use. But this never seemed to keep him from speaking out openly against injustice and hypocrisy when the truth required it.
   - Jesus' public challenging of injustice was very rarely against individuals, almost always against groups and group ways of thinking and acting that were wrong. In other words, it was against outlooks, attitudes, structures that were false.
   - Jesus' challenging of injustice, while strong, was never done to satisfy his own ego, nor with hatred, nor out of bitterness. It was simply to witness to the truth.
7. Our Call Today
   - We too, like Jesus, are called to witness to the truth, to challenge injustice.
   - Our struggle against injustice must above all be against the monstrous injustices that stalk our world: hunger and abject poverty and oppression and torture.
   - But, if like Jesus we are to witness to the truth, then we must challenge injustice also within the church; otherwise we are hypocrites.
   - Such criticism should be open and public only when quieter and internal representations have repeatedly achieved no effect, and when the matter is important enough to warrant it.

Nick Rieman SJ

CELEBRATION OF HEALING THROUGH A COLLECTIVE EXPRESSION OF TRUTH

Purpose: In order to appreciate and learn from the last few months' experience together, we will reflect on our growth and what has helped and hindered it. As a sign of our faith in the resurrection and belief in the Trinity's power to heal our society, we will also prepare a prayer service related to an issue of our concern.

Minutes

25   1. Begin with singing and praying.

Ask to recognize how the Lord has been at work in the community and to be grateful for all he will continue to do in and through you.

Reflect quietly on Revelation 21:1-8 and on the following questions:

a) How were you drawn to the Lord this week?

b) How has your awareness of who Jesus is expanded over the last three months?

c) Remember our community meetings (possibly read your journal for each meeting).

    i) In what ways were we in harmony with the Lord?

    ii) What seemed to divide us and turn us in on ourselves?

    iii) Is there any reconciling that needs to be done? If so, when? how?

    iv) What is the quality of our community's sense of humour gratitude, joy, generosity and service?

50   2. Share any of the above.

10   BREAK

277

60	3.	Organize a liturgy or prayer service (vigil) related to an issue in which you are involved. Possibly celebrate it in a significant public spot related to the issue. Could it be ecumenical and/or inter-faith, involving Jews, Hindus, Buddhists as well as some different christian denominations?
10	4.	Journal: How well did we listen and respond to each other this evening? For what are you grateful?
5	5.	Conclude by singing and prayer together.

Prayer for the Week:

(A) Awareness prayer.

(B) Scripture prayer:

Ask the Lord that we may co-operate effectively with all people of good will and learn to celebrate with hope, imaginative insight and freedom.

Zephaniah	3:14-18
Isaiah	51:1-3; 62:5
Luke	5:33-39

UNIT V
INTEGRATING GOD'S VISION OF RIGHT;
THE KINGDOM IN THE MAKING

Thrust: From reflecting on personal and social problems and doing justice on these levels, we now move to the Trinity's vision of right in the world and all creation. God has hopes, desires, a dream for us. The Lord's dream is one of wholeness, (salvation), and of right relationships (justice) within individuals, among all peoples, nature, the cosmos. He calls all to be one in him (Col. 1:9-20 and Ephesians 1:17-23).

When we move away from this, God constantly calls us back. This calling became most evident in Jesus' life and mission; fidelity to the call to draw all to the Father cost Jesus his life. Jesus took life, suffering and death seriously. What does it mean to take our lives, suffering and death seriously? (And with humour!) How can God's will, desire or dream be at work in that? In these next weeks, therefore, we will consider God's way of making creation right, his love that conquers even death.

Jesus' whole life became one of 'letting go', of letting the Spirit have full dominion over him. He was most human in depending completely on the Father, in saying yes in the absolute moment of life; that is, in death. His total emptying of self let God penetrate humanity fully, let God take over totally for resurrection, raising him up and Spiriting him. Because Jesus was so fully human embracing all humanity and creation, and because he was the Son of God, his yes is cosmic and given to us. All are called to resurrection, to become part of the new creation, new body with Jesus as its head, with full life in the Spirit.

Where do we meet this Jesus? The tomb is empty. We are sent to 'Galilees', everywhere, to proclaim the gospel, build up the kingdom through a variety of ministries, all empowered by the same Spirit. This is where and how we meet the living Lord!

This life - opening us up to the very heart of God - opens us to all cosmic reality, to the simplicity of right relationships in God. We celebrate this reality in life and liturgy. Celebrating Eucharist, for example, becomes a cosmic setting right, the total presence of God (in community, word and sacrament) re-humanizing the world, bringing persons and creation to their right end. Opening up to God's kingdom in our lives, (both in the gathering together in the kingdom and in the going forth to proclaim this victory of the Trinity's love) forms and transforms us into being a eucharistic people.

Process: Our approach is simply to be attentive to the Trinity's dream and Jesus' mission so that we may become followers. Because living the paschal mystery is central to this daily discipleship, we will actually follow the death-resurrection-ascension-pentecost event as our way of proceeding. Seeing how Jesus faced his death, can help us to face our own and to discover the Father's fidelity. Jesus' commissioning and empowering us with the Spirit becomes a source of strength and direction for us.

We will consider further what building the kingdom as well as what living and celebrating as a eucharistic people means. The theological and spiritual thrust of this unit deepens the foundation for better service.

Week 1 The Trinity's Dream: Making Creation Right

Week 2 Jesus' Following His Father's Desire Of Salvation For All

Week 3 Jesus Sets Right By His Trust In The Father

Week 4 Meeting The Risen Lord: Discovering The Kingdom

Week 5 Sent To Proclaim The Presence Of The Kingdom

Week 6 The Spirit's Gift: Responsibility And Ministry In The Kingdom

Week 7 Building Up The Body Of Christ: Covenant And Communion

Weeks 8-9 Covenant And Communion On A Global Scale

Week 10 Ways Of Celebrating Life In Jesus, Lord Of Creation

Week 11 About The Eucharist: Integrating All Life In Creation

Week 12 Giving Thanks For All Life In Creation

Goals:

- to experience how the Trinity is intimately concerned with human history, everyday realities and our future direction so that we may respond freely and co-operate wholeheartedly in Jesus' mission

- to share Jesus' total trust in the Father so that we will let him penetrate our lives completely

- to face the reality of death with recognition of our fear and hope so that we may see its meaning as Jesus does

- to realize that we meet the Lord in his body, the church, and that he empowers us to work effectively to build his kingdom of justice and love

- to ponder and treasure the wisdom and mystery of the kingdom of God

- to learn to celebrate with greater creativity, freedom and gratitude

- by listening well and responding in faith to become more of an open community

- to appreciate more of the mystery of covenant, communion, eucharist in life and liturgy

THE TRINITY'S DREAM: MAKING CREATION RIGHT

Purpose: We have reflected on the Trinity's vision of drawing ourselves and all creation to themselves. Within this, we realize that we have harmed creation; now, therefore, our focus is turned to the Trinity's desire to make right, to re-create or bring salvation. The purpose of this remembering is to strengthen us in God's way (in spiritual consolation) so that we are more trusting and willing to let more threatening issues surface without fear.

Minutes

15   1. Begin with prayer and singing.

Ask for the gift of appreciating the Trinity's way of making right and how we are invited to live accordingly.

Read Mt. 6:31-34 and reflect quietly on it.

50   2. Share any of what you experienced in prayer now or over the past week, and in the prayer service last week.

10   BREAK

45   3. Discuss:
   a) What image comes to you when you hear the word 'right' or 'justice'?
   b) What do you think is the Trinity's way of making right and justice? (Then refer, if necessary, to scriptural references on this at the end of the week.)
   c) What role is each of us invited to play in this?
   d) Read John 3:16-17. God offers us the kingdom; yet, the realization of it depends on our response, our acceptance or rejection of it. The Lord 'dialogues' with us and responds to each new reality of our lives with abundant

promise and the new hope of bringing all to unity in him (1 Cor. 15:28).

What does this mean for you?

15   4. Journal and sharing: What comments, ideas or sharing seemed to touch you this evening? (It could be in a quiet, affirming or a challenging, disturbing way.) What was our group experience this evening?

5   5. Prepare for the Prayer of the Week. What is helping members to take time for prayer?

10   6. Conclude with prayer and singing.

Prayer for the Week:

(A) Awareness prayer.

(B) Scripture prayer:

Ask for a deeply-felt appreciation of the Trinity's way of making right so that you may be strengthened to live accordingly.

> Genesis   1:26-27
> James   1:16-18
> Isaiah   58: 8-10

SOME SCRIPTURAL REFERENCES OF THE TRINITY'S VISION OF RIGHT AND JUSTICE

The Trinity is life. The Trinity loves life. The Trinity gives life lovingly. The life they are and give has a certain quality that cannot suffer alterations without the risk of promoting 'non-life', that is, death. That which is in the Trinity must be — for the sake of life itself — and it is right. The Trinity cannot, in faithfulness to itself, be other than the standard of life. This is a vital order that cannot tolerate change nor challenge, because as the absolute and ultimate fullness of life, the Trinity has done the best there ever will be. The Trinity's righteousness/justice is not therefore a sword dangling above everyone's head ready to smite whoever happens to stray outside some whimsical commandment. On the contrary, the 'doing right' of the Trinity is a gift, a gift of life in love, a gift that invites the receiver to abide in the realm of the Source, again for the sake of life itself. So when humanity contravenes the Trinity's law of life and adopts a 'death stance' (sin), the Trinity could either acknowledge the death desire of human freedom or rather, as in most cases, help humans overcome the death-producing action by giving them a new chance to live and act in a right relation with the Trinity. This is why in Hebrew literature the concept of 'justice' is so very close to the concept of 'holiness': being godly is not setting oneself apart but rather acting in a life-sustaining manner. To be righteous therefore is to turn self and others to real life rather than an illusion of it. It is against this background that history unfolds and that interventions are made.

1. The Lord is uprightness itself and justice.
   (Deuteronomy 32:4-6)
2. The Lord desires that justice should flow like water and integrity like an unfailing stream. (Amos 5:24)
3. The Lord intervenes to establish or give right order, justice, salvation (these are used synonymously). (Jeremiah 23:5; Isaiah 24:16, 54:14, 58:8-9)
4. The Lord's way of right is one of peace, of defense and saving for the poor. (Psalms 72:1-4, 82:1-4, 112:9, 140:12, 145:15-17, 146:5-9)
5. Justice is joy-filled, saving, bringing well-being.
   (Psalm 22:32, 89:17, 132:9; Isaiah 32:17, 53:11)
6. The Lord is a just judge, slow to anger and calling for repentance. (Psalm 7:10-12)
7. The Lord faithfully brings deliverance and vindicates his people. (Psalm 24:6, 36:7, 71:18-19, 85:11-14, 97:2)
8. Jesus is the righteous one; the one who vindicates and saves through his surrender in death. The Lord alone makes right. (Acts 3:12,16; 1 Peter 2:24, 3:18; 1 John 2:1-2; Romans 3:30, 5:17-18, 8:30; 1 Corinthians 1:30, 6:11)

9. Righteousness and justice (moral goodness) is the result of deliverance and forgiveness; it is conferred freely by Christ. (Romans 1:16-17, 3:24-26, 5:17-21)

10. The Trinity bestows righteousness, justice as life in the Spirit (Romans 8:10), light (2 Corinthians 6:14), peace (James 3:18), goodness and truth (Ephesians 5:9).

Justice or 'making right', therefore, is the free gift which the Trinity bestows so that we may share in the death and resurrection of Jesus, living in him and he in us. It is salvation, wholeness, the presence of the kingdom of God in our midst. This gift produces, in effect, right relationships and order between ourselves and the Trinity, and for us among each other and all creation. (James 1:13-18)

JESUS' FOLLOWING HIS FATHER'S DESIRE OF SALVATION FOR ALL

Purpose: We reflect on Jesus' example of compassion, caring and loving, his setting relationships and priorities in good 'order' before the Father and all people. The main question of the week is how caring for the human community, both locally and globally, fits with this.

Minutes

15   1. Begin with prayer and singing.

Ask to share Jesus' intimate affection for his Father in such a way that we will also share his commitment to the mission entrusted to him.

Reflect on John 3:16-17.

50   2. Share an awareness of the past week.

10   BREAK

50   3. Discuss:

a) Read Mt. 6:33 and John 3:16-17. What did this mean for Jesus' life?
   In your own words:
   i) What was Jesus' mission?
   ii) How did he become aware of it?
   iii) What did living it out involve for him? Why?

b) i) How did Jesus work through suffering and death?
   ii) How did this 'make right'? How did good come of it?

c) i) What do 'doing God's will' and 'obedience to God' mean?
   ii) How do caring and loving the human community (global and local) fit with this?

15   4. Journal: In what ways did you find a sense of harmony, support, new insights as you listened to others' sharing?

15   5. Conclude with singing and prayer.

Prayer for the Week:

(A) Awareness prayer.

(B) Scripture prayer:

Ask to share Jesus' intimate affection for his Father so that you may also respond generously in sharing his mission.

Romans   5:17-21
Hebrews   2:14-18
Hebrews   4:14-16, 5:7-9
Luke   22:24-27
Luke   22:39-46

(C) Gradually throughout the week, read chapter 13 of John's gospel noticing Jesus' love for his Father and his mission of service and his invitation to us.

JESUS SETS RIGHT BY HIS TRUST IN THE FATHER

Purpose: Following Jesus leads the disciple to participation in the paschal mystery. Our focus, therefore, is to reflect on our experience of letting go and to be with Jesus in his total trust in the Father even as he died. We also look at the meaning of death for followers of Jesus.

Minutes

15   1. Start with prayer and singing.

Ask for a great desire to share Jesus' total trust in the Father so that we will let him penetrate our lives completely.

Reflect on Philippians 2:5-11.

50   2. Share an awareness of the week.

10   BREAK

60   3. Discuss:

a) Remember examples of when you have forgotten yourself for another (others) in love, whether for a spouse, children or any others. What meaning did these experiences hold for you? In what sense did life come in the death (self-forgetfulness) itself? Ponder this. How does this relate to our ultimate death and meeting God?

b) What are some examples of Jesus' encouraging others to trust? What are some examples of Jesus' own trust in the Father? In others?

c) Of what did Jesus let go in his life and death?

d) Even sleep is a letting go, of conscious control for example. Yet that very act is itself not only renewing for us but essential for our well-being. What are some of the things of which you

i) have let go in the last year or two? Is

there any way you have grown to new life, compassion, wisdom, in and through these?

ii) now need to let go, for instance, of plans, hopes, favourite sin? Why?

iii) would find it hardest to let go? Why?

e) i) How does all this fit with God's dream (hopes, his will) for us?

ii) What is the meaning of death for followers of Jesus? What fear does it hold for you? Our society?

iii) How does this fit with our call to love one another and to assume responsibility for the human community and for the earth?

10   4. Journal: What happened within you this evening? What were you discussing when you experienced that? Possibly begin your next time of prayer with that experience.

5   5. Conclude with prayer and singing.

Prayer for the Week:

(A) Awareness prayer.

(B) Scripture prayer:

Ask for a great desire to share Jesus' total trust in the Father so that you will let him penetrate your life completely.

Luke	23:33-43
Luke	23:44-46
Mark	15:33-39
Luke	23:45-56
Wisdom	1:12-14

(C) During the week, gradually read chapters 22 and 23 of Luke's gospel.

MEETING THE RISEN LORD: DISCOVERING THE KINGDOM

Purpose: Neither Jesus' journey nor ours ends with death. Our sharing leads us from facing the reality of death to hope in God's fidelity. We discover that, like the disciples, we meet Jesus not in the empty tomb but 'in Galilee'; that is, where the good news is proclaimed by word and deed.

Minutes

15   1. Begin with prayer and singing.

Ask to meet the risen Lord as he leads us today and to respond to others as he does.

Reflect on Acts 2:32, 36.

50   2. Share some example of how your awareness drew you to the Lord and others, how it was was challenging, or encouraging for you.

10   BREAK

60   3. Discuss:

a) What happens when God takes over in Jesus? What does it mean for us?

b) What are some signs of our trust that God can conquer despair, suffering and death in us and our world?

c) Read and discuss what this means:
Mark 1:9, 14,15; Mark 16:6-7; Matthew 28:6-10, 16-20.

It is okay to go to the empty tomb, but the consistent message is to go to Galilee to meet Jesus. For Mark, Galilee is the place where the gospel is proclaimed. Even there, the disciples are not to stand looking into the clouds; they are sent to all peoples. Meeting Jesus is synonymous with announcing the gospel to all nations. If you are looking for Jesus, go to live among the nations; he is there already to meet you!

d) Consider: The risen Lord tells his followers 'Do not be afraid' and he gives them his Spirit, making them a community of his followers and sending them forth where he will be with them. And this mission will bear abundant fruit because it is a mission of love, love for every person in God. What does this mean for us?

10   4. Journal: What impressed you during the sharing?

Did you feel closer to any individuals and/or the community this evening.? Why/not?

What does this mean for you and for the community?

5   5. Conclude with prayer and singing.

Prayer for the Week:

(A) Awareness prayer.

(B) Scripture prayer:

Ask to meet the risen Lord as he leads you today and to be with him in responding to others as he does.

Acts   3:26
Mark   16: 6-7
1 Corinthians 15:35-46

(C) During the week, read chapters 14 to 17 of John's gospel, noticing Jesus' mission and his invitation to us.

SENT TO PROCLAIM THE PRESENCE OF THE KINGDOM

Purpose: We have pondered how the experience of meeting the Risen Lord is closely linked to the proclamation of the reign of God.

We will now consider how we are called to be part of this kingdom and to proclaim that it is already among us, though it has not yet been brought to completion.

Minutes

15 1. Begin with prayer (presence, thanksgiving, and light) and singing.

Ask for a heartfelt appreciation of the mystery of Christ among us so that we may build his kingdom of justice and love with confidence and courage in him.

Reflect on Acts 1:6-8, 2:32-34.

50 2. Share an awareness of prayer/life experience of the past week. Support each other with clarifications, gentle questioning, reassurance, whatever is appropriate for another follower of Jesus.

10 BREAK

40 3. Read and discuss:

i) In the Old Testament the task of the king was to set right, to do justice because of the power given him by the people and by God.

ii) Read and discuss the meaning of the following:
Luke 14:15-24; 13:18-21.

iii) The kingdom is salvation, life, (Mark 9:43,45; 10:17). It is the excessive love of God which makes itself felt in mutual acceptance of people, overcoming prejudices, and in the sharing of sadness and joy, in living community. It is also hidden in the ordinary events. It is mysterious and difficult to assess but truly at work in our midst. Ephesians 1:17-23.

iv) Jesus is now at the right hand of the Father; through his being Lord and sending his Spirit, the kingdom is to become a cosmic reality. Jesus' followers are to proclaim and build the kingdom of God. What does this mean? Read Luke 9:2,60; 10:12.

v) What are some symbols and images of the presence of the kingdom on earth, for example, body of Christ, covenant?

vi) Who are invited to communion in this kingdom? Luke 4:16-20, 6:20; Mark 9:37, 10:15; James 2:2-5; Matthew 25.

20   4. Journal: What did you experience this evening within yourself, in relation to the others, in response to the content and in terms of any of the process? What does this indicate for you and for the others? Share this together.

15   5. Conclude with prayer and singing.

Prayer for the Week:

(A) Awareness prayer.

(B) Scripture prayer:

Ask to appreciate and treasure the mystery of Christ among us so that you may help to build his kingdom of justice and love. Use each of the following as long as it is helpful:

What does it mean to build the Body of Christ? Who is part of it? The mystery is Christ among us. (Col. 1:27)

1 Corinthians 11:23-27 What does this mean?

| Luke | 24:44-49 |
| Luke | 6:20 |

293

THE SPIRIT'S GIFT: RESPONSIBILITY AND MINISTRY IN THE KINGDOM

Purpose: As we become more aware of the Spirit in our lives, we discover that we are called to intimacy with the Lord and sent out to continue his mission of proclaiming the good news and building his kingdom of love and justice. This evening we will consider the call and the mission, and the Lord's promise to be with us in it. It will be particularly important to 'root' or 'ground' this awareness in effective ministry.

Minutes

15   1. Begin with prayer and singing.

Ask the Lord to open us to hear his call and to respond generously in building the kingdom with him.

35   2. Share briefly from the past week. Note that the time is shortened for this tonight.

10   BREAK

40   3. Read the following alone or with a partner:

a) Read Exodus 2:23-4:17 and consider how the Lord took the initiative in responding to a need of his people, how Moses had some profound experience of knowing God, how God called Moses from among his people to be for them, how Moses tried various arguments against being sent on the mission but finally co-operated with God in leading the people from slavery to freedom.

b) Read Mark 3:13 and Luke 6:12-13. Consider the following notes on a literal translation of the original:

i) 'he summons' The original Greek is written in the present tense. His call is ever present and on-going.

ii) 'those whom he wanted himself' Jesus takes the initiative, freely calling whom he wants.

iii) 'he wanted' is best translated 'those he carried in his heart'. In his prayer during the night the Father had entrusted some people to Jesus, call is shown as loving action of a tender God; it draws people to himself. This parallels the Father's love for Jesus. Mark 1:11, 9:8; Isaiah 43:4 and Psalm 2:7-8.

iv) 'made them his companions': 'made' is the creative action of giving the capacity to live this new form of life. 'They were to be with him' is a good translation; their lives and destiny would be identified with his. They would share his mind and heart; that is, Jesus would be the basic disposition, love and driving force of their existence.

v) The entire statement is made in view of mission but it depends radically on being with Jesus. They are chosen 'so that they might be sent with power to cast out devils and to preach'.

vi) He calls them by name, personally.

c) The Spirit does the unexpected and ministry follows from that. Read Luke 2:1-4,22-24, 11:13; Acts 8:26-40.

Minutes

40   4. Discuss:

a) Part of the mission is gathering together those who have been dispersed. Consider people you know, and others who are 'near and far off' that is, close or distant from any experience of friendship, community, knowing the Lord, or even their own worth. How do you meet them? Is there mutual giving and receiving in the meeting? How?

b) What helps our community to be most energizing for us so that we truly are a healing, ministering community in Jesus' name, for each other and beyond ourselves? What is the source of this life?

c) What are the mission and ministry of the follower of Christ who is married, single, ordained, in a religious community?

10   5. Journal: What is the spirit or tone of our community this evening? What sparked various feelings you had?

10   6. Conclude with prayer and singing together.

Prayer for the Week:

(A) Awareness prayer. Include reflection on what you experienced in the meeting.

(B) Scripture prayer:

Ask the Lord that you may experience how he calls you to himself and how he is sending you to be for others.

Mark 3:13
Acts   2:1-4, 22-24
Luke 6:12-13
Luke 11:13
Acts   4:13

BUILDING UP THE BODY OF CHRIST: COVENANT AND COMMUNION

Transition and Purpose: Opening up to God's kingdom in our lives, (both in the gathering together in the kingdom and in the going forth to proclaim this victory of the Trinity's love) forms and transforms us into being a eucharistic people.

We celebrate Eucharist authentically in liturgy when we recognize our brothers and sisters, as well as the Lord, in the breaking of the bread. We celebrate the extent to which this is reality today. Humbly we come in faith to the Lord's meal, asking to be so incorporated into his Body that we may
– embrace our contemporary 'hour of darkness';
– be covenanted as God's people;
– find unity and reconciliation as a people (and peoples);
– be victorious over sin and its widespread consequences today;
– be transformed gradually, daily into more of a human community with the mind and heart of Christ for others;
– be empowered by the Spirit, missioned with and for others... even from within our weak, sinful state;
– be broken and poured out with/for others in consecration.

In the breaking of the bread (body) we recognize the Lord, (Luke 24:30,31) proclaim his death and remember him. We do this in memory of him.

In this union and self-gift with Christ we can pray and say with our lives, 'Your kingdom come'.

All of this is eucharistic living as well as eucharitic liturgy or celebration.

Eventually, death becomes our passage into full

incorporation into the body of Christ, the communion of saints; it is our complete surrender to the Father so that he can be God for us. It is covenant, communion and realization of the kingdom. It is eucharist!

This week, we will focus on the meaning of covenant and communion, as well as on symbols and images of them.

Minutes

15 1. Begin with singing and prayer.

Ask for a deep, heartfelt love for the entire body of Christ and a greater appreciation of what covenant and communion mean for us.

Reflect on Matthew 25:31-46.

50 2. Share any of the past week and what it indicates for you.

10 BREAK

50 3. Discuss:

a) What does 'being covenanted' with the Lord mean?

Whom does he covenant?

Read Exodus 19:3-8 and 24:3-8.

b) What is Jesus' covenant?

Read quietly Jeremiah 31:31-34; 1 Corinthians 11:23-29; Luke 22:14-20; John 13-17 (each read one chapter of this).

With and for whom does he make it?

How can we live and celebrate it?

c) What are various ways of being in communion with the Lord (entire body of Christ)?

d) i) What are our best (and most universal) signs, symbols, images of covenant and communion with the body of Christ? Include marriage, meals.

ii) What does it mean when we say eucharist is a sacrament? Of what is it a sacrament?

298

10   4. Journal: When did you feel most united with others this evening? (or distant) What was happening at the time? What does this indicate for you?

Reminder: Are you taking time for prayer daily?

5   5. Conclude with prayer and singing.

Prayer for the Week:

(A) Awareness prayer.

(B) Scripture prayer:

Ask daily for a heartfelt love for the entire body of Christ and a greater appreciation of what covenant and communion mean for us, individually and collectively.

DAY 1   Ponder your experience of covenant and communion with others. Ask the Lord to let you see the reality it symbolizes.

DAY 2   Reflect on Jesus' symbol of the breaking of bread and wine poured out as his farewell gifts to us. How are they gift? Talk with him about it.

DAY 3   Eucharist means that together we say 'Amen', yes, to this consecration of our lives to the Father and to all our brothers and sisters. Ponder this, asking the Lord to be with you enabling you to live this way in grateful generous response and/or showing you the extent of your fears and how he wants to transform you.

DAY 4   When have you been 'broken' and 'poured out'? When have you been with others who have been broken and poured out? 'As often as you do this, remember me'. Ask for the gift of a good memory to remember him in the dying whether it is in small or big ways.

DAY 5   'They recognized him in the breaking of the bread'. Luke 24:30-31. What does this mean in both liturgy and life?

DAY 6   Remember with compassion the multitude of needs in our world. Ask the Lord of the harvest to send labourers into his vineyard. Mt. 9:35-37.

COVENANT AND COMMUNION ON A GLOBAL SCALE

Purpose: Since covenant and communion are to be lived realities which in turn give us cause for celebration, we will consider urgent issues of our time and what kind of response we are able to make. We will also decide how we will continue this theme next week.

Minutes

15   1. Begin with prayer and singing.

Ask the great love for the body of Christ and a deeper appreciation of what call and covenant mean for us. We ask for the gift of being peacemakers at every level of interaction.

Reflect on 1 Corinthians 11:2-29, 12:12-13,27.

50   2. Share from an awareness of the past week. How was the Lord with you in that reality? How are you being sent to be more for others, even in your prayer?

10   BREAK

15   3. Reflect quietly:
a) What insights have been most meaningful to you over the last six weeks?
b) Choose a global issue of our time that concerns you and ponder how it relates to 3a).
c) Share on these.

15   4. a) Choose one issue for further study and discuss it in the light of Weeks 1-7, for example, nuclear disarmament. Refer to the excerpts at the end of this week's outline as an example of this.
b) Since next week(s) will focus on these issues completely, decide what approach you will take for your learning, sharing, action on it. The latter will probably emerge as you become acquainted with the issue.

5   5. Journal: What did you experience within your-
     self this evening? What does it indicate
     for you? How would you describe the
     group experience tonight. Share this.
     How does it fit with the basic thrusts of
     being rooted in love or fear (refer to
     III-10), to consolation or desolation
     (refer to III-8)?

5   6. Conclude by praying and singing together.

Prayer for the Week(s):

(A) Awareness prayer, particularly in regard to your own and
others' reactions to news or issues today.

(B) Scripture prayer:

Ask for a greater love for the entire body of Christ, a
deeper appreciation of what call and covenant mean for us,
and for the gift of being a peacemaker at every level of interaction.

1 Corinthians	12:12-27
Luke	24:13-35
Wisdom	1:12-14, 7:27-8:1, 11:21-27
Luke	1:46-55
Luke	1:67-79
The eucharistic prayers	

(C) Read and reflect on the articles 'An Example of Covenant
and Communion with the Body of Christ on a Global
Scale: Disarmament and Peace', and 'Bound Together for
Peace: New Abolitionist Covenant'.

AN EXAMPLE OF COVENANT AND COMMUNION WITH THE BODY OF CHRIST ON A GLOBAL SCALE: DISARMAMENT AND PEACE

Faith Reflection:

1. The Trinity create, sustain and guide our world and histo-

ry; they are passionately concerned with us and our world with love, peace, life, justice and mercy.

Desiring to forgive rather than destroy, they are faithful to their promise and will enable us to be victorious over evil.

2. Human nature is basically good, though weak. We are called to co-operate with all people of good-will in working for peaceful solutions to the problems of our time.

3. Sin is real and as such separates us from God, from the community and from ourselves. We are all sinners and are influenced by corporate sinful decisions which are often routinely made. The arms race is both reality and symbol of sins of ambition, despair, destructiveness and alienation. We recognize that preparation for war and war itself are the greatest sin and obscenity of our time; at the same time, we believe in the Trinity's presence with us, enabling us to bring order to a very disordered world.

4. Because the redeeming Christ is present in our midst, his kingdom is already mysteriously growing in among us. We can live in him and beat our swords into ploughshares, our spears into pruning hooks and not train for war anymore (Is. 2:5). This effort is grounded in the reality of our call to share his suffering.

5. We overcome sin through the Lord's gift of salvation within our real life situations. The socio-political and economic world is where the Trinity leads us to be active in the work of liberation. (Exodus 3 and 4)

6. Nonviolence is central to the gospel; we may not use evil means to achieve even a good result. Peace is the way. The love of the Trinity is a 'discovery' more energizing than any nuclear energy. Jesus' way of the cross is nonviolence, seeming failure; yet in it, God compassionately raises the body of Christ from death to life.

7. Technology is material reality and needs to be used in a right orientation, for the covenant and justice. If it is used for false 'security' or as a way of control, it is caught in the deception of being made an end in itself, rather than something that supports life.

'In 1976 the Holy See issued strong testimony to the United Nations condemning the arms race 'unreservedly.'

The testimony stated that the arms race 'is an act of aggression, which amounts to a crime, for *even when they are not used,* by their cost alone, *armaments kill the poor by causing them to starve.'* (emphasis in original) Regarding the strategy of deterrence, the testimony declared: 'The severity of the diagnosis is thus clear. In the eyes of the Church, *the present situation of would-be security is to be condemned.'*

(Peace, War, and the Christian Conscience, pg. 14, 1982, by Joseph J. Fahey.)

In Hiroshima, in 1981, Pope John Paul said, 'There is no justification for not raising the question of the responsibility of each nation and each individual in the face of the nuclear threat.'

The Canadian bishops joined U.S. bishops and citizens in condemning the decision of their government on the neutron bomb. 'We also ask members of the Catholic community and the people of Canada to oppose vigorously the build-up of nuclear arms by all nations.' October, 1981.

World Peace Prayer

Lead us from death to life,
 from falsehood to truth.
Lead us from despair to hope,
 from fear to trust.
Lead us from hate to love,
 from war to peace.
Let peace fill our hearts,
 our world,
 our universe.

BOUND TOGETHER FOR PEACE

(The story behind the New Abolitionist Covenant)

As the danger of the nuclear arms race has steadily grown, one thing has become clear: the need for a movement of Christian conscience to oppose the deadly momentum and to provide leadership for peace.

A small circle of Christians who saw that need began to meet and talk together almost a year ago. We met to deepen our fellowship with one another and to explore ways we might work more closely together. We came from five different groups, each working to re-establish the vocation of peacemaking in the churches: the Fellowship of Reconciliation, New Call to Peacemaking, Pax Christi, World Peacemakers, and Sojourners.

Our coming together was indeed an ecumenical event: Protestant, Catholic, and the historic peace churches; evangelical and liberal theological traditions; pacifist and non-pacifist. All had come to believe that any significant initiative for peace would have to be deeply rooted in faith. Our sessions were centred in prayer and theological reflection about our perilous situation. We asked how the new stream of Christian peacemaking now flowing here and there might become a mighty river of fervent prayer and costly action for peace in our time.

It became clear to us that we needed something more than another statement, and that one program of action wouldn't be adequate. The idea of 'covenant' emerged, perhaps because that was what was occurring among us. To covenant is to bind together for the sake of a common purpose; what if Christians would covenant together to abolish nuclear weapons as an urgent matter of faith? The covenant would not be a new organization but a new relationship among Christians for the sake of peace.

The historical precedent of the 19th-century abolitionist movement had become a great inspiration to us and served as an example of how faith could be applied to a fundamental moral question. In that day, Christian faith was made historically specific and played a significant role in the movement to abolish slavery. That testimony spurred us on.

What emerged finally was the New Abolitionist Covenant, which all five groups have made together and now offer to the churches. The covenant, found on the following pages, is comprehensive and calls for action on all levels: personal, congregational, and political. It begins in prayer and ends in public witness. The New Abolitionist Covenant expresses the deep conviction for peace that many of us feel.

Our hope is that it would draw Christians together into a vital relationship for the sake of peace. Our prayer is that it might focus and catalyze the movement of Christian conscience in our day to testify to the power of the gospel and turn the nation away from its present destructive course.

Let us covenant together as a sign of hope, as a step toward peace.

Jim Wallis

New Abolitionist Covenant

(Christian Edition)

In the name of God, let us abolish nuclear weapons.

The Christian faith must be demonstrated anew in each historical moment. The gospel is always addressed to the time in which we live. Christians must find ways to relate timeless but timely faith to their own situation, showing what they will embrace and what they will refuse because of Jesus Christ.

Some historical issues stand out as particularly urgent among the church's fundamental concerns. These overarching moral questions intrude upon the routine of the church's life and plead for the compassion and courage of God's people everywhere. Slavery was such a question for Christians in the 19th century. The nuclear arms race is such a question today.

Thousands of Christians from diverse traditions came to see that slavery was an evil that challenged the very integrity of their faith. They believed that for any person to claim ownership of another human being denied that each person is loved by God and made in God's image. These Christians began to preach that to follow Christ meant to run away from the institution of slavery, to refuse to cooperate with it, and to work

305

for its abolition. Though this seemed like an absurd, unattainable goal, they insisted that God required nothing less. They came to be called abolitionists.

Christian acceptance of nuclear weapons has brought us also to a crisis of faith. The nuclear threat is not just a political issue any more than slavery was: It is a question that challenges our worship of God and our commitment to Jesus Christ. In other words, the growing prospect of nuclear war presents us with more than a test of survival; it confronts us with a test of faith.

Nuclear war is total war. Unlimited in their violence, indiscriminate in their victims, uncontrollable in their devastation, nuclear weapons have brought humanity to an historical crossroads. More than at any previous time in history, the alternatives are peace or destruction. In nuclear war there are no winners.

We are Christians who now see that the nuclear arms race is more than a question of public policy. We believe that the wholesale destruction threatened by these weapons makes their possession and planned use an offense against God and humanity, no matter what the provocation or political justification. Through deliberation and prayer we have become convinced that Jesus' call to be peacemakers urgently needs to be renewed in the churches and made specific by a commitment to abolish nuclear weapons and to find a new basis of national security.

As the foundation of national security, nuclear weapons are idolatrous. As a method of defense, they are suicidal. To believe that nuclear weapons can solve international problems is the greatest illusion and the height of naivete.

The threatened nuclear annihilation of whole populations in the name of national security is an evil we can no longer accept. At stake is whether we trust in God or the bomb. We can no longer confess Jesus as Lord and depend on nuclear weapons to save us. Conversion in our day must include turning away from nuclear weapons as we turn to Jesus Christ.

The building and threatened use of nuclear weapons is a sin - against God, God's creatures, and God's creation. There is no theology or doctrine in the traditions of the church that could ever justify nuclear war. Whether one begins with pacifism or with the just war doctrine, nuclear weapons are morally unacceptable.

The God of the Bible loves the poor and demands justice for the oppressed. To continue to spend hundreds of billions of dollars in preparation for war while millions go hungry is a grievous failure of compassion and an affront to God. But by God's grace our hearts can be softened in order to heed the biblical vision of converting the weapons of war into instruments of peace.

When nuclear war is thinkable, folly and madness have become the accepted political wisdom. It is time for the church to bear witness to the absolute character of the word of God which is finally our only hope in breaking the hold of the political realities in whose name we march to oblivion.

In times past, Christians from many traditions joined together to oppose great social sin and point the way to change. We believe the growing prospect of nuclear war now calls for such unity of Christian response.

Our response as Christians begins with repentance for almost four decades of accepting nuclear weapons. Repentance in a nuclear age means non-cooperation with preparation for nuclear war and the turning of our lives toward peace.

Whatever we say to the government must be based first on what we have publicly committed ourselves to do and not to do in the face of a nuclear war. The fruits of our repentance will be made visible in our active witness and leadership for peace.

No longer trusting in nuclear weapons, we refuse to cooperate with preparations for total war. Trusting anew in God, we will begin cooperating with one another in preparations for peace. We covenant to work together for peace and join with one another to make these vital commitments.

1. *Prayer*

We covenant together to pray. Prayer is at the heart of Christian peacemaking. Prayer can change us and our relationships. Prayer begins in confession of our own sin and extends into intercession for our enemies, bringing them closer to us. We will pray, asking God to hold back the nuclear devastation so that we may turn from our folly. Through prayer the reality of Christ's victory over nuclear darkness can be established in our lives and free us to participate in Christ's reconciling work in the world.

2. *Education*

We covenant together to learn. Our ignorance and passivity must be transformed into awareness and responsibility. We must act together to dispel our blindness and hardness of heart. We will ground ourselves in the biblical and theological basis for peacemaking. We will become thoroughly and deeply informed about the dangers of the arms race and the steps to be taken toward peace. We will become aware of the churches' teachings on the matter of nuclear warfare.

3. *Spiritual Examination*

We covenant together to examine ourselves. To shed the light of the gospel on the nuclear situation, we will examine the basic decisions of our personal lives in regard to our jobs, lifestyles, taxes, and relationships, to see where and how we are cooperating with preparations for nuclear war. The church should be concerned with the spiritual well-being of its members whose livelihoods are now dependent on the nuclear war system. We will undertake a thorough pastoral evaluation of the life of our congregations in all these matters.

4. *Evangelism*

We covenant together to spread the gospel of peace. We will speak out and reach out to our friends, families, and Christian brothers and sisters about the dangers of the nuclear arms buildup and the urgency of peace. We will take the message to the other churches in our neighbourhoods, to our denominations, and to the decision-making bodies of our churches on every level. The cause of peace will be preached from our pulpits, lifted up in our prayers, and made part of our worship. We will offer faith in God as an alternative to trust in the bomb.

5. *Public Witness*

We covenant together to bear public witness. Our opposition to nuclear weapons and the imperative of peace will be taken into the public arena: to our workplaces, to our community and civic organizations, to the media, to our governmental bodies, to the streets, and to the nuclear weapons facilities themselves. A prayerful presence for peace needs to be established at all those places where nuclear weapons are researched, produced, stored, and deployed, and where decisions are made to continue the arms race.

The gatherings, events, and institutions of the churches will also become important places for our public witness. We will make our convictions known at all these places, especially on significant dates in the church calendar and on August 6 and 9, the anniversaries of the bombings of Hiroshima and Nagasaki.

6. *Nuclear Disarmament*

We covenant together to work to stop the arms race. In light of our faith, we are prepared to live without nuclear weapons. We will publicly advocate a nuclear weapon freeze as the first step toward abolishing nuclear weapons altogether. We will act in our local communities to place the call for a nuclear weapon freeze on the public agenda. We will press our government and the other nuclear powers to halt all further testing, production, and deployment of nuclear weapons, and then move steadily and rapidly to eliminate them completely.

We recognize a call from God to make these simple commitments and, through the grace of God, we hope to fulfill them. Rooted in the gospel of Jesus Christ and strengthened by the hope that comes from faith, we covenant together to make peace.

How to Use this Covenant

The purpose of the covenant is to place before the churches the abolition of nuclear weapons as an urgent matter of faith. The nuclear threat is a theological issue, a confessional matter, a spiritual question, and is so important that it must be brought into the heart of the church's life.

This is not a statement to sign but a covenant to be acted

upon. In other words, the purpose is not to gain signatures, but to encourage response. Find at least two or three others to spend an hour, a day, or a weekend with this covenant. Gather with your friends to make the covenant and then take it to your congregations, groups, and communities. We hope to see the covenant distributed widely, used locally, and result in action.

The covenant should be dealt with in a community process. These commitments cannot be carried out alone. Therefore, we encourage people to enter into supportive relationships with others for the purpose of prayer, reflection, and action. Our hope is that the covenant can strengthen existing groups working for peace and help create new ones.

Sojourners Magazine, August, 1981
P.O. Box 29272, 1309 L Street N.W.,
Washington, D.C. 20017

WAYS OF CELEBRATING LIFE IN JESUS, LORD OF CREATION

Purpose: In order to celebrate well the reality that Jesus is Lord and the blessings of the past few months, we will try to expand our creativity by brainstorming and imagining possibilities for celebrating different kinds of events.

Minutes

5   1. Begin with prayer and sharing.

Ask to see the depth of hope promised us by the Lord and to learn to celebrate this with creativity, freedom and gratitude.
Read Zephaniah 3:17-18 and Ephesians 1:19-23.

45   2. Share an awareness of the past week and how you discerned its meaning for you.

10   BREAK

10   3. Remember
   a) usual ways of celebrating in our society;
   b) brief overview of all that we have pondered together;
   c) how we meet each other and God in silence, word, community, events, signs or symbols, sacrament.

10   4. Brainstorm. What are some helps for celebrating well?

40   5. Lead the following:
   a) Use your imagination to see and discover other ways of celebrating, ways that express some of the depth of the life and hope we know and believe in because Jesus is Lord of the cosmos; our globe, family and colleagues are certainly a part of this.

311

b) Close your eyes and imagine celebrating (being with) in great freedom, freedom that is
true to the reality of the event: in birthdays
(pause a few moments), victory... marriage...healing...reconciliation...creation
and salvation...death...an anniversary.

c) Now choose one of these (pause) and we will
take 10-15 minutes to relax with this and let
any ways of celebrating emerge. You may
be, use, and do all you want!

d) Share these and what you experienced as you
did it!

Minutes

15   6. Choose any sacrament and imagine ways of celebrating it well. Discuss these together.

10   7. Journal: How did we experience the presence
of the Lord this evening? How do we
show our gratitude for such a gift?

5   8. Conclude with singing and prayer.

Prayer for the Week:

(A) Awareness prayer.

(B) Scripture prayer:

Ask daily to see the depth of hope promised us by the Lord
and to learn to celebrate this with creativity, freedom and
gratitude.

Ephesians	1:17-23 (and all of chapter 1)
Colossians	1:10-20
Philippians	1:3-6
Philippians	4:4-7, 12-13

ABOUT THE EUCHARIST: INTEGRATING ALL LIFE IN CREATION

Purpose: In order to celebrate well what we have been trying to live, we will recall and deepen our understanding of eucharist. Then we will plan a celebration that incorporates creative elements expressed in Week 10.

Minutes

10   1. Begin with singing and prayer.

       Ask to experience how the Trinity is with us and desires to strengthen us in hope; ask for the gift of celebrating the life and love they share with us in a spirit of creativity, freedom and gratitude.

       Read Ephesians 1:17-23.

30   2. Share briefly from the past week.

10   BREAK

30   3. Recall and deepen your understanding of eucharist by pondering and sharing together various aspects of this action; namely,

       – how it is a community celebration of covenant and meal

       – how it is an incorporation into the body of Christ

       – what building the kingdom means

       – who is invited to the kingdom, to the marriage feast

       – how it is a sign of unity that already exists, as well as a source of further unity

       – like all the sacraments, it can open us up to unity, harmony, salvation on every level of the cosmos. This necessarily involves re-integration of all brokenness.

       – how it is the presence of the Trinity and how our surrender and openness to God opens us up to communion with cosmic reality

- how God's people are mandated or commissioned and empowered (or enabled) to build a better world
- how real eucharist must be historical (that is, lived) to set things right. Words without action are empty.
- the meaning of agape (overflow of God's unconditional love for all in celebration).

60   4. Prepare a creative celebration of Eucharist that expresses its unique reality for you! You are welcome, of course, to invite whomever you choose! Might it include a pot luck meal and street dance...or...?!

5   5. Journal: How did we experience the presence of the Lord in community tonight? How do we express our response?

5   6. Conclude with singing and praying.

Prayer for the Week:

(A) Awareness prayer, noticing how you express gratitude and joy.

(B) Scripture prayer:

Ask the Lord to experience the depth of hope he offers us and to learn to celebrate this with creativity, freedom and gratitude.

Acts   6:1-2
Luke   14:12-14
1 Corinthians 11:17-29

UNIT V WEEK 12
GIVING THANKS FOR ALL LIFE IN CREATION

Purpose: So that we may unite our celebration of gratitude with Jesus, and express our covenant and communion with the body of Christ, we will celebrate Eucharist publicly, in a creative way that is relevant to our time. Invite others.

UNIT VI

WORDS TO ACTION: INTEGRATION THROUGH DECISION-MAKING

Thrust: Our attention has been focused on liberation at every level (physical II, emotional III, social IV, and spiritual V) from the personal to the cosmic dimensions. The questions of both 'liberation from' and 'liberation to' lead us to holistic growth in the multi-faceted mystery of our lives. Whatever generates faith-filled human living and lets God have full power over us is to be encouraged and developed with generous, disciplined fidelity and co-operation; whatever confuses, paralyses or destroys this life is deception and is not to be given either our energy, time or loyalty. It becomes evident that clarity of vision, and good decision-making are of utmost importance if we are to act effectively on the word of God, making it concrete in our lives. 'Doing theology' in this way (experiencing, reflecting, judging, deciding, acting in a faith context with hope and love) can become a way of life on the personal and communal level; its penetrating effects, however, go well beyond the contribution of any one individual. The community of the Lord empowers its members in an expanded way. In the Lord the community broadens its vision and finds the power to fulfill it because the Spirit of Jesus gives it life.

How can we as individuals and as a community decide our ministries? How can we help each other for mutual growth? How can we get in touch with the Lord? How can we be aware of our own needs? How can we implement what we see as God's way for us? This unit will meet these questions.

315

Process: We have consistently considered the vision of the Trinity, of Jesus and of the Christian. Now again we will consider the impact of dream and vision on our life and our daily decisions; self-knowledge (the human element) and the presence of the Spirit of Christ are very significant in both personal and group decisions. We will reflect, therefore, on both personal and communal history as they relate to decision making and our call to transform society. We will focus on actual decisions, reflect on our experience of these past months and celebrate together.

This unit is based on *Communal Graced History: A Manual of Theology and Practice,* by John English SJ.

Week 1 Following Jesus Today: Vision And Motivation

Week 2 Personal Decision-Making

Week 3 Personal Blessed History And Decision-Making

Week 4 Personal Disordered History And Decision-Making

Week 5 Discovering Our History Of Being Energized Or Built-Up As A Community

Week 6 Communal Disordered History And Decision-Making

Week 7 Forward Direction Of Hope In This Community's History

Week 8 The Community's Present State

Week 9 Heightened Consciousness Of The Harmony Between Our Graced History, Signs Of The Times And The Call To Transform Society

Week 10 Community Assistance For Personal Decision-Making (1)

Week 11 Community Assistance For Personal Decision-Making (2)

Week 12 Making Decisions About Our Response To Needs

Week 13 Community Evaluation

Weeks 14 to 16 Communal Discernment Regarding Our Future As A Community

Week 17 Preparing A Celebration Of Gratitude And Commitment

Week 18 Celebration Of Gratitude And Commitment

Goals:
- to become aware of the impact of our dream and vision on our life, and especially on our decisions in work, family, church or civic situations
- to realize in a deeply pesonal way the many blessing we have received individually and communally so that we will appreciate the Trinity's personal presence in our unique life-history and be filled with the desire to build with them the kingdom of love and justice
- to let this gratitude influence our decisions
- to be able to perceive better the 'signs of the times' and our present reality as a community
- to recognize and follow the presence of the Trinity in our communal history, as well as avoid movements that are evil and deceptive
- to see what interior experiences have led us to good and to wrong decisons
- to experience how community can aid individuals in their decisions
- to reflect on how we are in fact a community of followers of Jesus and to celebrate this together

FOLLOWING JESUS TODAY: VISION AND MOTIVATION

Purpose: Throughout our journey together, we have constantly re-focused our attention on the Trinity's vision and dream for us. Once again, we consider the vision of the Trinity, of Jesus and of the Christian; it is their love that empowers us to respond, to choose and act out of our deepest desires for good. As we remember, we are strengthened in good decision-making, in work, family, church and global situations. As preparation for our next theme of personal decision-making, our prayer for the week will focus on remembering our blessed history with the Lord.

Minutes

15   1. Begin with singing and praying (presence, thanksgiving, light).

Ask to follow Jesus with deep love and generosity within the reality of our times.

Reflect quietly on the hope the Trinity offers us. Ephesians 1:17-23.

50   2. Share any observation or awareness from the celebration (V-12) or from your Prayer for the Week.

10   BREAK

20   3. After reading the article, which is included after the outline for prayer, write down what you consider essentials of being a follower of Jesus. Share these. How would you express these as a group?

25   4. Discuss:

a) How has your preferred vision of Christian community changed over the last year? What is it now?

b) Read the following and see how they fit with your response to numbers 3 and 4 a):

Philippians   2:5-11
Mark   8:34-38
Mark   10:45
Luke   12:13-21
Luke   16:13
Luke   9:22-23
Luke   1:26-38

c) What difference does being a follower of Jesus make in today's world?

d) What might help you now to live as a disciple?

5   5. Prepare the Prayer for the Week; the same approach is used each day.

10   6. Journal: How has Jesus been with us? What is his invitation to you now?

15   7. Conclude with singing and prayer.

Prayer for the Week:

(A) Awareness prayer.

(B) Scripture prayer:

Begin by considering the following passages of scripture:
1 Corinthians   1:26-31
John   1:35-39.

Then with Jesus as your companion on the journey, relive your life. Remember elements in your life, trying to see and hear and touch them through the eyes of Jesus. Talk with him about their significance. Seek to realize in a deeply personal way the many blessings you have received so that you will appreciate the Trinity's personal presence in your unique life and be filled with the desire to build with them the kingdom of love and justice. Ponder over your history by considering *the blessings:*

- of your family background, childhood, school years, work years;
- from different persons, places, situations, apostolates and the historical state of the world;
- from different prayer experiences, emotional experiences, experiences of success and failure.

Often speak to the Lord, to the Father, to the Holy Spirit in questions and in appreciation.

(C) Reflection after prayer (review):

After this time of remembering your blessed history in company with Jesus, spend some time reflecting on these questions:

- How do you sense the Trinity's presence in these years?
- What is the continuous element in your relationship with the Trinity?
- What interpersonal response to the Trinity, to others, to yourself, keeps recurring that you now see as blessings?
- How do you foresee these blessings as continuing in the future?

For further reading:

BECOMING FOLLOWERS OF JESUS

It is rather fascinating to observe in all four gospels how rapidly Jesus gathers people around himself and gradually invites them to understand the unique richness of the Good News of the Kingdom. The relation Jesus undertakes with these persons is quite special. They will often call him 'teacher' (rabbi); yet Jesus' purpose is not to set up a school or to help them acquire some sophisticated knowledge about life. The content of Jesus' message is not an intellectual reality; it is nothing less than his *own* person, his relationship with the Father and the consequences of this for humankind. Jesus' companions were never expected to become teachers like Jesus. They were never expected to become experts on all that Jesus had said, nor to mimic or pantomime his conduct. They were never to be pupils, nor apprentices, nor students. They were simply expected to *follow* him (Mark 1:17-18, 8:34, 10:21, 28-30,52, 15:41).

The greek words used to describe the act of following could be loosely translated as 'to be with on the road', 'to walk or go behind'. This attitude is found almost exclusively in the gospels and reveals a reaction to the earthly Jesus during his years of ministry. But one must remember that the act of following Jesus is used by the gospel writers many years after Jesus' death and resurrection as an example for the reader who would want to accept Jesus as saviour and might not know what this entailed. Put simply, to follow Jesus is to express discipleship.

1. A first observation to make about this reality is that Jesus is the one who takes the initiative (Mark 1:17,20 and 2:14), who calls, even if there is a latent yearning in the the hearts of those who meet him (John 1:38-39). He does not wait for volunteers; nor does he force, cajole or coax.

2. A second observation would be that Jesus calls his followers to something radically new, unconventional yet deeply traditional; they are called not to the knowledge of the Law but to the service of the Kingdom. They are to become part of Jesus' mission of proclaiming the Good News, and of witnessing compassion (Mark 2:17) by drawing together people of good will and effecting change in society.

3. The new option proposed by Jesus involves being critical of accepted practices, of rejecting the false values of society; it also involves letting go, giving up securities, ambitions, power, success and ties with the past. This might prove to be very painful (Mark 10:21-22). There can be no sitting on the fence, no split-decisions. The response must be whole-hearted and receive top priority. It is the unconditional discipleship of the one who makes God the only necessary goal of one's life, remembering that the reward will be great (Mark 10:28-30, Philippians 3:7-11).

4. Because Jesus was fully obedient to the Father, nothing less can be expected from the follower. If the master suffered, and took up his cross out of love, then his followers will be invited to do the same (Mark 8:34), to give up their lives and personal advantages out of love of God and neighbour (Mark 12:30-31).

5. A follower can never outshadow or outpace the leader. S/he will always be on the path of learning, of discovering, of venturing, of becoming, of being continually re-molded by Jesus. The race is never truly over while on this earth (Philippians 3:13-17, Hebrews 12:1-2) and there are no 'time-outs' (Mark 13:23, 32-37).

6. The purpose of the followers is not to 'know' the master with their heads only, sharing insights about his teachings. The followers are invited to enter into a special relation with Jesus: a relation of their bodies (as part of creation, see Unit II) and of their hearts (Unit III), a relation seeking concern for all (Unit IV), a relation based of the vision of faith (Unit V). Followers are bound to Jesus in his journey of liberating both creation and people; they are invited to become attached to his person, to become one with him, to be in him (Galatians 3:28), seeing, acting, feeling and loving in his place, having his Spirit to guide them. They are to be 'his body' the way that he as risen Lord communicates to others.

'Come and see' said Jesus. It sounded simple enough. No sales pitch, no guilt trips, just a simple open-ended invitation to come and spend some time with him (John 1:39). Jesus then invites a fellow named Philip to come with him. Interestingly, this same Philip then turns around and repeats the words of Jesus to his friend Nathanael: 'Come and see' (John 1:46). Many people became followers because Jesus invited them through others to come and see, to walk with companion pilgrims and searchers down the road of life. So it is that followers never cease their questing until the glory of Christ is revealed in their persons (Romans 8:18) and all creation.

322

PERSONAL DECISION-MAKING

Purpose: We will consider how our interior life leads us either to react compulsively or to respond out of our deeper desire for good. We are reminded, therefore, of the fully human element of our choices even as we remember the significance of the presence of Christ and his way as we make decisions.

Minutes

15   1. Begin with prayer and song.

Ask to realize in a deeply personal way the many blessings we have received so that we will appreciate the Trinity's presence and be filled with the desire to build with them the kingdom of love and justice.

Reflect quietly on your prayer of the past week in light of
a) What happened to you in this prayer?
b) What experiences of these years of your history are present to you now?
c) What feeling does this arouse in you?
d) How will you express yourself in the sharing?

50   1. 2. Share any of the above.

10   3. Reflect quietly on what you experienced in the sharing:
a) What impressed you as the others shared?
b) Where did you experience affective harmony with others as they spoke about this history?
c) What gave you new insights about this church-community?

10   BREAK

20 4. Quietly and spontaneously answer
   a) List many of your goals.

   Star those that are most essential for you;
   e.g., by the time you die, which will have
   been most important?
   Check any that require some decision on
   your part or by others.
   b) List about 15 choices you have made in the
   last few days. Beside each of the items mark:

   + choices made out of habit
   x choices made with full consciousness that
     you were making a choice
   * half and half

   For example: + put on a new pair of socks
                 * agreed to visit relatives on
                   Sunday
                 x contracted to buy a house.

   c) What is your normal style of making decisions; for example,
     — I wait until the last moment and avoid
       thinking about it; then I choose arbitrari-
       ly.
     — I ask many questions explicitly, get hold
       of variables, work out the pros and cons
       and try to deduce my decisions logically.
     — I respond intuitively (gently or leaping
       into it?).
     — I hate to think clearly about it.
     — I use the pleasure-pain principle and
       choose what appears to be less painful.
     — I usually choose because of deep feelings.
     — I let circumstances dictate decisions.
     — I try to see whether it fits my inner core.
     — Other:

324

d) Is there a difference in the way you make decisions in the different areas in your life?
— between small decisions, large decisions
— personal decisions and work-related decisions
— personal decisions and other public-re-
lated ones (for example, purchasing,
working on a committee, joining a volunteer group, responding to requests for
your time . . .).

e) With what kinds of decisions are you more
— careful
— at ease
— secular
— spiritual
— efficient
— logical
— impatient.

f) How did you make significant decisions in
the past?
— choice of school
— career
— vocation: single, married, religious life,
priesthood
— spouse, community
— change of job.

John Veltri SJ

30   5. Share regarding the above:

What did you notice about the way you make
decisions?

How would you describe your approach to decision-making?

10   6. Prepare for prayer during the week.

5   7. Conclude with prayer and singing.

Prayer for the Week:

(A) Daily awareness prayer.

(B) Daily scripture prayer:

Ask to appreciate in a deeply personal way the many blessings you have received so that you may be encouraged by the Trinity's presence in your life and filled with the desire to build the kingdom of love and justice with them. Read one of the following passages:

Luke 24: 1-8
Luke 24: 9-12
Luke 24: 13-35

Ponder your history by considering your decisions at different stages in your life, with the various people who touched your life and within your work. Be with the Lord as you remember them anew.

PERSONAL BLESSED HISTORY AND DECISION-MAKING

Purpose: The next weeks presume that our history is significant when we make decisions in a faith context, that all history can be part of salvation history, that decisons should be made when one is experiencing spiritual consolation, that the Trinity is deeply involved in drawing us to themselves and that we experience this mainly in our affective life. It is also helpful to realize that these suggestions image the Trinity as dynamically involved in our history. They gift us with freedom to love; we trust the Trinity's promise to let grace be more powerful than evil. The dynamic includes experience, reflection, articulation, interpretation, and action.

This week, therefore, focuses on remembering spiritual consolation in our personal history, recalling what consolation means and applying this to our discernment.

Minutes

15   1. Begin with singing and prayer.

Ask to remember moments of spiritual consolation in your life and to discover how the Trinity have been with you; ask confidently for the gift of discernment!

Reflect quietly using Jeremiah 31:3.

50   2. Share any aspect of your Prayer for the Week.

10   BREAK

50   3. Reflect on and then share the following:

a) Recall your experience of prayer and insights (possibly reread your journal for these!) from:

327

Unit I, Weeks 6, 7 and 8 on your life-experience of confidence, growth, generosity.

Unit III, Weeks 8, 9 and 10.

What are signs of the Holy Spirit at work in you?

b) What interior experiences led you to make good decisions and to act on them throughout your life?

c) Where are you 'rooted' and does this present decision (if you are making one) fit with this? Do you see any pattern emerging?

10   4. Journal:

a) What impressed you as others shared this evening?

b) Where did others' sharing lead you to feel in harmony with them?

c) What gave you new insights about this church community and what gave you a new sense of union?

10   5. Prepare the Prayer for the Week.

5   6. Conclude with a hymn and prayer.

Prayer for the Week:

(A) Awareness prayer.

Reread your journal from Unit I, Weeks 6, 7 and 8 and Unit III, Weeks 8, 9 and 10 and ponder how the Trinity has been with you.

(B) Scripture prayer.

Luke 24:36-43
Luke 24:44-49
Luke 24:50-53
Mark 16:16-20

PERSONAL DISORDERED HISTORY AND DECISION-MAKING

Purpose: So that we may grow in discernment, we seek to let Jesus reveal our sinfulness to us and how he was present through this painful history. This not only leads us to pray for forgiveness and healing and the grace to forgive others but also alerts us to avoid similar deceptions in the future.

Minutes

15   1. Begin with singing and prayer.

Ask to experience how the Trinity has been with you throughout your life and is now with this community for your growth and healing.

Reflect quietly using Mark 11:22-25.

50   2. Share any aspect of prayer or awareness from life experience.

10   BREAK

45   3. Reflect on and share some of the following:

     a) Remember Unit 1, Weeks 6, 7 and 8: times that were difficult, not together for you, and Unit III, Weeks 8, 9 and 10: what are signs that something is not right, not of the Holy Spirit but more of temptation or tending to evil for you?

     b) What interior experience led you to wrong decisions and to act on them?

     c) What patterns lead to poor decision-making for you?

10   4. Prepare the Prayer for the Week.

15   5. Journal: Are you trusting or fearful of the community? How do you show this? What helps/hinders us in the sharing?

5   6. Conclude with prayer and singing.

Prayer for the Week:

(A) Daily awareness prayer.

(B) Daily scripture prayer:

Begin by reading one of the following:

Mark 14:44-46	Mark 16: 9-11
Mark 15:14-15	Mark 16:14-15
Mark 15:20,29,32	

Then with Jesus as your companion on the journey recall the historical state of the world and the locality you have lived in and relive the sinful aspects of your life. Remember these elements in your life trying to see and hear and touch them in the love of Jesus who reveals their sinfulness to you. Seek to realize in a deeply personal way that Jesus was present with you through this painful history. Pray for the grace of sorrow and healing. Seek forgiveness and the grace to forgive.

You may do this by considering the:

● sinful history of your childhood

● sinful history of your adolescence

● sinfulness flowing from your successes

● sinfulness flowing from your failures

● sinfulness flowing from your sense of rejection

● sinfulness flowing from different places, situations and structures of which you are a part

● sinfulness flowing from your emotional experiences.

Often speak to the Lord, to the Father, to the Holy Spirit in questions and appreciation.

(C) Reflection after prayer (review):

After this time of remembering your sinful history in company with Jesus, spend some time reflecting on these questions:

● Do you perceive any pattern in your sinful history?

● How has the Lord brought you through your sinful history? What dimensions in you still need forgiveness or healing?

330

DISCOVERING OUR HISTORY OF BEING ENERGIZED OR BUILT-UP AS A COMMUNITY

Purpose: In the last weeks, we have remembered our personal blessed and disordered/sin history so that we could be more aware of and grateful for the way the Lord leads. We move from individual experiences that are shared, to focus on our communal attitudes, spirit and graced history. Our hope, therefore, is to discover in a deeply personal way, the many blessings our community has received so that we will appreciate the presence of the Trinity in this history and see better how to further our community's work for the kingdom of love and justice in the future.

Minutes

15   1. Start with prayer and singing.

Ask to appreciate the presence of the Trinity in our history so that we may see how to further our work for the kingdom of love and justice in the future.

Reflect on your prayer and awareness of the last week in light of John 15:13-15.

a) What happened to you in this prayer?

b) As you reflect on your history, how do you sense that the promises of God are still operating or active?

c) What does this mean as you look to the future?

50   2. Share any of your awareness of this week. Pray and sing together, sharing a sign of peace.

10   BREAK

45   3. Ponder quietly and then share at length, gently
         moving more deeply into the questions on our
         community experience of light and grace:
      a) What have been our greatest blessings?
      b) How can this remembering and the insights
         we have received help us to make good deci-
         sions as a community?

10   4. Journal: What happened within you as you lis-
                 tened and shared this evening? How
                 did you experience increased apprecia-
                 tion of our community's history? How
                 were you drawn closer to others?

10   5. Prepare the Prayer for the Week.

10   6. Conclude with singing and prayer.

Prayer for the Week:

(A) Awareness prayer.

(B) Scripture prayer:

Begin with one of the following passages:
         Proverbs   8:30-31
         Luke   10:23-24
         Luke   13:17
         Luke   17:7-10

Then unite yourself with Jesus as he speaks the words of
John 15:13-15 and recall the recent history of our community, seeing, hearing and touching it. Speak with him
about the significance of these years. Seek to realize in a
deeply personal way the many blessings our community
has received so that we will appreciate the Trinity's personal presence in our history and better see how to further
our community's work for the kingdom of love and justice
for the future.

Do this by considering:

● The historical state of the world during these years.

- The significant persons of these years.
- The apostolic works and the growth within the community.
- The personality, spiritual experiences, choice of lifestyle of our community in these years.
- The highlights for you in this history.

  Often speak with the Lord as this history unfolds before you.

(C) Review of prayer:

After your time of prayer, reflect on how the Trinity was present and how the community grew. How did persons respond to their life situation and difficulties? How do you judge success and failure now? How do you sense the promises of God are still alive for us?

COMMUNAL DISORDERED HISTORY AND DECISION-MAKING

Purpose: So that we may learn communal discernment, we now focus on the disordered history of the community, asking to see both how this was influenced by society and how it contributed to the sinfulness in society. We will celebrate a short service of reconciliation as well.

Minutes

15   1. 1. Start with prayer and singing.

Ask for deep awareness of how the Trinity is leading our community with love and of how we respond.

Reflect quietly on Wisdom 11:26-12:2.

30   2. Share any awareness of the history of light of this community and what it now means for you.

10   BREAK

20   3. Quietly ponder:

a) Ask for an awareness of the sin dimensions in our community history so that we may unite ourselves with the community sense of sorrow, need for forgiveness and healing. Then remember with the eyes, ears and touch of imagination, the persons, places and situations in which we expressed or promoted sinful ways, attitudes or structures.

Sense the gradual growth of the community with its tensions, fears, domination, paralysis, cowardice, pride, competition, resentment, compulsion, anything that leads to turning in on ourselves, or was harmful to our relationships with others.

What were some of our main weaknesses/ sin?

Can you own your part in this sinful history?

What is the relationship of these areas to what is happening in society/church today?

What is the significance of our sinful history for the future?

b) Prepare for sharing by reflecting on what happened to you in this prayer. How do you see the vision of this community as part of your present call? What feelings did this reflection arouse in you?

40   4. Share any of the above.

30   5. Continue this healing, this reconciling of bringing darkness to light by reading, sharing prayers of sorrow, forgiveness, gratitude, praise and petition as it is appropriate. Stand, join hands and pray the Our Father together. Sing a hymn in gratitude for God's merciful love.

Prayer for the Week:

(A) Awareness prayer.

(B) Scripture prayer:

Ask the Lord for light to see the significance of the pattern of our sinful history for the future, how he has brought our community out of its sinful history in the past and, finally, what dimensions of our community's history both within itself and in its relationship to others still needs forgiveness and healing.

Wisdom	11:23-12:2
Luke	17:4
Luke	11:7-11
Luke	11:34-35
Deuteronomy	8:11-20
Baruch	2: 5-8

FORWARD DIRECTION OF HOPE IN THIS COMMUNITY'S HISTORY

Purpose: We desire to recognize how the Lord calls us beyond ourselves for others and to concretize our vision within the reality of our situation and our deeper social consciousness. We also desire to expand our world view.

Minutes

15   1. Begin with prayer and singing.

Ask to recognize how the Trinity are leading us today.

Reflect quietly on your awareness of the past week in the light of John 17:20-23.

50   2. Share any part of your awareness.

10   **BREAK**

10.   2. In silence, remember whatever you can of the history of the world, and church, in the last twenty years and what differences these have made in your life (individually for your family and for this community), for example, consider various movements, ministries, renewal groups, efforts toward developing social consciousness. Speak with the Lord as this history unfolds before you. Also consider with him how he brings success out of failure, strength out of weakness, humility in times of success and courage in times of failure. How are the promises of God being fulfilled and what hope do they offer? What does this mean for us as we look to the future?

30   4. Share any of this in groups of three.

15   5. Journal and sharing:

How did we experience an increased sense of union and identity as a community as we listened to the others' sharing? What was in harmony with the way the Lord leads us?

10   6. Conclude with prayer and singing.

Prayer for the Week:

(A) Awareness prayer, remembering what you experienced in the community and possibly following the same kind of approach but reflecting on your family or work experience.

(B) Scripture prayer:

Read a passage:

Philippians	3:8-10
2 Corinthians	12:5-10
Psalm	127:1
Habakkuk	3:17-19
Baruch	2:31-3:7

and then recall the history of the world and church (in the last 10-20 years), seeing, hearing and touching it. Speak with the Lord about the significance of these years. Since the promises of the Lord last forever, ask to recognize how he is still leading you within these changes into the future. Ask also for light to see how he is bringing success out of failure, strength out of weakness, humility in times of success and courage in times of failure.

THE COMMUNITY'S PRESENT STATE

Purpose: This week, we focus on the signs of the times in order to see our present world, church, personal and communal life more clearly. We will consider negative and positive movements within these from the perspective of the poor, marginalized and oppressed.

Minutes

20   1. Start with prayer and singing.

Ask for increased ability to read the signs of the times from the perspective of the poor, marginalized and oppressed. In the light of Luke 12:49-50 consider the negative and positive movements in the world, church, your personal family life, our communal life. Speak with the Lord about them.

50   2. Share any awareness from the past week.

50   3. Discuss and write down, from the perspective of the poor, marginalized and oppressed:

     a) What criteria do you use for considering movements 'negative' or 'positive' in the world, in the church?

     b) What do you perceive as tendencies that lead to breakdown in the world, church, your family, our community?

     c) What do you perceive are the signs of the Holy Spirit at work in the world, church, your family, our community?

15   4. Journal: What experiences of this history are present to you, your family and community now?

What feelings does this arouse in you?

How did you experience a greater sense of union and identity with our community as you listened to the others share?

10   5. Conclude with prayer and singing.

Prayer for the Week:

(A)Awareness prayer.

(B)Scripture prayer:

Ask for increased ability to read the signs of the times and to perceive our present state from the perspective of the poor, marginalized and oppressed.

Use one of the following:

Luke   12:49-50
Hebrews 12:1-4
Romans 12

HEIGHTENED CONSCIOUSNESS OF THE HARMONY BETWEEN OUR GRACED HISTORY, THE SIGNS OF THE TIMES AND OUR CALL TO TRANSFORM SOCIETY

Purpose: By remembering again the negative and positive movements in the world, church, our personal and communal life, we desire to discover how the Lord is calling us to transform society. As we sense harmony between what is happening in society, work, family and what we know is graced history for us, we know what to work for/against. The sense of rightness and peace in the community energizes members to respond generously and courageously to these needs.

Minutes

15   1. Begin with prayer and singing.

Confidently ask the Lord for the gift of discernment so that we may recognize and follow the positive movements in our communal history; we also ask for the grace to recognize movements within us that are deceptive and act against them.

Reflect on 1 John 4:1-2.

50   2. Share an awareness of the past week, a negative or positive one and why you would call it that.

10   BREAK

40   3. Discuss from your perspective:

a) What qualities do you see in contemporary movements in the world, church, family, our community?

b) How are these movements in tune with our history?

        c) How are they not in tune with our graced history?

        d) How do they harmonize with our blessed history? With our sinful history?

        e) How are they an expression of call?

10   4. Contrast #3 with your response to VI-8, #3.

10   5. Journal: What does our awareness mean for us?

           How is the Lord leading you now?

           Where did you find a sense of harmony, support, new insights as others shared their prayer and reflections?

15   6. Conclude with prayer and singing.

Prayer for the Week:

(A) Awareness prayer.

(B) Scripture prayer:

Confidently ask the Lord for the gift of discernment so that you may recognize the positive, blessed movements in your history in relation to world, church, family and community; also ask for the grace to recognize movements that are deceptive and act against them. Ask for the same gift for our community.

        1 John   4:1-2
        Romans 8:14-17, 24-27
        Galatians 5
        Mark   8:18

COMMUNITY ASSISTANCE FOR PERSONAL DECISION-MAKING (1)

Purpose: It becomes increasingly evident that not only clarity of vision is important for followers of Jesus in today's world, but also that good decision making is of utmost importance if we are to act effectively on the word of God, making it concrete in our lives. We have considered how the community of the Lord empowers its members in ways that go beyond the contribution of any one individual. We remembered that in the Lord the community broadens its vision and finds the power to fulfill it because the Spirit of Jesus gives it life.

This week, our purpose is to use this gift of community to assist members with any important decisions they may have. We will consider one possible approach; it would be used, obviously, only when the issue or the conclusion is not clear. It has the advantage of helping people sort out their mixture of values and preferences and be in touch with community wisdom. By doing so with community participation, members also tend to get in touch with their affective movements more quickly.

Minutes

15 1. Begin with prayer and sharing.

Ask for compassion and wisdom that we may assist each other in making decisions which help us apply our christian values to the everyday realities of our lives.

Reflect on Mark 9:41.

50 2. Share an awareness of prayer and life experience of the past week.

10 BREAK

10   3. Consider quietly how the Lord is calling you now regarding your vocation, career, ministry (at home or elsewhere) or, for example, whether to do a retreat and/or the Spiritual Exercises of St. Ignatius, or any other decision. Name the questions for yourself.

5   4. Share (simply by naming it) any decision you now need to make.

10   5. Introduce communal aids for personal decision-making (refer to the outline that is included after the Prayer for the Week).

15   6. Choose one person's question (with his/her consent of course) and respond to it as suggested in the outline at the end of this week.

15   7. Journal: How does your experience this evening harmonize with our blessed history? Share this.

10   8. Conclude with prayer and singing.

Prayer for the Week:

(A) Awareness prayer.

(B) Scripture prayer:

Ask for compassion and wisdom that you may assist others and be open to their participation in preparing for decision-making which would help us apply our christian values to the everyday realities of our lives. Use the following:

Mark 10:35-40
Mark 10:41-45
Mark 10:46-52
Acts   2:42-47

On one day, reflect on and fill out the columns for the issue chosen by the group (Step 6).

COMMUNITY ASSISTANCE IN PERSONAL DECISION-MAKING

Prayer:

Because faith, openness and sensitivity to the Spirit's action are key attitudes for discernment, proceed in a prayerful way, asking for the Lord's light, to be purified to follow his way and for inner freedom to move either way on an issue. Remember individual and communal blessed and sin history so that you may be more in touch with the Lord's way of leading you with his promises and fidelity. This enables you to trust the Lord and companions, and to sense whether your affective response as you proceed are in harmony with the consolation the Lord gives or not.

Continue as follows:

1. State the problem or decision to be made.
2. Clarify the issue, searching out background facts and sharing feelings that pertain to it. As this is done, surface alternative responses.
3. Select the key aspects of the issue and prioritize them, if necessary, in order to decide what the key issue is.
4. State the issue clearly and briefly as a positive statement, and then in its negative position.
5. Outline four columns for #4; for each side, list advantages and disadvantages for me (and, possibly, for us as a couple); for example,

I/We Need A Second Job		I/We Do Not Need A Second Job	
Advantages For Me/Us	Disadvantages For Me/Us	Advantages For Me/Us	Disadvantages For Me/Us

344

6. Each member of the group takes the issue home to pray about it (or do it quietly during a meeting) and fill in the columns according to his/her insights on the issue. We remember here the importance of filling this in with empathy; feeling with the person and considering his/her personality (strengths and weaknesses) and situation. We also pray for the guidance of the Holy Spirit and the grace of freedom.

7. A week later at the next meeting (or later in the same meeting), each person gives the results of his/her reflective prayer, simply reading all the columns, not giving advice. It may be helpful to give the written points to the person(s) at the end of the evening. The community supports the person/couple in prayer but is not involved in any more of the discernment.

8. The person/couple making the decision pray and discern the Lord's will, decide and ask the Lord for a confirmation of the decision.

   This same process or some adaptation of it may be helpful within families; for example, as a way of approaching decisions with a teenager.

COMMUNITY ASSISTANCE FOR PERSONAL DECISION-MAKING (2)

Purpose: We will complete our participation in assisting member(s) with individual decisions.

a) Extra weeks following this same approach for communal decision-making could certainly be included as members need to make decisions. The entire exercise could be completed within a meeting, simply by taking some quiet time to consider and fill in the advantages and disadvantages; sharing them would follow immediately.

b) Another important concern for the community is how its members minister to others. Because there are so many needs, generous people may tend to over-commit themselves. We suggest that the community consider the needs of their locality, the gifts (qualities, time, energy) of members and then participate together in deciding on commitments. It is important, of course, to remember family needs, issues of work and the civic community and international concerns (ecology, human rights, peace groups) as well as parish renewal groups. All of these are service to the church.

Begin the process for 'b)' if no further personal decisions are brought to the fore; if the latter does arise, follow 'a)' and do 'b)' when (and if) it is appropriate.

Minutes

15   1. Begin with prayer and singing.

Ask to recognize what is best for us as a community so that we may follow Jesus and be filled with desire to build his kingdom of love and justice with him.

Reflect on Luke 11:6-11.

50   2. Share awareness of the past week, being aware of how the Spirit is leading this community. Respond to the Lord together in your own way.

10   BREAK

30   3. Share the results of your reflections (four columns of advantages and disadvantages, VI-10, article #6) on the issue decided last week by the group. Note that the person(s) who sought the help initially now take(s) this for prayer and discernment. The community or group itself does not make the decision; it assists the person who is making the decision and continues to pray for that person. At times the group will help the person to weigh the findings; often it becomes obvious where the Spirit is leading. The group remains silent as to the final decision.

30   4. If no further individual decisions are raised now, discuss:
   a) What are the needs of our locality (issues of work, parish and civic community)?
   b) What international concerns need our participation (ecology, human rights, peace groups)?
   c) How is it best for our community to respond? Consider the qualities, time and energy available to the members and group as a whole; family needs must, of course, be a priority as well. The purpose of doing this is to choose well in view of abundant needs, to affirm some in present commitments, and support others either to withdraw from excessive involvement or to become involved further, as it is appropriate for individuals.

　　　　　d) Is there a need to which our community is able to respond as a group (as a whole or by delegating some members)?

10　　5. Journal: What happened in you and the community this evening?

5　　6. Conclude with singing and prayer.

Prayer for the Week:

(A)Awareness prayer. Include reflection on your present involvement in local and international needs in view of the qualities, time and energy you have.

1. How do you use your gifts of personality, talent, energy and time; for example, some may give too much time for personal leisure and body fitness, and others too little for good health. Where is the call of the Lord for you?

2. What signs of the Spirit show that your involvements are Spirit-led? What questions do you have about them?

3. How would your family and community answer numbers 1 and 2 for you? How do you know this?

4. In view of all this, how is the Lord inviting you both to intimacy with him and to effective ministry with/for others?

5. How would you respond to numbers 1 and 2 for each community member if s/he asked you?

(B) Scripture prayer:

Ask to experience how the Lord is leading you now so that you may respond generously.

　　　　　　　Acts 3:1-8
　　　　　　　Acts 4:5-22
　　　　　　　Acts 4:23-24, 29-31
　　　　　　　Acts 4:32-35

MAKING DECISIONS ABOUT OUR RESPONSE TO NEEDS

Purpose: In order to make wise choices about how we respond to needs, we continue the process started last week and conclude by commissioning members in their ministry, or praying for the group in its communal service.

Note: it may be helpful to use the process outlined in VI-10,11 to assist some with these decisions; if it is a group decision refer to VI-14.

Minutes

15   1. Begin with prayer and singing.

Ask for wisdom to see what is needed around us and to discern how the Lord is calling us to respond.

Reflect on Acts 6:2-7.

50   2. Share an awareness from prayer this week and what it means for your daily life. (or vice versa!)

10   BREAK

50   3. Continue last week's process of reviewing our individual and communal response to needs. Extra meetings may be needed for this.

15   4. Conclude by praying and singing together, including some form of commissioning; each member would state it for some other member in any informal way, such as, 'We support you, *name*, in your decision to . . . , and affirm the way you are using your gifts of being able to . . . We pray that . . . .'

Prayer for the Week:

(A) Awareness prayer.

(B) Scripture prayer:

Ask to be filled with Jesus' spirit of wisdom, generosity and love that you may be with him for others.

> Acts 5:12-21
> Acts 5:27-42
> Acts 9:1-30

COMMUNITY EVALUATION

Purpose: In order to be more aware of and grateful for the Lord's blessing, as well as clarify and correct any ways in which we have conflict or need, we will reflect on our interaction and direction. This can help us to prepare for our decision next week; namely, whether we will continue community meetings or not.

Minutes

15   1. Begin with prayer and singing.

Ask for wisdom and insight to see the Lord's way for us and respond generously.

Reflect on Acts 14:21-23, 27-28.

50   2. Share awareness and its impact on your life.

10   BREAK

55   3. Do an evaluation together, possibly using the following questions:

a) What essentials do you think need to be covered in an evaluation by a community of followers of Jesus? List them and respond to them now or after evaluation.

b) How can we evaluate whether we are translating our willingness to call ourselves 'christian' into effective action, saying it more with our lives; e.g., are we learning to forgive and accept forgiveness more obviously in daily practice?

c) How did we share Jesus' mission in this process?

d) What signs are evident that we are a community of followers of Jesus? (If we were put on trial for being christian, would there be enough evidence to convict us?)

e) What effect have we had on others in this process and what influence have society, other groups, and individuals had on us?

5   4. Journal: What did you experience that was in harmony/ disharmony with our graced history?

15   5. Conclude by praying and singing together.

Prayer for the Week:

(A) Awareness prayer.

(B) Scripture prayer:

Ask for the grace you, your family and community need.

Acts	15:1-4
Galatians	6:6-16
Ephesians	4:1-16
Ephesians	4:17-32

COMMUNAL DISCERNMENT REGARDING OUR FUTURE AS A COMMUNITY

Purpose: If the group does not have a clear sense of the rightness of their continuing to be a community together, it would be important to clarify any questions involved and discern together whether to continue to meet or not. If you are a community of lay christians not linked to the world community of Christian Life Communities, it would be good to encourage serious consideration of this. The article 'Communal Discernment' may be helpful for both decisions.

Minutes

15   1. 1. Begin with prayer and singing.

Ask for a grateful heart and a good memory to remember all that the Lord does for us, to recognize how he is leading us and for the inner freedom to follow this.

Reflect on Ephesians 2:4-10.

50   2. Share an awareness of prayer from last week and its relation to your daily life.

10   BREAK

55   3. Begin the following discernment(s) now and continue for the next weeks (until the process is complete).

a) Ask the community if there is a clear sense of whether it is good for us to continue to commit ourselves to each other in community as we have been doing. If not, discern this together. Refer to the article, 'Communal Discernment: Seeking the Truth Together' which is included after the prayer outline.

353

b) If you desire to continue as a community and are not linked to the world community of Christian Life Communities, you are encouraged to consider it seriously. The procedure for communal discernment would be the way of proceeding for this. A description of Christian Life Communities and the General Principles are included, as well as addresses of centres from which you can receive further information and assistance.

10   4. Journal: What signs of harmony/disharmony did we experience this evening? From where did these arise?

30   5. Conclude with prayer and singing together.

Prayer for the Week:

(A) Awareness prayer. For one week, note your interior affective experiences when you are considering linking with the world community of Christian Life Communities. If the decision is not clear to you, take the opposite position (of not joining them) and note what happens. Which position puts you in harmony with your graced history? How?

(B) Scripture prayer:

Ask for freedom to follow Jesus as a generous disciple and for his light in this decision.

John 8:12
John 17:17-23
John 17:26
John 16:33

In the review of prayer, note which decision you were tentatively holding, as well as what happened in the time of prayer.

COMMUNAL DISCERNMENT: SEEKING TRUTH TOGETHER

Because faith, openness and sensitivity to the Spirit's action in each member and the community are key attitudes for discernment, proceed in a prayerful way, asking for the Lord's light, to be purified to follow his way and for inner freedom to move either way on an issue. Remember individual and communal blessed and sin history so that you may be more in touch with the Lord's way of leading you, with his promises and fidelity. This enables you to trust the Lord and companions, and to sense whether your affective responses throughout the process are in harmony with the consolation the Lord gives or not. (Possibly refer to III-8 on consolation/desolation and apply this to the community spirit in moments of reflection.)

Continue as follows:

1. Express the issue as an open question, for example, how and through what activities can you keep your thrust, interest, and commitments in your community alive, true to the gospel and in touch with your concerns as well as those beyond yourselves? Clarify the issue, considering relevant factors, research, influences, possible implications or consequences, feelings and values of the group about these.

2. Brainstorm for possible solutions.

3. Prioritize the alternatives given, at least selecting the key aspects or possibilities.

4. Take one of these possibilities and state it as clearly as possible. Clarify any further questions or necessary information about it; following the example given in #1, consider the General Principles of Christian Life Communities and what joining their world community would mean.

For both this statement and for its opposite stance, list the advantages and disadvantages; for example,

Our community will commit ourselves as a Christian Life Community		Our community will not commit ourselves as a Christian Life Community	
Advantages For Me/Us	Disadvantages For Me/Us	Advantages For Me/Us	Disadvantages For Me/Us

5. With time for quiet prayerful reflection, each member fills out the options.

6. Share the points listed for the first option, even if they repeat what another has contributed.

7. Take time for prayerful consideration of the first option.

8. Share the points given for the second option.

9. Prayerfully consider these points.

10. Each person shares his/her preferred decision and states the reason briefly. Any further insights are added to the list of advantages and disadvantages.

11. If consensus seems to be reached; that is, if all the members agree with or can accept the decision, it is taken for confirmation to the Lord (during the coming week).

    NOTE:

    a) Consensus: The facilitator may recognize consensus as it emerges during the sharing and simply say this to the community and ask for explicit recognition of it. Some groups determine before starting the process what they consider adequate consent to be; for example, 85% of the membership.

    b) Confirmation is experienced interiorly as the individuals and community sense the harmony of this decision with the Lord's action in their lives; are you energized, generous and at peace in view of this reality and the call to be a follower of Jesus?

12. If there is not consensus, further clarification, stipulations, alternatives or adaptation may be required before coming to a decision that all can support.
    As you 'live with' this decision, is it right for you? Is it supported by legitimate authority? Outward success or failure neither confirms nor denies whether a decision is according to the Lord; there may be need for re-evaluation and a new decision, however, as circumstances change.

13. Share how the decision was confirmed or questioned.

14. Take time for prayer and singing in gratitude for the ways the Lord is leading, for the marvels he will work in you and through you for others.

CHRISTIAN LIFE COMMUNITIES

What is it?

Christian Life Communities is an international federation of small groups of committed (mostly Roman Catholic) Christians who seek to integrate the realities of lay experience of Ignatian Spirituality with basic Christian community, and a mission of proclaiming the gospel of justice and love.

It is neither a religious community, nor a secular institute but rather a lay directed, Ignatian-based movement, which calls members to unite their human life in all its dimensions with the fullness of Christian Faith. The movement is shaped by a charter of General Principles which delineate in broad strokes the vision of CLC.

What does the CLC way of life mean in practical terms?

Our way of life commits our members to seek, with the help of the community, a continuing, personal development that is spiritual, apostolic, and human. In practice this involves frequent participation in the eucharist, an intense sacramental life, daily practice of personal prayer, (especially prayer based on sacred scripture) discernment by means of a daily review of one's life and regular spiritual direction, an annual interior renewal in accordance with the Spiritual Exercises, and a love for the Mother of God.

Each member is further challenged to simplicity, in all aspects of living, in order to more closely follow Christ and to preserve interior liberty in the midst of the world. This demands of each an apostolic commitment to the renewal of the structures of society, and an effort to strive to develop human qualities and professional skills so as to become ever more competent and convincing in his/her witness.

Finally, each member assumes the responsibility for participating in the meetings and activities of the group, and each helps and encourages the other to pursue his/her personal vocation, always ready to give and to receive advice and aid as brothers and sisters in the Lord.

Why join CLC?

All baptized Christians have a vocation to reveal the healing, reconciling power of Christ in our world. There are many gifted ways of doing this. Christian Life Communities is one way for men and women who desire to have a part in building the kingdom of God in our world in the last quarter of the twentieth century. It is a way that is both traditional and new. It is an invitation to men and women who are professionals and looking for a way of bringing gospel values to their profession, to men and women in business and commerce who want to bring Christ to the marketplace, to men and women in the factory who want to show others the dignity of Christ the worker, to men and women in politics who believe that Christ speaks in the halls of legislatures, courts and executive offices, to men and women in the home who believe that Christ is the center of every family and each family member's life.

In short, men and women who desire the spiritual freedom to speak and act in Jesus' name in this world will find a home in Christian Life Communities.

What does CLC mean by community?

Community is the interaction of a group in such a loving way that members become 'at home' with one another, able to trust the care and reverence of each other, and able to extend a gospel quality love that heals while revealing Christ in the world.

Christian Life Communities gather at many levels but the experience of human affection spans the levels to create bonds which are basic to the personal growth and apostolic service of members.

Christian Life Communities have developed formation tools for enabling new groups to get started or existing groups to become CLC's. Men and women come to CLC for a variety of reasons. Some come to have a companionship (community), some come to find a deeper, freer relationship with Christ (spirituality), some come committed to a vision of changing the world and desirous of finding others equally committed. Some come to find a simple structure that enables the integration of an active and contemplative life in relationship to others. For whatever reason people come, formation and growth of persons and communities is a life-long process. While our communities are not exclusively prayer groups, discussion groups, scripture study groups, self-help groups or issue action groups, there are dimensions of all these at various times in any community's history.

What is Ignatian spirituality?

The impetus of Christian Life Communities is a spirituality that is Ignatian. Very simply this means that CLC recognizes that the saving action of the Christ is the work of all baptized Christians who are empowered by the same Spirit that enabled Jesus of Nazareth to reveal the unconditional, compassionate love of the Father. St. Ignatius of Loyola, a 16th century basque nobleman experienced a specific conversion in Christ and a subsequent growth to freedom that he recorded in the Spiritual Exercises. This process has been recognized by the Catholic Church as a powerful tool for bringing men and women of generous spirit to a total interior freedom. This freedom is the basis for discovering the always-loving will of God rooted in the human heart and traced in human desires, affections and intellectual considerations. This spirituality therefore is characterized: by a presupposition of the Trinity's love for individual persons; by a willingness on each person's part to seek the Trinity's presence in all dimensions of life; by a willingness to discern prayerfully day by day what it is God is calling me to do in my own particular corner of the world; by an openness to a spiritual guide(s) or friend(s) who can assist me in my interior listening, and, finally, by a willingness to engage actively in the work of Christ in death and resurrection to effect a kingdom of justice and mercy.

What does CLC mean by mission?

Each CLC member sees him or her self as engaged in the work of Christ to proclaim a gospel of love, and to address that which is most urgent and universal in our time. The proclamation of the gospel, however, cannot be accomplished only in words. It requires, rather, that the Christian actively engage in deeds which express and effect a more just society in this world. The traditional works of mercy, (feeding the hungry, clothing the naked, etc.) have not changed; we realize, however, that God is asking us to challenge *why* people are hungry, naked, uneducated, oppressed, or driven by the millions to despair. For a CLC member the reality of a broken world is at his/her place of business or profession, is among his/her family and friends, is in the town jail, is permeating various nations' commitments to armaments and violence as valid means of solving problems, and is in his/her own heart if unreconciled to any other human being. The mission is wherever and whenever a CLC member hears the gospel command to love as Jesus did and takes it seriously.

Internationally

The World Federation of Christian Life Communities is presently comprised of over 50 member national federations. The World Movement is directed by a General Assembly of delegates from all member nations which meets for two weeks every three years.

Themes of World Assemblies over the last decade indicate the deepening vision of our vocation in Christ:

1973 – Augsburg, Germany – A community at the Service of the Liberation of the Whole Person and of all Persons.

1976 – Manila, Philippines — Poor with Christ for a better service: The Vocation of CLC in the Mission of the Church.

1979 – Rome — Toward a World Community at the Service of One World.

1982 – Providence, R.I., U.S.A. – This is what is asked: To act justly, to love tenderly and to walk humbly with your God.

The day-to-day work of the World Community, including providing training programs, the task of communications liaison among member communities and with the broader Church; and publishing a monthly journal Progressio, falls to an international Secretariate presently staffed by the Vice-Ecclesial Assistant(s), an Executive Secretary, and assistant(s).

GENERAL PRINCIPLES
CHRISTIAN LIFE COMMUNITIES

Because our movement is a way of Christian life, and not a rigid organization, these principles are to be interpreted not so much by the letter of this text but rather by the spirit of the gospel and the interior law of love.

This law, which the Spirit inscribes in our hearts, expresses itself anew in each situation of daily life. It respects the uniqueness of each personal vocation and enables us to be open and free, always at the disposal of God. It challenges us to see the serious responsibility we have as Christians; it inspires us to labor unceasingly for solutions to the problems of our times; and it impels us always to work generously with all people of good will for peace and progress, charity and justice, liberty and dignity for all.

AIM AND CHARACTERISTICS

Aim of Christian Life Communities

Our groups are Christian communities which aim to form a people for service. We seek to develop and sustain men and women, adults and youth, in their commitment to the service of the church and the world in every area of life: family, work, professional, civil and ecclesial. To prepare members more effectively for this apostolic service, especially in their daily environment, each Christian Life Community is formed of people with similar ideals who are willing to work together, and each community organizes itself to meet the demands of vital Christian living for its members. Our communities are for all who feel a more urgent need to unite their human life in all its dimensions with the fullness of their Christian faith, especially for those concerned with temporal affairs. Thus we seek to achieve this unity of life which is a response to the call of Christ from within the world in which we live.

Sources of Spirituality

The spirituality of Christian Life Communities is centered on Christ and on participation in his paschal mystery; it draws from the sacred scriptures, the liturgy, the doctrinal development of the church, and God's self-revelation in the needs of our time. We hold the Spiritual Exercises of St. Ignatius as a specific source and as the characteristic instrument of our spirituality. Our vocation calls us to live this spirituality which opens and disposes us to whatever God wishes in each concrete situation of our daily existence. We recognize especially the necessity of personal prayer and spiritual direction as indispensable for seeking and finding God in all things.

Sense of Church

Union with Christ expresses itself in union with the church where Christ is here and now continuing his mission of salvation. By learning constantly to be sensitive to the signs of the times and the movements of the Spirit, we become better able to encounter Christ in all persons and in all situations. Conscious that we are the church, we participate in the liturgy, meditate upon the Scriptures, contribute to its doctrinal development, collaborate with our spiritual shepherds, and share with them genuine concern for the problems and progress which the whole church and all of humanity face today. This sense of the church impels and sustains in us concrete personal and group collaboration in the work of building up the kindgom of God.

Bond of Community

Our gift of self finds its expression in the commitment to a particular, freely chosen community. Such a community, centered in the eucharist, is a concrete experience of unity in love and action. For each of our groups is a community in Christ, a part of his mystical body; our members are bound together by our common commitment, our common way of life, our deep concern for all our brothers and sisters, and our recognition and love of Mary as mother of all people. Our responsibility to develop the bonds of community does not stop with our own group but must extend to the National and World Federations of Christian Life Communities, our parishes and diocesan communities, the whole church and all people of good will.

Apostolic Life

We have received, as the people of God, the mission of being witnesses to Christ by our attitudes, words, and actions before all people. We are convinced that in our Christian Life Communities we must consecrate ourselves first of all to the renewal and sanctification of the world. To accomplish this, we help each other give an apostolic sense even to the most humble realities of daily life. Through our spirituality, which makes possible personal and communal discernment, we become aware of what is most urgent and universal; we are moved to work for the reform of the structures of society, participating in efforts to liberate the victims of all forms of discrimination and especially to abolish differences between rich and poor within the Church. Our life finds its permanent inspiration in the gospel of the poor and humble Christ so that we work in a spirit of service to establish justice and peace among all people.

Union with Mary

Since the spirituality of our groups is centered on Christ, we see the role of Mary in relation to Christ; she is the image of our own collaboration in his mission. Mary's cooperation with her Son began with her "fiat" in the mystery of the Annunciation-Incarnation. This cooperation, continued all through her life, inspires us to give ourselves totally to God in union with Mary, who by accepting the designs of God became our mother and the mother of all. Thus we confirm our own mission of service to the world received in baptism and confirmation. We venerate the Mother of God in a special manner and we rely on her intercession in fulfilling our vocation.

Centers for Christian Life Communities

1. *World Center:*
   World Federation of Christian Life Communities,
   C.P. 6139, Borgo S. Spirito 5, 00195 Rome, Italy

2. *French-Speaking Canada:*
   Fédération Nationale des Communautés de Vie Chrétienne,
   4100 Avenue Vendome, Montreal, P.Q. H4A 3N1

3. *English-Speaking Canada:*
   Christian Life Community President,
   c/o Loyola Retreat House,
   Guelph, Ontario, N1H 6J9

4. *U.S.A.:*
   National Federation Christian Life Communities,
   3721 Westminster Place,
   St. Louis, Missouri 63108

PREPARING A CELEBRATION OF GRATITUDE AND COMMITMENT

Purpose: We desire to plan a celebration in hope and gratitude for the way the Lord is leading us. If some members are discontinuing, we need an appropriate conclusion after the depth of sharing we have experienced together. If we are joining the world community of Christian Life Communities, we will include a commitment service within it. We can also begin to consider our goals, hopes, needs and resources as we set our community direction for the coming months. Included also is the "Shakertown Pledge" as an option for our consideration and support; it is included after the commitment for CLC.

Minutes

15   1. Begin with prayer and singing.

       Ask the Trinity for the gift of gratitude for their presence with us and the ability to celebrate this well.

       Reflect on Philippians 1:3-9.

50   2. Share awareness of prayer and daily life. How are we more at ease and trusting in our relationship with the Trinity and others?

10   **BREAK**

30   3. Aware of all the themes we have experienced together, plan a celebration of hope and gratitude, with a commitment service if this is appropriate. A suggestion is included after the prayer outline.

30   4. Begin to consider goals, hopes, needs, resources
and practical possibilities for future meetings.
Reflecting on the methodology of *Becoming
Followers of Jesus* may help.

15   5. Conclude with prayer and singing.

Prayer for the Week:

(A) Awareness prayer.

(B) Scripture prayer:

Ask the Trinity for the gift of gratitude for their presence
with us and the ability to celebrate this well.

Colossians	1:27-29; 2:2-3
1 Thessalonians	5:12-18
2 Peter	3:8-10

AN EXAMPLE OF THE COMMITMENT MADE BY CHRISTIAN LIFE COMMUNITIES IN GUELPH, ONTARIO, CANADA

After the homily, the celebrant, will invite members to
make their commitment:

1. *Within the Circle of the Local Community*
   a) Individually

   I, (name) , commit myself to you, (group name) Christian Life Community.

   b) Together

   As a member of the Canadian English-speaking CLC, I
   commit myself to seek, with the help of our community,
   a continuing, personal development that is spiritual,
   apostolic, and human. I understand that this involves
   the willingness to share my interior life with others so
   that by individual and communal discernment, I may

with the community, in the spirit of the Spiritual Exercises be responsible for, and realize, the upbuilding of the kingdom of peace and justice in today's world. I choose to live according to the General Principles of Christian Life Communities.

2. *The Entire Assembly* (all communities)

   As members of the English-speaking Canadian federation of Christian Life Communities, approved by the international federation at the 1982 world assembly, we realize a more global expression of our commitment; our responsibility to develop the bonds of community does not stop with our own group but must extend to the national and world federation of CLC, our parishes and diocesan communities, the whole church and all people of good will.

   To help us with this, we call upon some of our members to form an executive in order to develop our federation under the basic responsibilities of formation, communication, interior life, and faith-justice.

3. *The Executive*

   We, the executive, of the federation, accept the responsibility you have given us and we realize that carrying it out will involve continual dialogue with you.

THE SHAKERTOWN PLEDGE

1. *Origin of the Pledge*

   The Shakertown Pledge originated when a group of religious retreat center directors gathered at the site of a restored Shaker village, near Harrodsburg, KY. A number of us were personally moved by the global poverty/ecology crisis we saw all around us, and we covenanted together to reduce our levels of consumption, to share our personal wealth with the world's poor, and to work for a new social order in which all people have equal access to the resources they need. We have since been joined by others.

   We believe that all people of faith should consider this Pledge. We have taken it not just because it is the right thing to do, and not just out of enlightened self-interest, but because of our deep religious conviction.

2. *The Pledge*

   Recognizing that the earth and the fulness thereof is a gift from our gracious God, and that we are called to cherish, nurture, and provide loving stewardship for the earth's resources.

   And recognizing that life itself is a gift, and a call to responsibility, joy, and celebration,

   I make the following declarations:

   a) I declare myself to be a world citizen.
   b) I commit myself to lead an ecologically sound life.
   c) I commit myself to lead a life of creative simplicity and to share my personal wealth with the world's poor.
   d) I commit myself to join with others in reshaping institutions in order to bring about a more just global society in which each person has full access to the needed resources for their physical, emotional, intellectual, and spiritual growth.
   e) I commit myself to occupational accountability, and in so doing I will seek to avoid the creation of products which cause harm to others.

f) I affirm the gift of my body, and commit myself to its proper nourishment and physical well-being.

g) I commit myself to examine continually my relations with others, and to attempt to relate honestly, morally, and lovingly to those around me.

h) I commit myself to personal renewal through prayer, meditation, and study.

i) I commit myself to responsible participation in a community of faith.

3. *What Would it Mean to Take the Shakertown Pledge*

Many people are attracted to the sentiments expressed in the Shakertown Pledge, but are not sure just what the Pledge might mean in their own lives. Here is a brief discussion of each item in the pledge.

a) *I declare myself to be a world citizen.*

Recognizing that we are citizens of one world can have a profound impact on our daily lives. Those who make this declaration should begin to think of the needs of all the people of the earth, and adjust their lifestyle, their social vision, and their political commitments accordingly. We must go beyond our family, village, regional, and national loyalties and extend our caring to all of humankind.

b) *I commit myself to lead an ecologically sound life.*

Through this we pledge that we will use the earth's natural resources sparingly and with gratitude. This includes the use of the land, water, air, coal, timber, oil, minerals, and other important resources. We will try to keep our pollution of the environment to a minimum and will seek wherever possible to preserve the natural beauty of the earth.

Concretely, this should mean that we will participate in local recycling efforts. It means that we will try to conserve energy and water in our own homes. It means that we will try to correct wasteful practices in our communities, schools, jobs, and in our nation.

c) *I commit myself to lead a life of creative simplicity and to share my personal wealth with the world's poor.*

This means that we intend to reduce the frills and luxuries in our present lifestyle but at the same time emphasize the beauty and joy of living. We do this for three reasons: First, so that our own lives can be more simple and gracious, freed from excessive attachment to material good; Second, so that we are able to release more of our wealth to share with those who need the basic necessities of life; Third, so that we can move toward a Just World Standard of Living in which each person shares equally in the earth's resources.

Concretely, anyone who takes the Pledge should sit down with their family and review their present financial situation. Each item of expenditure should be looked at carefully and unnecessary or luxury items should be reduced or eliminated. The surplus that is freed by this process should be given to some national or international group which is working for a better standard of living for the deprived. This surplus should be a regular budgeted item from then on, and each member of the household should endeavor to see how this surplus can be increased. In the future, families and individuals who have taken the Pledge might consider meeting together in "sharing groups" to discover new ways in which community and co-operation can free up more resources for the poor.

d) *I commit myself to join with others in reshaping institutions in order to bring about a more just global society in which each person has full access to the needed resources for their physical, emotional, intellectual, and spiritual growth.*

This compliments and enhances our commitment to share our personal wealth with those who need it. Wealthy nations such as the United States need to "develop" those parts of their economies that are wasteful and harmful in ecological and human terms. Wealthy nations must reduce their overconsumption of scarce re-

370

sources while supporting the ecologically wise development of the poor nations to the point where the basic needs of all "spaceship earth" passengers are met equally.

We commit ourselves to use our political and institutional influence toward these goals. This means that we will support those candidates who will do the most for the poor both here and abroad. It may mean that we will engage in lobbying, peaceful demonstrations, or other forms of "direct action" in support of the transfer of more of our resources and skills to the developing lands. It means that we will oppose and attempt to change those aspects of our economic system which create an unjust distribution of wealth and power here and abroad. This also means that we will support efforts to bring religious, intellectual, and vocational freedom to peoples who are being denied these basic human rights.

e) *I commit myself to occupational accountability, and in so doing I will seek to avoid the creation of products which cause harm to others.*

This most certainly means that we will not allow our labor to go into making products which kill others. It should also mean that we will take a close look at what we are producing to determine if it is safe, and if it is ecologically sound. We should also consider our choice of a career, and whether it contributes concretely to a better world for all humankind. If our present occupation does not do so, or is only marginally helpful to others, we may decide to change it, even if we earn less money as a result.

f) *I affirm the gift of my body, and commit myself to its proper nourishment and physical well-being.*

Many of us in the developed (or over-developed) countries desecrate the "temple" of our own bodies through overeating or through consuming nutritionally "empty" foods. Also, through our meat-centered diets we con-

371

sume protein in its most wasteful form, depriving people in other lands of desperately needed protein. (See *Diet for a Small Planet*, by Frances Lappe, Ballentine paperback.)

Serious attention to this point would mean: A. a commitment to maintain our weight at the normal, healthy level; B. a reduction in the consumption of animal protein in our diets; C. a regular attention to healthy physical exercise; D. a reduction in consumption of empty calories, especially in "desserts," candy, pastries, alcohol, and other food products which contain great amounts of refined sugar.

g) *I commit myself to examine continually my relationships with others, and to attempt to relate honestly, morally, and lovingly to those around me.*

We will seek to understand and improve our relationships with others, and to treat each person as our neighbor. We will try to affirm and nurture the gifts and talents of others. We support the development of the small group in religious life — since here many people are learning new ways to communicate their love, their needs, their hopes and dreams, and their anguish. The small groups have also been helpful in enabling people to see more clearly how they affect others.

h) *I commit myself to personal renewal through prayer, meditation, and study.*

For many people, "prayer" and "meditation" are alternate terms for the same process of turning one's thoughts toward God. We believe that deep and continuing personal renewal can result from a discipline of prayer or meditation, and from reading and reflection. We encourage each person to find their own individual spiritual discipline and practice it regularly. For a start, we would suggest setting aside time twice a day for prayer or meditation.

i) *I commit myself to responsible participation in a community of faith.*

We believe that God not only has a relationship with each of us individually, but also collectively — as a people. One of the obligations — and joys — of living our faith is that we are called to worship together with others. We recognize that common worship and the support of a community of common beliefs are essential to an active, creative, joyous life. Concretely, this means participation in a church synagogue, or "house church," or other worship group.

UNIT VI WEEK 18

CELEBRATION OF GRATITUDE AND COMMITMENT
(to Christian Life Community and/or any other way you desire to renew your commitment within the church)

CONCLUDING NOTE

At this moment of our journey, we also humbly recall Jesus' words, "You foolish people! So slow to believe the full message of the prophets! Was it not ordained that the Christ should suffer and so enter into his glory?" (Luke 24:25-26) We recognize ourselves and how slow we are to believe the full message.

Every ending marks a new beginning. We remember the many blessings of the Lord as he has led us along his way and brought us back to himself in community when we have lost the way. We also rejoice in his abundant promises: "I know the plans I have in mind for you – it is Yahweh who speaks – plans for peace, not disaster, reserving a future full of hope for you" (Jeremiah 29:11) and "Now I am making the whole of creation new" (Revelation 21:5).

"Now I am revealing new things to you,
things hidden and unknown to you,
created just now, this very moment;
of these things you have heard nothing until now,
so that you cannot say, 'Oh yes, I knew all this'.
You had never heard,
you did not know,
I had not opened your ear beforehand."

(Isaiah 48:6-8)

As we move forward in hope, our lives continue to touch themes, concerns and issues similar to those we have explored but it will always be new because we change. We are being transformed by the Trinity who love us profoundly and invite us not only to share ever new depths of intimacy with them but to do this as a human community rejoicing in, grateful and responsible for all creation, their gift to us.

In our communities we will be "doing theology" and discovering how the Lord is revealing what "libertion" requires of us and promises to us both in our separate localities and in our global village. It is important to share this good news and to hear how the Lord of history is working his wonders in other areas. All of those who have co-operated in developing this approach invite you to share with us your comments and experience.

Finally, it is with deep wonder, awe and silence before the Lord that we now thank and praise him for all he is doing in and through you.

"Glory be to him whose power, working in us, can do infinitely more than we can ask or imagine; glory be to him from generation to generation in the church and in Christ Jesus for ever and ever. Amen."

May your journey be filled with the Lord's ever-surprising presence!

EXTRA READING FOR EACH UNIT

UNIT I:

English, John SJ, *Choosing Life*, Toronto: Paulist Press, 1978.

UNIT II:

Kavanaugh John SJ, *Following Christ in a Consumer Society*,
New York: Orbis Books, 1981.
Segundo, Luis SJ, *Grace and the Human Condition*,
Maryknoll, New York: Orbis Books, 1973.

UNIT III:

Baars, Conrad M.D., *Feeling and Healing Your Emotions*,
Plainfield, New Jersey: Logos
International, 1979.
Johnson, Robert, *He: Understanding Masculine Psychology*,
New York: Harper & Row, 1974, 83 p.
She: Understanding Feminine Psychology,
New York: Harper & Row, 1976, 72 p.
Linn SJ, Dennis & Matthew, *Healing Life's Hurts:*
Healing Memories Through Five
Stages of Forgiveness, Toronto,
New York: Paulist Press, 1978.
Linn, Mary Jane, Dennis, Matthew, *Healing the Dying*,
Toronto, New York:
Paulist Press, 1979.
Pope John Paul II, *On the Mercy of God*, 1980.
Powell, John SJ, *Fully Human, Fully Alive*,
Argus Communications. (or any of his)
Sanford, John, *Invisible Partners*,
New York: Paulist Press, 1980.
Segundo, Luis SJ, *Our Idea of God*,
Maryknoll, New York: Orbis Books, 1974.
This Community Called Church.
Maryknoll, New York: Orbis Books, 1973.

UNIT IV:

Baum, G. *Priority of Labour*,
      N.Y.: Paulist Press, 1982

Brown, R. et al, *Mary in the New Testament*,
      Toronto: Paulist Press, 1978.

Cassidy, R., *Jesus, Politics and Society: A Study of Luke's
      Gospel*,
      Maryknoll, New York: Orbis Books, 1978.

Mische, Patricia & Gerald, *Toward a More Human World
      Order*,
      New York: Paulist Press, 1977.

Nolan, A., *Christ Before Christianity*,
      New York: Orbis Books, 1980.

Roy, Paul SJ, *Building Christian Communities for Justice*,
      Toronto, New York: Paulist Press, 1981.

Vatican Documents
Statements by Canadian Bishops:

    Formation of Conscience, 1974.
    Sharing Daily Bread, 1974.
    Northern Development: At What Cost?, 1975.
    From Words to Action, 1976.
    A Society to be Transformed, 1977.
    Witness to Justice, 1978.
    Fullness of Life, 1978.
    Strangers in our Midst, 1979.
    Unemployment: The Human Costs, 1980.
    One in Christ Jesus, 1980.
    On the Neutron Bomb, 1981.
    Ethical Reflections on the Economic Crisis, 1983.

    Canadian Conference of Catholic Bishops
    90 Parent Avenue, Ottawa, Ontario
    K1N 7B1

Papal Encyclicals:
    Peace on Earth, John XXIII, 1963.
    On the Development of Peoples, Paul VI, 1967.
    On Human Labour, John Paul II, 1981.

Synodal Document: *Justice in the World*, 1971.

We encourage in Canada,

1. Participation in the
   Canadian Urban Training Project for Christian Service,
   51 Bond Street,
   Toronto, Ontario
   M5B 1X1.
   Their courses are held in several cities.

2. Use of the Social Justice Curriculum for High Schools available from the
   Christian Movement for Peace,
   427 Bloor Street West,
   Toronto, Ontario,
   M5S 1X7.

   It is excellent for adults as well. Because it is experience based, it could be used for many meetings to reflect on our work experience. You could follow our usual introductory approach of reflecting on experience in the light of faith and then follow the suggested format on issues; such as, unemployment, unions, industrial disease and injury, conditions of farm work, coke workers in Guatemala, problems of clerical workers. 'Ten Days' booklets (1980 & 1981) on work are also excellent for this.
   Ten Days for World Development,
   Room 315, 85 St. Clair Avenue East,
   Toronto, Ontario,
   M4T 1M8.

3. Reading autobiographies and biographies of people who lived with similar values to those expressed in this book; for example,
   Cassidy, Sheila, *Audacity to Believe*. London: Collins Press, 1977.

UNIT V

Donovan, Vincent CSSP, *Christianity Rediscovered,*
    New York: Orbis Books, 1978.
Segundo, Luis SJ, *Sacraments Today,*
    Maryknoll, New York: Orbis Books, 1974.

UNIT VI

English, John SJ, *Communal Graced History:*
    A Manual of Theology and Practice,
    Ottawa: CRC Publication, 1981.
        324 Laurier Ave. E.
        Ottawa, Canada

Schemel, George, SJ, and Sister Judith Roemer, "Communal Discernment",
Review for Religious, Volume 49, Number 6, Nov./Dec., 1981, pp. 825-836.